Groupwork with Offenders

Groupwork with Offenders

edited by

Allan Brown and Brian Caddick

Whiting & Birch Ltd
London
MCMXCIII

© Whiting & Birch Ltd and Contributors, 1993

Published by Whiting & Birch Ltd, PO Box 872, Forest Hill, London SE23 3HL, England.
USA: Paul & Co, Publishers' Consortium Inc, PO Box 442, Concord, MA 017422.

British Library Cataloguing in Publication Data.
A CIP catalogue record ins available from the British Library

ISBN 1 871177 52 9 (cased)
ISBN 1 871177 41 3 (limp)

Printed in England by Short Run Press, Exeter

CONTENTS

Part One

Contexts and Issues

1

Groupwork with Offenders:
Approaches and Issues

ALLAN BROWN AND BRIAN CADDICK

There is a long tradition in the Probation Service, and elsewhere in the criminal justice system, of working with offenders in groups (see for example Barr's 1966 survey). A wide range of groups have been reported including: activity groups aimed at diverting young people from crime, pre-discharge groups in prisons, sex offender groups, support groups for the families of offenders (and others affected by crime), social skills groups, groups with the general aim of rehabilitation, and so on. The latest available evidence (Caddick, 1991) indicates that the use of groups in the probation service – particularly in direct work with offenders – is now probably more extensive and more varied than it has ever been.

We have noted elsewhere (Brown and Caddick, 1991) that despite this tradition, there is comparatively little discussion in the literature of the models, values, aims and characteristics of groupwork with offenders. There is also scant acknowledgement that national policies determining the scope and focus of work with offenders can have a significant impact on the shape of groupwork that is offered. Our awareness of this omission led most recently to the preparation and publication of a special issue of the journal *Groupwork* (4(3),1991), which contained nine papers dealing with the use of groups in working with offenders. Reactions to that special issue confirmed our view that there is interest in and a need for material which charts current activity, reflects on the context and the issues, illustrates new developments and points to much needed ones. Here we extend our earlier work by bringing together a wider collection of papers: some new, some previously published and some – amongst the latter – modifications from their original form.

Although we would agree that there is scope for an 'authored', as distinct from an 'edited' book on groupwork with offenders, we have chosen an edited book in this instance for several reasons. Firstly, as groupwork with offenders takes place in a wide range of settings (prisons, hostels, day centres and elsewhere in the community), there is a need for a book which reflects this fact. Not many individuals, and certainly not ourselves, have the range of experience and understanding needed to cover all these settings. It was therefore both necessary and desirable to adopt an approach which allowed those with pertinent experience in particular settings to speak for themselves. Secondly, there are significant differences in practice method and perspective which in our view are most vitally illustrated by actual practice accounts. Thirdly, with many of the developments in groupwork over the past decade, there has been a process of evolutionary change – sometimes accompanied by policy debates – which those with the closest involvement are best able to set out and comment upon.

Where we have placed a boundary around the content and breadth of the book is in its almost exclusive focus (all chapters except that by Towl) on the use of groups by workers in, or closely linked to, the Probation Service. In Britain as elsewhere the Probation Service is one of the principal agencies charged with responsibility for working with offenders. Most of its professional workers hold social work qualifications: much of their work has a formal statutory relationship to the courts. Probation workers are thus faced daily with the complex interplay of 'care' and 'control' which, among other things, makes their use of groups in working with offenders of special interest. Recent policy developments, culminating in the 1991 Criminal Justice Act, are likely to be of great significance in pointing up the care/control duality, particularly the new expectations sentencers and managers are likely to have of the role of groupwork in 'community penalties'. All of these factors, plus our own interests, influenced our decision to make groupwork in the Probation Service our main focus.

Groupwork is not of course the only method used by the Probation Service: one-to-one work – initially associated with a concern to 'advise, assist and befriend', but now used for many purposes – has been and continues to be a central activity. Even so there seems to be wide contemporary agreement about using groups to work with people who, because they have offended and often because of their life circumstances, face a variety of demands and difficulties. It cannot be said that the appeal of groupwork rests on clear and systematically established evidence that its use with offenders is effective in meeting either their needs, or the interests of agencies which provide the facility. Nevertheless there is a considerable social science literature, now stretching over many years and encompassing many thousands of studies, which shows that small groups, through their interactive processes, can provide opportunities for challenge, support, learning and influence, as well as for sharing, empowerment and joint action (Hare, 1962; McGrath and Altman, 1966; Shaw, 1971; Smith, 1980; Douglas, 1983). There is also the persuasive impact of personal experience which – on reflection and by the very nature of our social lives – cannot help but confirm the potency of group membership in influencing our attitudes, perceptions, behaviours, sense of support and of common purpose. It is not at all surprising then that the use and potential of groups should be so widely accepted.

Groupwork is however a generic term which covers a range of models, purposes and practice ideologies. There are, in fact, some sharply contrasting approaches and their differences not only reflect debates about the causes of, and most appropriate responses to offending; they also have a significance in terms of recent policy developments. A few examples will illustrate the range of approaches.

Social Skills and Offending Behaviour groups (see Priestley and McGuire, 1978; McGuire and Priestley, 1985) are two of the most commonly encountered forms of groupwork with offenders. Each tends to be offered as a structured, short-term programme and each is used as a means of promoting individual change. But here the similarities end. Offending Behaviour groups are geared towards developing a capacity in individual members to avoid acting in an unlawful way; Social Skills groups focus on developing skills and abilities which the members do not possess but which they need if they are to engage in work, social or personal activities in a more productive and successful way. In the first, attention is directed towards anti-social behaviour and its reduction; in the second, the emphasis is on pro-social behaviour, the establishment of which is regarded as crucial if a person is to avoid further offending.

Both of these groups are examples of what Papell and Rothman (1966) have called 'remedial' groupwork: each is directed towards eradicating an individual condition – deviant attitudes and actions on the one hand, skills deficits on the other. But while the two approaches may thus be said to be individualistic in orientation, they nevertheless derive from very different views about the nature of offending. Implicit in Social Skills programmes is the belief that people who are disadvantaged by a lack of skills are unlikely to participate fully in society and more likely to find themselves on the periphery where criminal activity is a condition of survival and/or acceptance. Behind Offending Behaviour groups is the idea that offenders can be helped to understand the consequences of their unlawful actions, be made to see that they are accountable for these, and encouraged to make different behavioural choices in the future. It is the notions of accountability and choice which place this approach on the justice side of the 'justice versus welfare' argument (Raynor, 1985; Hudson, 1987). With its emphasis on overcoming disadvantage, the Social Skills approach is much more in keeping with the welfare philosophy.

Standing in contrast to each of these is an example reported by Mullender and Ward (1985) which, in Papell and Rothman's terminology, would be classified as a 'social goals' group. This was a group for 'teenage lads who had offended together on the council estate where they lived'. With a probation officer and two others acting as group facilitators, these young people identified factors which they felt had contributed to their offending — factors like limited leisure facilities on the estate and poor relationships with the police. They then planned and carried through a campaign aimed at changing these conditions, the success of which provided the impetus for further joint projects. Rather than attending to deviant behaviour or skills deficits, the group focus was on certain environmental disadvantages which the members shared. Yet the programme was not welfarist: the principles guiding the work were ones which emphasised member definition of the issues and group empowerment in the pursuit of wider external change. Mullender and Ward (1991) have provided a fuller conceptualisation of the 'Self-Directed' model in another publication in this series.

Quite similar ideologically to the above model, but with a different origin and emphasis, are groups which set out to empower people who experience structural disadvantage specifically because of their race or gender. Some groups of this kind, particularly for women offenders, are currently being offered by the probation service, usually as a result of the initiative of female workers (see Mistry, 1989, reprinted here). The difference from say fifteen years ago is that whereas then welfare, child care and mothering tended to be emphasised, now the focus is on the empowerment of women in the face of their frequent marginalisation in the criminal justice system and their oppression in the wider society.

The Papell and Rothman classification includes a third category which, in the context of groupwork with offenders, is also meaningful. This is the 'reciprocal' approach in which the group becomes the arena, and the worker the facilitator, for some form of mediation between the group members and other interested parties or groups, often the agency or the wider society. A variation on this theme – in that the mediation occurs in a kind of inter-group situation between different categories of group members – is illustrated by a group described by Nation and Arnott (1991). These workers provided a programme in which offenders and victims of crime met face-to-face for some sessions of the group. Given that it was an intention that this experience would promote a change in the offenders' attitudes towards offending, these particular sessions obviously had something of a remedial character. But there was also a reciprocal dimension in that the members were afforded an opportunity to re-establish a social connectedness and the victims to express and perhaps expel feelings of anger, fear and damaged trust. The practice ideology is in this case quite complex, combining features of individual culpability and need with restorative (rather than retributive) notions of justice which themselves are founded on the idea of a wide social contract (Harding, 1982; Davis et al., 1987).

The diversity illustrated by these examples naturally prompts questions. Is any one approach better than another? As has already been mentioned, there is no systematically established evidence on this point. Given their contrasting views on the nature of offending, are they essentially incompatible approaches? This rather depends on how far one takes the view that people offend for different reasons and may therefore require different responses, or combinations of responses, to break out of labels, lifestyles or sets of circumstances which are likely to lead to further offending. Has such diversity a future? This is unclear if not doubtful, given certain policy developments over the last decade.

In the 1980s probation areas were urged, through discussion papers which led to a Statement of National Objectives and Priorities (HMSO, 1984), to continue to develop ways in which a larger proportion of offenders – inevitably more serious offenders – could be dealt with by non-custodial measures. The political considerations behind this policy were, in part at least, the need to reduce pressure on an already overcrowded prison system and cut the costs involved in maintaining a person in prison. As it turned out, a reduction in the prison population was not achieved and there has been a tendency, in more recent policy documents, to imply that the Probation Service failed to convince the courts that the community-based programmes on offer were effective in controlling and altering an offender's motivation to commit further crimes. Thus the last years of the decade saw a growing governmental emphasis on the need for tougher non-custodial alternatives – or 'community sentences' as they are now to be known – and a clear assertion of a 'just deserts' approach in dealing with offenders. Indeed, the direction of governmental thinking is neatly summarised by the titles of some of the White and Green Papers which emerged from the Home Office during this period: Punishment, Custody and the Community (HMSO, 1988); Supervision and Punishment in the Community (HMSO, 1990a); and Crime, Justice and Protecting the Public (HMSO, 1990b).

In relation to groupwork, the significance of these developments lies in the apparent sanctioning of a particular approach. This can be found in the chapter of the White Paper dealing with the supervision of offenders by the Probation Service where it is stated that:

> Offenders should be made to face up to the harm they have done and learn how to avoid repeating it...Typically this kind of supervision involves regular meetings of a group of offenders led by a probation officer. The group follows a course of planned and structured discussions, examining the causes and consequences of the offending by each member of the group and how offending can be avoided in the future (1990b, p 36).

The value of such an approach, the White Paper goes on to suggest, is that offenders are 'more likely to respond positively if they are treated as responsible for their own actions, rather than as powerless victims of upbringing, circumstances or defects of personality' (p 36). Thus, while the probation officer should make an assessment of 'other aspects of an offender's way of life which may contribute to the pattern of offending: for example, lack of education, unemployment, addictions' and then '...put together a programme of action to help the offender out of these difficulties', it will nevertheless be '...unrealistic to expect sudden or dramatic change' as a consequence.

It is of course doubtful that workers attracted to any particular model would argue its virtues in terms of a capacity to encourage sudden or dramatic change. But the point to grasp here is that a specific form of groupwork – which is remedial and justice orientated – is being promoted and others downplayed.

Elsewhere, too, the White Paper gives short shrift to mediatory programmes by pointing out that: 'Financial reparation to victims is already available through compensation orders and reparation to the community through community service orders' (p 24). In brief, there is not a great deal of encouragement to make full and considered use of the potential of groupwork methods, and it might even be argued that the responsibility previously given to probation officers to assess and provide the most appropriate ways of working with those whom they supervise – and undoubtedly Offending Behaviour and similar groups would figure here – is being reduced and channelled. It is not clear what the result of this will be: policy, after all, is not the sole determinant of what imaginative and committed workers may provide. But policy is intimately linked to resourcing and, in this climate, the emerging challenge for probation officers who want to maintain and extend groupwork practice, and the perspectives which inform it, will be to demonstrate how the approaches which they wish to pursue merit adequate resourcing because they are at least as effective in achieving productive outcomes.

The range of papers in this book indicates both the diversity of contemporary groupwork in the probation service and the pressures on practitioners to concentrate on the kind of groupwork most obviously consistent with these current policy imperatives. We shall therefore now consider some of the practice issues which are identified by authors here and elsewhere, which highlight the tensions facing professional social workers undertaking groupwork in an agency which is becoming ever more integral to the control imperative of the criminal justice system. A professional perspective in a bureaucracy requires that practitioners have enough freedom from dictat to pursue new and creative approaches provided these can be shown to be consistent with agency objectives.

Nearly all groupwork writers (see for example Whitaker, 1976) emphasise the fundamental importance of a facilitative context for effective practice. This includes the organisational, physical and psychological environment of groupwork programmes. Groupwork on the scale evident from our national survey (Caddick, 1991, and in this volume) needs a sound organisational base, designed specifically to create a facilitating and well resourced environment for effective and diverse practice.

Two papers in this collection indicate what can be achieved, quantitatively and qualitatively, with proper organisation. Ashe describes how one prison consciously reorganised to provide a 'needs-led' groupwork programme as part of a through-care policy. Eight different group programmes were set up and resourced, offering prisoners real choice according to their needs and circumstances. Similarly, in a fieldwork setting in Newcastle upon Tyne (see Mackintosh), groupwork has been organised centrally enabling a comprehensive and varied programme of many kinds of groups to be offered to offenders in the city. Among other things, this allows women's and other groups for defined populations to be offered in a way which would not be feasible for a single fieldwork team. Significantly the resourcing of the Newcastle model is possible because it is one of the Intensive Probation Programmes partially financed by the Home Office.

The need for suitable organisational and physical arrangements for groups is clear, but equally important is the psychological climate. By this we mean a work culture which validates working with people in groups as at least as 'natural' a method as working with them individually. Sadly this does not always happen, particularly if the groupwork is in any way unconventional, and practitioners are left either to continue in the knowledge that they do not have a full mandate, or alternatively to abandon the idea altogether. It is important that the political pressures mentioned earlier do not become organisationally backed constraints and disincentives to imaginative and innovative groupwork programmes with offenders.

A major practice issue in groupwork with offenders is the difficult question of compulsion versus voluntarism. This is by no means a new issue, but there are increasing statutory pressures to coerce people into groups thereby running the risk of reducing the offender's commitment to change and development through personal decision. Some groupwork authors (see for example Garvin, 1981) regard compulsion as incompatible with the fundamental principles of groupwork practice, and voluntarism is strongly supported by some authors in this volume (see Canton et al.; Mistry; Mackintosh; Towl; Ashe) not only for philosophical but also for pragmatic reasons – it seems to work and in their experience achieves at least as good an attendance rate as compulsion does.

This matter is a complex one when working with offenders in the probation context, because the comparison is often between different forms of supervision/sentence all of which have elements of compulsion once the probation order is made by the court. For example, a condition of residence at a probation hostel may not stipulate compulsory attendance at groups, but in practice there can be all sorts of subtle and not so subtle pressures to participate in various group events. We have no easy solution to this dilemma, except to observe that if a group is to have any impact on offending behaviour, what really matters is that the offender is motivated to participate actively (see Behroozi, 1992): it is not enough simply to be physically present.

The next issue which illustrates the trend towards reducing the scope for diversity of approach has been characterised as 'package v process'. Undoubtedly there has been a growing emphasis on groupwork 'packages'. The attractions are obvious: for the busy practitioner there is a ready made programme with pre-packed exercises telling him or her what to do each session, and for sentencers and managers there is the reassurance of something tangible and specific. Earlier we identified several types of groupwork with offenders, each associated with different aims: learning social skills; confronting offending behaviour; social action; empowerment; and reparation. It is interesting to observe that whist some of these approaches differ profoundly in ideology and purpose, none of them proclaims the primacy of group process. Yet this element of group interaction and group development is seen by many writers as the core element of mainstream social groupwork (Papell and Rothman, 1980).

The essence of 'classical' groupwork is the facilitation of the chemistry that develops between members as they build a group which creates the conditions for positive change grounded in a climate of mutual support and strength. Group process influences behaviour and feelings in a group all the time; to ignore it is to be unresponsive to individual needs, avoiding both the risk and creativity that openness can bring. Package and process are not of course mutually exclusive: what the worker – and members – need is to be able to draw flexibly on a repertoire of ideas, activities, exercises and techniques in ways which are congruent with the needs of the group, not to fit the group members into a straightjacket of predetermined packages.

In this book Earnshaw traces the evolution of a probation centre programme from a person-centred 'process' approach to something much more structured and programmed. The evidence on reconvictions suggests the latter method is at least as effective as the former, although the author presents the change with an apparent touch of regret that external pressures have led to this change in emphasis. Two other authors – Mark writing about another day centre, and Mulvie about groups in a hostel – have held on to an approach which emphasises feelings and relationships, the former drawing on a psychodynamic framework and the latter on a humanistic perspective. Our impression is that this is becoming less common and less tolerated by agency management. However, notwithstanding political and agency pressures, we anticipate a possible swing of the pendulum back to a 'rediscovery' of the inseparability of a person from his or her behaviour, as a basis for real change. This would be no more than a confirmation of the essence of social groupwork practice.

Another reason for diversifying groupwork programmes is the need to ensure that whatever pattern is established does not discriminate against the needs of minority groups. In this context we are thinking particularly of female and black offenders, as they are frequently marginalised in groups in the probation service. At the end of his paper, Senior juxtaposes the twin developments of those routinised group approaches which are instrumental, rule-conscious and staff-driven, with the new radicalism of empowerment and anti-oppressive approaches (see Mistry, and Badham et al.), suggesting the latter offer a potential source of innovative and creative groupwork. Interestingly, the latest 'National Standards' (Home Office, 1992) give prominence to an anti-discriminatory perspective as part of their requirements for practice under the 1991 Criminal Justice Act. Perhaps, as suggested by both pieces on the Miskin groups for female offenders in Mid-Glamorgan (Jones et al.; Thomas), there is a possible resolution in which the imperative of focusing on offending behaviour and the justice approach, creates a context for legitimising the empowerment of group members. By this we mean that, paradoxically, confronting and examining the reasons for offending behaviour not only faces the offender with responsibility for her/his own behaviour, but also opens up awareness of the centrality of social and discriminatory forces in the generation of offending behaviour, without defining the offender as victim as in the welfare model. There is much truth in the view that anti-racist and anti-sexist practice are no more than good practice, and perhaps therein lies the clue to a way out of these groupwork 'cul-de-sacs'.

Finally, a word about the organisation and contents of this book, which we believe presents a broad and informative picture of current practice so far as groupwork with offenders in the probation context is concerned. The range of papers has been selected partly to reflect the rich diversity of approaches and practice ideologies, but also because some of the authors indicate some possible ways forward on the issues discussed above.

· The two remaining papers in Part 1 offer an important general backcloth to what follows. Caddick's survey indicates, inter alia, the already existing variety of groups for offenders, as well as some of the gaps which need to be filled. Senior traces the historical developments in groupwork with offenders, highlighting the increasing policy constraints on practitioners, but also sensing opportunities for exploiting and building on the serious attention being given to anti-discriminatory groupwork.

The rest of the book is divided into two further Parts. The first collects together nine papers on groupwork in 'institutional' settings, and the latter seven papers on a range of groups in 'fieldwork' settings.

The four based on penal establishments between them demonstrate a remarkable commitment to support, dignity, empowerment and anti-discrimination, showing that this is possible in the harsh conditions of imprisonment. They range from the rationale and organisation of a comprehensive diverse programme of voluntary groups (Ashe); to a self-directed group offering some degree of choice and empowerment in a young offenders institution (Badham et al.); to a voluntary 'culture' group run on holistic principles designed to help prisoners address values issues (Towl); to an 'open' discharge group in a large prison, demonstrating the imaginative and creative use of exercises to address a policy directive, whilst remaining sensitive to anti-discriminatory issues (Fisher and Watkins).

The other five papers in Part Two suggest that the increased contact available in the complex group living contexts of hostels and probation (day) centres leads to greater involvement of staff in the lives of the group members, and a consequent awareness of the need for more person-centred group approaches. In the two hostel accounts, Mulvie emphasises the importance of process and versatility in staff roles, and Sapsed stresses the opportunities presented in a residential context for working at confronting sexist and racist attitudes in both residents and staff. Probation centres will continue to be a key resource following the implementation of the 1991 Criminal Justice Act, with much of the work being carried out in groups. Here we present experience from three centres (Earnshaw; Mark; Hill et al.), each working in significantly different ways with offenders who attend intensive daily programmes over a three month period. In addition to the psychodynamic and humanistic perspectives of Mark and Mulvie respectively, Hill et al. describe an approach with cognitive and person-centred elements which also meets the requirement to tackle offending behaviour. Even during the period of preparation of this book, there has been a significant shift nationally towards the more widespread use of cognitive methods (Ross et al. ,1986) which are rapidly being introduced in some centres and which raise in acute form some of the 'package v process' issues discussed earlier.

Part Three includes seven papers on 'fieldwork' groups. This selection does not include such well-known approaches as induction/assessment groups and groups for people whose offending is drug or alcohol related. Yet those that are included amply demonstrate the considerable variety of groupwork that is possible in the probation service: the commitment to anti-discriminatory practice; the concern with providing and enabling choice; and the careful thought given to preparing, carrying out and constantly evaluating groups.

In addition to the points previously made about the advantages of the organisational framework described by Mackintosh, it is worth mentioning that, as with Canton et al., most of the Newcastle groups are three or four day 'block' events rather than once-a-week groups over a longer period. This question of the optimum time-frame for different kinds of groups is a crucial practice issue: the benefits of concentration versus the gains of group contact sustained over a longer period. In this context it is interesting to note Cowburn's point that the Nottinghamshire Probation Service, having recently reviewed their policy on groups for sex offenders, have decided to sustain the groupwork over a much longer period, with a series of weekly half-day sessions spread over eleven months. This also accords with the special provisions in the 1991 Criminal Justice Act for this type of offender.

Three papers focus on groups for female offenders. Those by Mistry (writing from a feminist perspective) and by Jones et al. (the 'Miskin' group) describe the struggle to establish the principle of specialist groups for women in which their needs come first, as distinct from the marginalisation they so often experience in mixed offender groups. Thomas takes an agency-wide view in demonstrating how the success of the Miskin women's group has empowered women staff throughout the organisation, and radically changed the whole agency policy towards female offenders. Caddick's research and other evidence suggest that this battle for recognition of the particular needs of women has begun to have an impact.

By contrast, the picture regarding group provision for black offenders – not just in field settings but in all the settings dealt with in this book – is very worrying. Caddick's survey indicated that less than 1 per cent of all groups run are for black offenders only, yet there is at least one black person in no fewer than 61 per cent of the 1500 groups surveyed. This almost certainly means that many groups are being run with only one or two black members, with the almost inevitable marginalisation of their particular needs and interests. Unfortunately it has not proved possible to include a chapter on groups for black offenders in this book, reflecting the dearth of such groups at the present time. There is an urgent and pressing need for this subject to be addressed by researchers, theorists and most importantly by agencies and practitioners. Statements about anti-racism and anti-discriminatory practice are meaningless unless they are translated into practical policies. It is not for example satisfactory for a decision to be taken not to include 'singleton' black members in groups if the organisation does not also arrange access to suitable black only groups. A choice for black offenders between marginalisation in mixed groups or possible disenfranchisement from certain group-related sentences is manifestly discriminatory.

The other three types of groups included in the fieldwork section are: a group for motoring offenders (Hutchins) which whilst based on a programme package is developmental in the sense that it is responsive to changing needs and experience; a group for violent offenders (Canton et al.) emphasising membership by consent and demonstrating a viable alternative to prison for serious offenders; and groups for male sex offenders, with the author (Cowburn) emphasising the importance of establishing practice principles with an explicit value-base. All three relate to clearly identifiable types of crime which cause serious hurt and anxiety to the general population. Effective well thought out groupwork responses as illustrated in these examples are an essential resource.

We end this introduction with a brief but important comment. We are very pleased that the contributors to this book have provided such a broad and detailed picture of groupwork – and the issues surrounding it – in the probation service. But it needs to be emphasised that this collection of chapters is not meant to be either an exhaustive or a definitive account. What we have sought to do is produce a book which illustrates the vitality of groupwork practice with offenders, and which gives support and encouragement to the kind of discussion, analysis, confidence and creativity through which groupwork can be developed and extended, yet at the same time remain valid, principled and enabling.

Allan Brown and Brian Caddick (co-editors), Bristol University

2

Using Groups in Working with Offenders: A Survey of Groupwork in the Probation Services of England and Wales

BRIAN CADDICK

INTRODUCTION

It is now 25 years since Hugh Barr published *A Survey of Group Work in the Probation Service* (1966) and both the service and ideas about groupwork have changed and developed a good deal since then. Legislative action and intention (the Criminal Justice Acts of 1972 and 1982; the more recent 1991 Act) and Home Office policy initiatives (for example, the *Statement of National Objectives and Priorities,* 1984, and the later Green and White papers: *Punishment, Custody and the Community,* 1988; *Supervision and Punishment in the Community,* 1990a; and *Crime, Justice and Protecting the Public,* 1990b) have significantly affected the focus, aims and activities of probation workers in relation to offenders. Meanwhile groupwork in the UK has, for its part, continued to move beyond its early reliance on psychodynamic theory and therapeutic method so that, today, practitioners have a wider and more ideologically diverse range of concepts and approaches on which to base their practice. There are good reasons, then, for taking a fresh look at the scale and nature of groupwork in the probation service so as to establish a more up-to-date benchmark and to assess the scope for new developments and directions.

Such is the main purpose of this paper, which presents the results of a questionnaire survey on the use of groupwork with offenders in most of the probation services of England and Wales during 1989. (This survey was carried out by Brian Caddick and Allan Brown of the Department of Social Work at Bristol University.) Of the 56 services approached, 43 replied to the questionnaire and supplied information on some 1500 groupwork programmes. These numbers are themselves an eloquent expression of the changes since Barr's original study, for he found that only about a quarter of the services in England, Scotland and Wales made use of a group approach in work with offenders, and his analysis suggested that only a very small number of groups were being run. On the strength of this comparison, and despite the traditional and continuing importance of one-to-one involvement between probation officer and individual offender, it could perhaps be argued that the probation service is the agency most actively involved in the practice of groupwork in Britain today.

That groupwork seems to have found increasing favour in the probation service could be interpreted in a number of ways. For instance it is a widely promulgated view, stemming from the findings of researchers and the observations of workers in many fields, that the small group is a useful medium for promoting support, enabling change, conveying new knowledge and developing new skills. This collection of virtues ties in well with what many probation officers would see themselves as trying to achieve in their work with offenders and, indeed, with what many standard statements of the purpose of probation imply. It is hardly surprising, then, that as training courses have given more attention to groupwork as a social work method, there are clear signs that more and more officers have sought to make use of its apparent potential in their work.

But there are other, less comfortable explanations. The small group may have many enabling features but it can also be used for the purposes of control, restraint and enforcing conformity to prevailing norms and, as argued by Senior elsewhere in this book, official pronouncements about the agency's statutory role in providing a service to the courts have increasingly underscored these interests. It could be, then, that the growth in the use of groupwork in the service simply reflects a continuation by other means of the containment and treatment ideology which has often been said to inform traditional one-to-one work (Walker and Beaumont, 1981). Alongside this, and perhaps complementing it, a professional pre-occupation with developing new and distinctive methods of working might also have come into play as the profile of probation officers has itself been raised over the past 10-15 years.

But it is possible that this may be too stark an assessment and it is, in any case, one which drifts rather too close to the unsubtle notion that there are few (if any) circumstances in which control and personal change are valid objectives. Take, for example, groupwork aimed at changing and promoting control in individual offenders whose crimes are of a violent or sexual nature. Though pervasive social attitudes concerning male dominance are undoubtedly implicated, the personal behaviour of these offenders is an immediate and accessible focus for change and it would be unusual, to say the least, if none of this sort of work was found to be occurring in an agency which has been given more and more responsibility for managing serious offenders in the community. In fact, of course, there are accounts which attest to the existence of this kind of groupwork (e.g., Weaver and Fox, 1984; Eldridge and Gibbs, 1987; Mackintosh, this book).

It also needs to be noted that there exists a small but growing literature on groupwork with offenders where social action in the environment and/or the exploration of the broad social - as opposed to presumed personal - factors which lie behind offending are the principal aims. Mullender and Ward (1985), for instance, have described a group for young offenders where the approach was to help the members:

> ...work together as a group to improve leisure facilities on the estate, the lack of which had been, in the [members'] view, an important factor in the causation of their offences (p.166).

Two papers by Badham and his colleagues (Badham et al., 1988; 1989) provide further evidence. In the first of these, projects with a groupwork base are described where the aim for the workers was to maximise:

> ...(the members') control over their own lives by increasing their confidence to act on their own ideas, to use resources available to them and to make their needs known to those who have power over resources (p.240).

The second paper deals with a group in a youth custody centre in which the members were:

> ...encouraged to define their own issues and take action on them. The workers' standpoint was that difficulties the young prisoners faced were not necessarily the result of 'personal inadequacies'.

Instead, their practice reflected an understanding that 'social and economic factors, racism and sexism are major forces contributing to young people's problems' (p.28). Mistry (1989), writing about a group for women offenders, noted as one of its central themes the exploration of offending behaviour within a framework which recognised 'that offending is closely related to socio-economic factors, changing roles of women in society, personal history and poverty...' (p.149). The Jones et al. paper included in this book provides yet another illustration of groupwork with offenders in which empowerment, allied to self-control, is the primary goal.

What might be taken from this is that groupwork in the probation service is not, on the face of it at least, a 'single model' phenomenon. But it is not actually known whether, in practice, there is a significant variety of approaches and, if so, whether one or two predominate. Nor is it clear whether particular settings (field offices as against day centre or prison settings, for instance) adopt particular approaches, how far the needs of particular client groups (women, black people) are recognised and acted upon, whether the time invested is an adequate reflection of the outcomes sought or is instead determined by other considerations. The findings which are presented below are not always unequivocal in regard to these issues but, as will be seen, a discernible picture emerges and some important pointers for change are indicated.

METHOD

The method by which information was obtained was a single page, previously piloted questionnaire, sufficient copies of which were supplied to all 56 services in England and Wales for circulation to the first line managers of team/staff groups in all sections of the agency providing a direct service to users. The settings surveyed therefore included field offices, probation/day centres, divorce court welfare offices, hostels, community service offices, prisons and 'other' settings (such as court teams, student training units, specialist teams, etc.). The questionnaire asked respondents to indicate whether or not groupwork was being carried out in their team and, if so, what type(s) of groupwork, whether that groupwork was with offenders or with others (an example of the latter might be a group for prisoners' partners, say, or a support group for volunteer workers), and the primary aims of the group(s) listed. Additionally, details were sought about the length of groupwork programmes, the frequency of sessions and the number of workers typically involved; about member composition in terms of gender and race; and about whether other teams or other agencies had a hand in running the groups. The information to be given was for a specified period - January to December 1989 - or another substantially overlapping 12 month period if that was easier.

As has already been mentioned, 43 of 56 services replied. Those services which did not generally gave current heavy workloads or re-organisation activities as the reason for not doing so. (There certainly was no suggestion that groups were not being run in these agencies.) The number of questionnaires returned for each of those services which did supply information varied from 28 to 100 per cent, with an overall average for these agencies of some 60 per cent. Material on 1463 groups for offenders was provided.

Not all of the results from the survey will be reported here. In particular, groups in which the members were not offenders are not discussed, although it is worth mentioning briefly that there is considerable activity of this sort being carried out. There are, for example, groups for people experiencing divorce, groups for training and supporting community service supervisors and others who have taken on a voluntary role in the agency, support/ action groups for staff and for the partners or families of people who are in prison, and so on. One consequence of leaving these aside will be that divorce court welfare and community service settings will not enter into the analysis. Thus it is important to say at this point that a significant amount of groupwork does take place in those settings, but not - as far as the survey revealed - planned groupwork with offenders.

FINDINGS

Prevalence of groupwork

Only 16 per cent of the responses received recorded that there had been no groupwork in that particular team/staff group over the period surveyed. Indeed, for the 84 per cent indicating that groupwork had been carried out, most of the responses received listed more than one example. The picture is not uniform, however. There are probation agencies in which groupwork is very common and others where it is rather less so. There are also a few agencies in which most of the groupwork taking place is provided by a special unit offering that service to the rest of the agency. But despite these variations, it is clear from the results that groupwork is not the marginal activity it was when Barr conducted his original survey.

Programmes and aims

The main findings concerning the kinds of groupwork practised are set out in Table 1. Of the nearly 1500 groups said to have been run, 70 per cent were easily classifiable into the 12 types listed and, in the main, the labels used in the table are the ones given by the respondents. However it should be noted that the 'life and social skills' category not only includes sessions designated as such, but also separate programmes dealing with, for instance, cookery, money management, personal relationships, literacy, job search and so on. The same is true for the 'activity' classification, where entries such as arts and crafts, sports sessions and the like have been placed. The 'residents' label seemed to best characterise hostel groups known variously as weekly house meetings, living groups, hostel group, community sessions and, of course, residents' meetings. Lastly, the 400-odd groups not included within the table represent an extraordinary diversity of offerings, many of which are 'one-offs' or, when clustering is possible, define categories which individually account for considerably less than two per cent of the overall total (examples would be 'drop in' and 'reporting' groups).

The 12 categories which have been listed are arranged according to frequency of mention, the bracketed figures showing this as a percentage of the 1463 groups registered in the survey. For each of the 12, the three most frequently mentioned aims are also given and these too are differentiated in terms of level of importance (with *** signifying the most prominent of the three, and so on downwards). Taken together these data permit a somewhat crude, but nevertheless interesting, analysis to be made: six of the types listed - offending behaviour, alcohol education, motoring offenders, sex offenders, drugs/addiction, control of anger and temper - are pretty solidly concerned with changing or controlling unacceptable or problematic behaviour and jointly account for 36 per cent of the groups run. But five of the others - life and social skills, activity, women's, temporary release and residents' - appear to be directed towards providing developmental or enabling experiences and these forms collectively account for 31 per cent of the total. Behaviour control is, it would seem, the objective of a significant proportion of groupwork in the probation service, but it is not the whole story.

Another noteworthy feature is that the aim of promoting insight and understanding shows up as the one most widely shared over the categories listed. Of course the term 'insight and understanding' is not very precise in this context and might just

Table 1
Types of groupwork offered and their principal aims

Type of groupwork	Principal aim of group programme								
	a	b	c	d	e	f	g	h	i
Offending behaviour (12)		*	***		**				
Life & social skills (11)	**			***				*	
Alcohol education (10)	*		***		**				
Activity (8)				**		***		*	
Women's (7)					*		***	**	
Motoring offenders (4)	*		***		**				
Sex offenders (4)		*	***		**				
Temporary release (3)	***			*	**				
Induction (3)	***	**			*				
Drugs/addiction (3)			***	*	**				
Control of anger and temper (3)			***	*	**				
Residents' (2)	***							*	**

Key:
a= supply information; b = assessment; c= behaviour change; d = develop skills;
e = insight and understanding; f = leisure activity; g = support; h = empower;
i = group action for wider change.
*** = most frequently cited aim   ** = second most frequently cited aim
* = third most frequently cited aim
(figures in brackets indicate prominence of group type as a % of total no of groups recorded)

as easily be applied to groupwork focusing on personal conduct or culpability as to a programme in which consciousness-raising about the structural factors associated with crime is an important element. Only in the case of women's groups, where the two other principal aims are support and empowerment, is there a suggestion that it is the latter which is meant. For most of the others the former is more likely, given the pairing with the aim of behaviour change. Thus the practice ideology, if it can be called that, appears broadly individualistic in outlook or, in groupwork model terms, primarily remedial (Papell and Rothman, 1966).

This is also apparent in another way. Despite examples cited in the introduction of this paper, it is clear from Table 1 that the survey provided no evidence of any substantial use of the social action model of groupwork (Mullender and Ward, 1985; 1991). Only in the case of residents' groups, run exclusively in hostel settings, did the aim of group action for change in the wider community receive significant mention and it is fairly obvious that the community which these respondents had in mind was the somewhat bounded one of the hostel itself (though that should certainly not be taken as unimportant). It is perhaps worth pointing out that, like other groupwork approaches (see, for instance, Brown and Seymour, 1983), the social action model has developed in a particular part of the country and, unfortunately, two of the services in that area did not participate in the survey. And yet even if they had done so and each had registered considerable use of the model, the overall message would still have been that social action groupwork with offenders is not widespread.

Programmes and settings

Table 2 gives several pieces of information on a setting-by-setting basis. Included are figures showing the total number of groups reported to have been mounted in each of service settings listed, and it is obvious from these that the field and probation/day centre locations together account for about two-thirds of the groups run. Additionally the table shows - in order of decreasing importance - the five most prominent kinds of groupwork mentioned in each of the settings (with the bracketed figures which follow indicating the 'popularity' of each kind of group as a percentage of the total number of groups run in that setting).

In terms of the kinds of groups offered, the picture is remarkably similar from setting to setting, although there are some obvious differences - for instance, lifer support groups are run only in prisons and residents' groups are run only in hostels. Order of prominence is more varied across settings but a more interesting contrast emerges if the same rough and ready classification as used before (groupwork aimed at providing enabling or developmental experiences vs groupwork concerned with changing or controlling unacceptable behaviour) is applied. This reveals that in field settings, for the five kinds of groups

Table 2
Most frequently offered groups in different probation service settings

Setting	Most frequently offered groups*	
Field team *n = 589*	1. Offending behaviour	(14)
	2. Alcohol education	(14)
	3. Women's	(10)
	4. Motoring offenders	(6)
	5. Activity	(6)
Probation/day centre *n = 473*	1. Life & social skills	(20)
	2. Offending behaviour	(12)
	3. Activity	(10)
	4. Alcohol education	(8)
	5. Women's	(5)
Hostel *n = 142*	1. Residents' group	(18)
	2. Life & social skills	(17)
	3. Activity	(13)
	4. Offending behaviour	(11)
	5. Alcohol education	(6)
Prison *n = 211*	1. Alcohol education	(11)
	2. Life & social skills	(10)
	3. Temporary release	(10)
	4. Lifer support group	(10)
	5. Induction group	(9)
Other *n = 48*	1. Activity	(17)
	2. Life & social skills	(17)
	3. Alcohol education	(10)
	4. Offending behaviour	(10)
	5. Women's	(8)

n = total no. of groups run in the setting
*figures in brackets indicate prominence of group type as a % of the total no. of groups offered in that setting

mentioned, more than twice as many behaviour change programmes are mounted in comparison to enabling/ developmental type groups. But in all of the other settings the emphasis is reversed: for the five kinds of groups listed in each case, around twice as many enabling/developmental programmes (or more) are actually offered.

The explanation for this difference must, at least in part, be found in the different sorts of involvement that the non-field settings permit. In day centres, hostels, special groupwork units and (to a varying degree) prisons, contacts between officers and offenders are likely to be more immediate, more intense, more frequent and possibly more spontaneous. Under such circumstances a fuller sense of the whole person can develop and the idea of focusing on a behaviour, rather than the person and his/her broad needs can become much less tenable. The fact that life and social skills groups feature strongly in all except field settings lends weight to this view.

That said, it is noteworthy that there are more women's groups run in field teams than in all the other settings combined. This no doubt reflects the reality that more women offenders are dealt with by field-based officers, but it also shows that groupwork aimed at empowerment and support is practicable in a setting which otherwise appears to rely heavily on behaviour-focused groupwork packages.

The time dimension

Douglas (1979) has pointed out that the time dimension in groupwork is a crucial but often unconsidered one. Process is certainly, though not wholly, related to time and for this and other reasons time will have a bearing on the value of a group for its members. There is, of course, no simple way of defining the appropriate number of sessions a programme should contain and in any case this is bound to vary between members. The same is true for the frequency of sessions and their length as well. But the matter is worth considering anyway, not least because the time element is a central feature of an offender's sentence.

Analysis of the survey data shows that - while block programmes exist - virtually all of the kinds of groups listed in Table 1 were commonly offered on a weekly basis (though in the hostel and prison settings there were generally no consistent patterns). It is hard to know what to make of this 'one session a week' approach. In the field setting it no doubt helps many members to manage other aspects of their lives (e.g., child care, employment) and may thus be consciously supportive. But it inevitably facilitates surveillance over a longer period and, in that sense, is reminiscent of weekly reporting. Since there is no good reason to suppose that all of the kinds of groups listed in Table 1 are most effective when offered on a one session a week basis, questions can be raised about programme flexibility, about the value to members of a spread-out, as against a concentrated experience, and about whose needs are being served (programme organisers or members). In the answers to such questions there may be further implications concerning, for instance, the degree to which the conditions and basic understandings central to the use of a social action model of groupwork actually exist (Mullender and Ward, 1989).

From the information supplied about the usual number of sessions in a programme, some fairly clear distinctions between the groups in Table 1 can be made: offending behaviour, alcohol education, motoring offenders, temporary release, induction, drugs/addiction and control of anger and temper groups tend to include ten or fewer sessions; women's groups and sex offenders' groups generally involve many more sessions; life and social skills groups fall somewhere between these two poles and activity programmes and residents' meetings tend, not surprisingly, to be provided on a rolling, open-ended basis.

These distinctions prompt one or two speculative observations: it may be that ten or fewer group sessions can significantly affect a person's motivation to drink excessively, drive dangerously, act violently, etc, but since that evidence has yet to be adduced, there is the possibility that the existence on the shelf of certain groupwork packages, or organisational or sentencing interests are the real determining factors. The time allotted to sex offenders' groups is probably more realistic, whether seen in insight development, surveillance or behaviour change terms. With women's groups there seems to be a proper recognition that the exploration of offending activity in the context of structural oppression requires some time to address and to consolidate.

Group facilitation / joint provision with other agencies
Time is a resource whose use must be planned carefully and, of course, the same is true of staff. What the survey responses make clear is that the probation service is prepared to invest staff resources in the running of groups. Two or more facilitators were used with 87 per cent of the 1463 groups run and, within this category, paired co-leadership was the most favoured approach (67 per cent of the total). Unfortunately the survey was not designed to elicit detailed information about other aspects of group leadership - for instance, whether consultancy was provided or used, whether special consideration was given to issues of race or gender in the forming of co-working partnerships, whether group facilitation was primarily a matter of choice or expectation, whether there were special considerations in linking particular workers to particular groups (e.g., women facilitators for women's groups) - or, indeed, why co-working as opposed to single leadership was chosen in the first place. These are all points which deserve further investigation, not least because of the light this would shed on the thoroughness with which the service, and the workers themselves, attend to some of the fundamentals

of effective groupwork practice.

Information was supplied, however, on the extent to which personnel from other non-probation agencies shared or assisted in the running of groups. Overall, 23 per cent of the 1463 groups mounted were in some degree joint or cooperative ventures although there was considerable variation between settings. That is, almost half the groups run in prisons, but only about one in six of those run in field and day centre settings, were with the involvement of workers from some other agency. This is another area in which further research is warranted. From a purely practical point of view, the involvement of others with different knowledge, skills and perspectives might be thought to be wholly beneficial in terms of its consequences for group members. On the other hand, it is highly unlikely that the members themselves have any say in a matter which could also have the consequence that other agencies and individuals become privy to personal information about members which they need not, and might prefer not to disclose. In short, the extent to which shared groupwork is also ethical groupwork needs to be looked at.

The issue of joint groupwork with other agencies also touches, though somewhat tangentially, on current concerns about the possible future role of probation officers. Following the publication of a discussion paper setting out the Government's interest in encouraging independent sector involvement (*Partnership in Dealing With Offenders in the Community,* 1990c), there has been a good deal of debate about how far other agencies might be contracted in to work with offenders. This debate is conducted mainly around the issues of privatisation, the possible dilution of state provision and responsibility, and the conversion of probation officers into case managers more involved in negotiating with other agencies than with using their skills in direct work with offenders. There is an additional argument that, because they can be developed as packages, groupwork programmes will be the easiest to hive off. Some therefore will see the finding that there is already a level of sharing as the thin end of the wedge, although - in the event that the Government pursues its stated course - sharing rather than contracting out groupwork may seem to many to be a preferable option.

Gender and race considerations

Table 3 presents the findings concerning the gender and racial composition of the groups mounted. The broad context from which these data derive is one in which there has been a growing

Table 3
Group composition by gender and race

Group composition	Prominence
Women only	7
Men only	48
Mixed gender	45
Black members only	less than 1%
White members only	39
Mixed race	61

(The figures show groups of a particular composition as a % of the total no. of groups recorded in the survey)

recognition that women and black people coming into contact with the criminal justice system experience discriminatory treatment (Carlen and Worrall, 1987; Worrall, 1990; NACRO, 1986; Crow, 1987; Fletcher, 1988). This has led probation agencies to formulate and issue anti-discrimination statements and, in some cases such as the monitoring of social inquiry reports for sexist or racist assumptions, to engage in affirmative action. However statements of intent are by no means a guarantee that anti-discriminatory practice will be established, encouraged or thoroughly thought through.

When it comes to groupwork with women and with black offenders there are many important considerations but two, in particular, stand out: Does the programme address the experiences and needs of the members in a way which recognises the discriminatory pressures which they bear and which may well have played a part in their current situation? Is the membership composition of the group such as to allow these issues to be attended to? (It is known, for instance, that in mixed gender groups men tend to dominate and women to defer and/or take on a stereotypically supportive role.)

It must be said that the figures in Table 3 raise serious concern about the anti-discriminatory element of groupwork practice in the Probation Service. There are, it is true, definite indications that a number of women offenders are being offered women-only groups. And this, taken together with the material presented in Table 1, suggests that the group programme and group composition considerations mentioned just above are being attended to in some degree. Even so the figures for mixed gender groups, when reflected against the fact that there are proportionally fewer women convicted of offending, imply that many women offenders find themselves a minority in such groups. This is certainly worrying and the position for black offenders is even more so. *Only three of the 1463 groups registered in the survey were black membership only groups.* It is impossible to accept that groupwork which gives such scant attention to race as a crucial compositional factor is seriously addressing the real experiences and consequent needs of black offenders and, in light of the considerable over-representation of black offenders in the criminal justice system, this finding is painfully ironic.

None of this is to say that there are no circumstances in which mixed groups for men and women members, or black and white members, could be valuable. Nor is it to say that there are no common experiences linking men and women or black and white people who find themselves enmeshed in the criminal justice system. Finally, it is certainly not being suggested that the whole of anti-discriminatory groupwork practice is encompassed and defined by the use of women only, or black membership only groups. But the existence or non-existence of such groups conveys something important about the service's attention to anti-discriminatory practice and about its approach to offenders generally. More will be said about the latter below.

OVERVIEW AND CONCLUSION

There can be little doubt that, in today's Probation Service, groupwork has a significant presence. With the creation and eventual extension of the training centre/day centre model (see Earnshaw, this book) and with policy changes which incorporated participation in groupwork schemes into certain sentences (Criminal Justice Act 1982), this was bound to happen in some degree. But as the survey shows, groupwork is by no means confined to the probation/day centre setting and has, in fact, emerged as a vital activity across almost all settings in the service. From estimates provided by respondents to the survey questionnaire it appears that several thousands of offenders experienced membership in groups run by the Probation Service over 1989. Barr's cautious view, expressed in the conclusion of his report on groupwork in the probation service over 25 years ago, was that groupwork may have a bigger part to play in work with offenders '...or it may turn out to be of comparatively restricted value' (1966, p.74). Whether through agency directive or practitioner initiative the emphasis, most emphatically, has been on the former.

But what sort of part is groupwork playing and from what perspective is it being offered? Broadly speaking there appear to be two main kinds of groups: those concerned with the modification of offending or offence-related behaviour and those whose objectives lean more towards providing developmental or enabling experiences for the members. The fact that each occurs to roughly the same extent suggests that the notion that groupwork in the Probation Service is used essentially as a controlling device is, as yet, somewhat overstated. Of course it has to be acknowledged that for many offenders the court will expect contact to be maintained between officer and offender for surveillance (as well as other) purposes and group membership can be a way of ensuring this through required attendance. But it would seem inappropriate to identify this as the essence of the use of groupwork since a court requirement about contact will apply to whichever method officers adopt in such cases and so it is, in effect, a feature 'by definition'. It is, nonetheless, an important element affecting the process of groupwork with offenders and interestingly there are signs (in the papers by Hutchins, Ashe and Mackintosh in this book) that the principle of voluntary group membership is being recognised and - in places - put into practice. Moreover, there are indications that the level of attendance in such groups is, if anything, enhanced.

When it comes to the perspective from which groupwork is being offered, the differentiation noted above between behaviour changing and developmental/enabling groupwork begins to blur. There is a strong indication - mainly from the information on group aims - that groups in both of these categories share the same broad practice perspective. That is to say, attention is focused on the needs, experiences or behaviours of members as individuals and not on their needs, experiences or behaviours as people in, and affected by, a socio-cultural context. Clearly, women's groups are the exception to this and, in a lesser way, residents' groups as well. But together these two account for less than 10 per cent of the groupwork offered.

These indications on perspective are probably the most disquieting to emerge from the survey. They suggest that, to a very considerable extent, the service and many of its groupwork practitioners have failed to engage with the idea that the conditions of disadvantage which lie behind a good deal of offending can be as much to do with a socially created lack of power and choice as with a personal insufficiency of skills, or an inability to control or consider the consequences of one's behaviour. The wider significance of this is that it adds to a concern as to whether the service will be able to withstand the more punitive elements of government proposals for its work in the 1990s. But at the more specific level of groupwork, three things in particular are highlighted by it. First, for as long as this perspective prevails there seems little likelihood that the social action model of groupwork will receive the attention it deserves. This is disappointing because the scope for its application in all probation settings and with a wide variety of offenders is undeniable. Second, since a premise on which women's groups have been established is that the socio-cultural context does bear meaningfully on women who offend and should be a focus of attention in work with them, there must be some uncertainty as to whether the use of such groups will grow much beyond what the survey has revealed. (A paper by Mistry [1989] provides a pertinent illustration of the attitudes which can be encountered in mounting such groups.) Third, and again for as long as this perspective prevails, there seems very little chance that black offenders coming into contact with the Probation Service will be offered group conditions, and therefore groupwork programmes, in which their relevant experiences as black people can be raised, acknowledged and addressed.

It is not groupwork per se which sets these limitations. Historically speaking, the 'social goals' side of the method has as deeply rooted a foundation as the 'remedial' (though perhaps more in America than in the UK). The policy context is, of course, crucial since it creates and enforces expectations and determines the availability of resources. And yet it has to be said that the policy context is not the only influence or the sole arbiter. After all, women's groups were not the consequence of a policy directive or managerial enlightenment but of the initiatives taken by the workers who set them up. This shows that another key element in the future development of groupwork in the Probation Service will be practitioners themselves and, in particular, the extent to which their outlook can be broadened. In this respect it is as well to remember, first of all, that it is with training that much of the responsibility lies for shaping and strengthening a worker's practice ideology and, secondly, that the Home Office has recently questioned the value of links between probation and social work training. It seems there was an idea that, by doing away with or reducing the latter, there would be more likelihood of producing officers who would:

...implement programmes in the way envisaged by the courts...take full account of the need to protect the public...gear [their] work more and more towards...firm and constructive work with offenders - getting them to face up to the harm they have done and helping them reintegrate into the community... (Home Office, 1990a, p.6).

Were this to happen, groupwork in the Probation service would not disappear; it is now too well established for that to happen. But its form would narrow and the plurality of approaches needed to work in a just and productive way with offenders would not only fail to expand beyond its current, rather modest level: it might well be lost altogether.

Brian Caddick, Bristol University. This chapter is reprinted from Groupwork, *1991, 4(3)*

3

Groupwork in the Probation Service: Care or Control in the 1990s

PAUL SENIOR

INTRODUCTION

Groupwork has always struggled to be located in mainstream probation work. This has not been because of a shortage of opportunities for work in groups nor because it has lacked proponents. But the widespread use of a set of techniques and approaches which utilises the group as a medium for mutual support or for social or personal change and development has nevertheless been hard to establish. To see why, it is helpful to look at the contribution of groupwork in the context of three historical phases: pre-1972, where groupwork was clearly marginal to probation practice; 1972 to 1984, where a distinct growth of groupwork occurred; and 1985 into the 1990s, where groupwork has moved closer to centre stage but perhaps more as a means of community control. Understanding these historical phases helps to put the debate about the future role of groupwork into sharper relief but I must emphasise that I am using these phases as an heuristic device only and do not intend to imply that they are water tight compartments.

Before 1972: casework in groups and compensatory activities

Although small scale, the rise of groupwork in the wider field of social work had its adherents in the probation service. It was mainly practiced as an additional tool to individual family casework, psycho-therapeutic in theoretical commitment and at the end of the day marginal to individual practice. Both organisationally and in terms of training, groupwork posed no threat to the dominance of individual casework approaches at this time (see Barr, 1966).

Its 'add-on' nature can also be seen in the presence of groups which were primarily forms of compensatory activity for deprived and disadvantaged groups (e.g. prisoners' wives groups or outward bound activities for young adults often run by support or volunteer staff). There was little concerted effort to use these groups for anything other than mutual support, or in the vague hope of change by a process which, in another context, Collins and Behan (1981, p.89) have dismissed as stemming from:

...the view that an offender has only to be put deep into the country for him to mop up virtue by some obscure process of moral osmosis as he labours up to his ankles in manure.

The only other real evidence of groupwork at this time is that which went on as an attachment to probation under mental treatment orders (Lewis, 1980). Thus, whilst groupwork existed, it was marginal both as a method of practice and as a sentencing strategy of the courts.

1972 to 1984: voluntary or compulsory groupwork– still a social work choice

The decade between the two Criminal Justice Acts witnessed a huge spurt in groupwork activity, engendered by legislative changes and encouraged by training and the use of a new set of techniques (i.e. social skills training). One could almost sub-title this period the 'Age of Priestley and McGuire'! (1978; 1983; 1984). The Children and Young Persons Act 1969 and the 1972 and 1982 Criminal Justice Acts gave legislative weight to groupwork endeavours, particularly through intermediate treatment (Section 12, 1969 Act); and supervised activities orders (1982 Act). The development of Schedule 11 in the 1982 Act was particularly intended to sanction groupwork approaches of all kinds. This included both the development of day centres (under Schedule 11, 4b conditions) and specialist groupwork activities such as alcohol education and sex offender groups (under Schedule 11, 4a conditions).

Brown et al. (1982) noted that 'during the decade (1970-1980) groupwork has become more widely recognised as a method of social work in Britain'. But they went on to point out that this was still only haltingly reflected in social work training. Even so, the ways in which groupwork developed in the service were varied and prolific and included a wide range of targets.

The particular foci included intermediate treatment groups, induction to probation groups (Brown and Seymour, 1983) and a variety of day centre programmes (both voluntary - Burney, 1980 - and otherwise through the day training centre experiments).

Specialist endeavours also expanded, including groups for sex offenders, alcohol education, groupwork in prisons and hostel groups. Task-focused groups such as literacy, education, employment and motor projects, self-help projects (e.g. women's groups) and more idiosyncratic developments (such as drama groups) all had their adherents too.

Many of these groups were 'artificial' and time limited, created via the demands of a caseload or sentencing process and often task-centred. Willis (1986) has identified elsewhere that probation officers see problem-solving activities and practical advice as their crucial helping task and this was reflected in groupwork projects of this time. As Willis stated 'the business of probation, it appeared, was all about the provision of help'.

Thus, although the external context for the creation of these groups was the apparatus and values of the criminal justice system, the motivation of individual probation officers derived more from their beliefs about the personal and social benefits of groupwork for their clients than from any crude correctionalism. In other words, intrinsic reasons for groupwork were mixed in with extrinsic demands arising out of the court process. This duality was a constant tension for groupworkers.

One result of this duality was a certain ambivalence by managers about groupwork developments which, in allowing for the co-existence of a mixture of aims, provided space for innovation. This enabled, by default maybe, the potential for a radical practice to develop (Senior, 1985; Mullender and Ward, 1985). This radicalism did not extend to a more embracing anti-oppressive approach - a task awaiting the 1990s and discussed below.

It is this tradition of client-centred groupwork which is under threat. The application of the legislative context to practice has meant that developments have occurred not simply as a useful method of social work intervention but also as an organisational form, via court orders. In the current historical phase this duality has become increasingly significant.

The late 1980s: groupwork centre stage as a means of control?

The 1982 Act as I have suggested did give legislative support for developing groupwork but in a context which sanctioned and demanded the 'toughening' of probation orders. The use of conditional attendance for groups in the 1980s became a vigorous debate in probation circles (McLoone et al., 1987). There developed a split between practitioners over the New Right emphasis on containment as a central objective of supervision.

This highlighted the tension between form and method so that, for instance, the liberal and essentially voluntaristic approach of Priestley and McGuire was adapted to a correctional emphasis.

Drawing on the work of Denman and other juvenile justice practitioners (Denman, 1982; Thorpe et al., 1980), an offence-specific practice developed (exemplified by the title of McGuire and Priestley's new book *Offending Behaviour*, 1985). These developments were not necessarily unwelcome to those on the other side of the argument. As Carlen (1990) has noted, women in prison welcomed the chance to focus on offences rather than attempts to mould them into traditional domestic stereotypes. Nevertheless it became noticeable that there was a decreasing appreciation by practitioners of the dynamics of the groupwork process and a concentration on the task rather than the process. Put at its crudest, the groupworker had to have a stock of exercises on the shelf, get them down and do them. Time was thus occupied or, as Blagg and Smith put it, 'the correctional curriculum .... gave social workers and their clients something to do rather than something to talk about' (1989, p.111).

This approach to groupwork dovetailed with the wider world of training embodied by government training agencies such as the MSC and its successors. This produced some high quality training materials (see the *Staying Out* pack, Nottinghamshire Probation Service for instance), but unless groupworkers were skilled enough to use the group process appropriately, opportunities for personal development of clients were missed and crucial work left undone.

Whatever its merits as an approach, offence-specific groupwork emerged in the late 1980s as the new solution to offending and as a core element in a package of assistance and control. We can see it highlighted by the Audit Commission and in the curriculum of Schedule 11 programmes in probation centres and groupwork elsewhere (see Caddick, this book). Indeed the methods used with offenders in groupwork are, ironically, increasingly being adapted for individual work. This is particularly evident in juvenile justice where insufficient numbers force practitioners into individualised offending behaviour programmes. But the trend is clear. Groupwork has become characterised by compulsory attendance and defined by the tightening of controls on curricula. Increasingly the aim is to service the court's needs not those of the offenders. The question is: How will this trend move forward into the 1990s?

PROBATION OFFICERS: SOCIAL WORKER, BROKER OR SCREW?

As we analyse the major papers of the early 1990s, two main themes can be identified as reflective of the intended changes to be imposed by government, with a third largely inspired by other, grassroots sources. These are: greater accountability, changing definitions of probation practice and (some) commitment to equal opportunities. What do these themes entail for probation practice in general and groupwork in particular?

Greater accountability

Since coming to power in 1979, the government has espoused a philosophy of reducing state involvement in the public sector. Paradoxically we have actually seen increased central control by the use of measures such as forms of quality assurance, and increased financial oversight through 'value for money' exercises and cash limited budgets. The means of achieving this goal for the probation service is by possible restructuring; enhanced oversight from probation inspectors; national standards; central control of training and financial scrutiny. These contextual changes clearly have the potential to limit severely the freedom of local services and, in turn, individual groupwork practitioners.

The movement towards a version of the industrial models of 'management by objectives' has characterised the late 1980s. Starting from the *Statement of National Objectives and Priorities* in 1984 and moving on to Financial Management Initiatives, Performance Indicators and Information Systems, this trend has threatened to curtail the freedom of practitioners. With action plans (e.g. Annex A to *Punishment, Custody and the Community*, 1988) and greater scrutiny of budgets, there is an enhanced managerial role for middle managers over practice. But since the vagaries of individual casework practice are not easily measured within this approach it is not surprising that action plans and project developments, and thus service publicity, have alighted on group ventures. Groupwork programmes offer saleable commodities easy to portray for ministerial visits! As long as they are tied to the operational imperatives on managers (and there's the rub) they can be guaranteed funding and support. It seems likely that those groups which cannot demonstrate clear connections to service objectives will get squeezed even more for both funding and officer time. An example of this effect has been the fate of women-only groups, which in addition suffer the oppression of striving for existence in a male-dominated organisation. As Carlen notes, their continuance has been hampered by 'sexism, financial restrictions and the contemporary political prejudices against any purely deterrent and non-punitive work in probation' (1990, p.73). Close appraisal of practice will also come through the definition of national standards for social inquiry reports, supervision in the community, probation centres and parole. It would seem that controls on groupwork programmes via core curriculum requirements are not entirely distant possibilities.

But it is not simply via agency structure or national standards that accountability will be enforced. The Home Office has recently turned its attention to placing its own imprint on training at both qualifying and post-qualifying levels. Basic training has been critically scrutinised by the Coleman Report (1989), negatively commented upon by the Davies research (Davies, 1989), threatened by the recent Green Paper (*Supervision and Punishment in the Community*, 1990a) and circumscribed by the recent Home Office/CCETSW paper (1990). For in-service training a move from a regionally-based and locally controlled operation (via the regional staff development offices and in-service units) to control via Home Office regional coordinators and a national probation staff development unit has been recommended (Hadjipavlov et al., 1991). It can reasonably be asked: What sort of groupwork training and practice will be encouraged and sanctioned?

CHANGING DEFINITIONS OF PROBATION PRACTICE

It is regarded as quaintly traditional to hark back to the well-established objectives of probation supervision to 'advise, assist and befriend'. An increasing criminal justice emphasis in government papers has reworked those objectives into diversion from custody, preventing re-offending, reparation to victims and reintegration into the community. These goals will, it is argued, help achieve the transcendent, if elusive, goal of reducing the prison population. This will not apparently be achieved by any increase in supportive client-centred groupwork. Instead practice will have to orient itself towards these new objectives, which means, (as I suggested earlier), that 'confronting offending behaviour' will become the key focus for work. (The aggressive macho language seems to reflect neatly this new era!).

In my brief review of the history of groupwork above, I alluded to this development in the 1980s, although it was less trenchantly expressed and indeed came largely from within the social work profession and the juvenile justice field in particular. But the vogue words 'confronting offending behaviour' are now centre stage. Consider for instance the terms set for the 1988 action plans arising from the Home Office initiative *Tackling Offending:*

> Programmes should always focus on working with offenders to *confront their offending* and to examine, with them, the circumstances of their offending and the effects on their victims... this might be pursued [through] a) *'Offending Behaviour'* groups... and b) Groups on self-control, social skills, alcohol education... (Home Office, 1988, author's italics).

It is this conflation of form and method which particularly characterises the direction in the papers. The growth of monitoring functions through new orders, packages, and temporary release programmes means the nature of the engagement with clients is predetermined by statutory contact through courts or prisons. This aspect will be further affected by the introduction of national standards and such mechanisms for eligibility as Risk of Custody Scales in determining client access. Thus the boundaries of groupwork are set by surveillance needs not client needs.

The Home Office paper *Partnership in Dealing with Offenders in the Community* (1990b) also envisages changes for the role of the probation officer from social worker to broker, with time increasingly being spent as a resource manager negotiating packages with the 'independent sector'. The spectre of privatisation looms and the control over the conduct and content of groupwork programmes could be transferred to other agencies. A key question will be: Who does the groupwork?' It has been suggested that these moves are designed to coerce the Probation Service into the delivery of tougher alternatives to custody (Ryan and Ward, 1990). If the service fails to deliver, the 'independent sector' will step in.

If this approach gains ground then the focus of groupwork could shift quite dramatically as the test of the effectiveness of the Action Plan has suggested. This test is: diversion from custody; reduction in reoffending; cost-effectiveness; participation of ethnic minority and female offenders. Its concern with quantifiable goals rather than quality may lead to increased participation of ethnic minority and female offenders without corresponding attempts to understand their needs. Thus it does not contain any goals which are more recognisably to do with problem-solving, social work or social action.

EQUAL OPPORTUNITIES

Though 'equal opportunities', as a policy, is supported by the Home Office, in the Service, through NAPO and by individual practitioners, its meaning and intention varies greatly among these groups and rarely tends to be as radical as the terms anti-racist, anti-sexist or anti-oppressive imply. Still, it is round the issues of race and gender that the most thinking and some action has occurred. Race issues have tended to lead services into equal opportunity policies and training but the impact on service delivery is as yet unclear. The main focus at a national level has been on race issues, although even this is rather a muted theme in the Government papers. (It is notable, for instance, that the Home Office has insisted on a race policy statement from all services but has left the initiative mainly to local discretion).

Recruitment is a central issue if services are to progress towards a multi-racial service. For instance intermediate treatment has always been dominated by white men as have activity programmes for young adults. This can mean at a service delivery level that the kind of activities which are given prominence in groups also reflects a male-dominated, able-bodied and white ethos. This in turn will lead to low take-up of groups by black people and women.

One strategy used by women probation officers has been to develop women-only groups (Mistry, 1989). Pat Carlen discusses the development of women-only groups and the usefulness of their existence. But she rightly cautions optimism by outlining four major sources of threat to their continuance. Those include:

...familial ideologies that still propagate the notion that a woman's place is in the home; male chauvinism within probation together with a prejudice against groupwork in general; current government policies on criminal justice that are inclined more towards punishment than towards the rehabilitation of offenders and the prevention of crime; and contemporary conservative ideologies that favour individualistic rather than collectivist responses to social problems... (Carlen, 1990, pp.85-86).

Carlen does nevertheless document some considerable activity in this area which is not replicated in the case of black-only groups, a rare phenomenon, nor is there evidence that groups are run which give central attention to the differential needs of white and black offenders. With little staff support and institutionalised racism, the opportunities for black offenders to get an equitable and relevant service appears a long way off (see Caddick, this book).

There remains a clear need for training which can help staff identify shortcomings in current groupwork practice and work towards forms of groupwork which respond to the real needs of disadvantaged groups. Issues of race and gender need much attention but so, too, do key areas of discrimination such as age, disability and the concerns of gay men and lesbians. There are, however, some positive signs. For instance, groupwork programmes focusing on motor car thefts and handling aggression have developed which begin seriously to challenge the sexist stereotypes of the attenders. Hopefully, social work training will ensure such issues are given greater centrality although this could be limited if probation officers become the brokers and the face-to-face work transfers to those not given the opportunity of such training.

A committed approach to anti-oppressive matters will have profound implications for groupwork practice. This is an important exercise in its own right and needs to be developed more thoroughly by all groupworkers. It must include staffing issues; co-working; challenging discriminatory behaviour as part of group norms and rules; incorporating race and gender awareness into programmes; more focused groups - e.g. women's groups, black groups and so on.

CONCLUDING THOUGHTS

I: the dangers for the 1990s

I have suggested that groupwork has simultaneously expanded both as a method of social work practice and as an organisational form for the delivery of non-custodial options. There remain opportunities for innovative practice but they are limited by the context I have tried to describe. Before referring briefly to those positive options I want to reiterate some of the implications for groupwork of current governmental policies:

1. The current vogue is for narrow operational and measurable goals, what McWilliams (1990) terms 'instrumental' rather than 'expressive' goals. This is bound to act as a curb on creative practice and breed a uniformity of provision.
2. The lack of attention given to equal opportunities, coupled with the faulty notion that it is about sameness rather than fairness, means that it will continue to be hard to justify groups where empowerment or social action are principal aims.

3. Groups which are tied closely with the wishes of the sentencers and the requirements of the new Criminal Justice Act will inevitably push the service to embody the concerns of routine oversight rather than the merits of social work intervention. This desire for net strengthening increasingly drives the form of the group - high time commitments; strict enforcement of rules; increased use of breach; programmes driven by staff not attenders; core curricula - as it is perceived by policy makers as the necessary accompaniment to diversion from custody.
4. As probation officers take on the role of brokers rather than service providers, the standard and the form of groupwork provision, and the nature of the commitment to it, may change.
5. To the extent that training - basic, post-qualifying and in-service - is altered to reflect uncritically Home Office interests, there must be doubt that groupwork in the service will be able to sustain or re-establish a prior tradition of creativity and innovation.

II: the potential for innovation and change

Despite the pessimistic outlook of the previous section the potential for broad policy initiatives to be diluted - even subverted - at a grassroots level remains. It is in this policy space that workers can continue to innovate and maintain some of the liberating benefits of groupwork, ideas that I have developed elsewhere (Senior, 1985). There is no doubt that an ability to resist management directives is getting harder but, even within Schedule 11 groups for instance, there is still the freedom to plan curricula. In my experience programmes continue to exhibit much variation. Even in intensive probation programmes, the embodiment of the *Punishment in the Community* ethos, enormous variety in the programme content is becoming evident (Mair, 1991).

Groupwork has the potential to allow groups of normally disenfranchised offenders to find a voice and sometimes collectively redefine their problems as shared political experiences. We can empower our clients through such groupwork and avoid the individualising and pathologising evidenced in traditional groups. Maintaining a focus on structural issues and social goals as an aim of groupwork is thus vital. This can be assisted by giving central attention to anti-oppressive approaches to practice both in terms of programme content and by effective and open co-working partnerships between men and women and black and white workers. In fact, the organisation takes a risk in promoting equal opportunities because it creates a space where more radical actions can be attempted. This space must be used.

Although research has an uncertain influence on practice we also need to know more about what it can tell us about the apparent success of 'offending behaviour groups'. Policy-oriented groupwork demands evaluation which takes as its starting point the needs and concerns of the recipients and how far these are successfully addressed. This can be small scale and practitioner initiated.

It is ironic and disappointing that after struggling to get accepted as a viable method, groupwork now runs the risk of being highjacked for different goals. I have tried to set out the dangers and indicate the ways by which they might be resisted. Ultimately it is the action of practitioners in maintaining and developing innovative practice around the policy spaces which needs to be encouraged if further intrusions into groupwork structure and method are to be resisted.

Paul Senior, Senior Probation Officer, Nottinghamshire Probation Service/Lecturer, Nottingham Trent Polytechnic. This chapter is reprinted from Groupwork, *1991, 4(3)*

Part Two

Groups in Prisons, Hostels and Probation Centres

4

Meeting Prisoners' Needs Through Groupwork

MIKE ASHE

CONTEXT AND BACKGROUND

HMP Lindholme is a prison which has a CNA (Certified Normal Accommodation) of 800 adult male convicted prisoners who are deemed suitable for category C conditions because of their low security risk. The prison has inmates from across the north region, and the population includes about 60 life sentence men, 20 of whom are in a category D annexe and aiming at release targets in the near future.

The prison population changes at the rate of about 30 each week. Within this context the prison managers have tried to develop a number of services for meeting the throughcare needs of inmates, one part of which is the provision of problem-focused groups.

In many prisons the welfare of inmates is largely a matter for wing-based probation officers and inmates gain access to the services they provide by putting in a welfare application which a probation officer then processes. The inmate quite often has very few other ways of resolving an identified need except through the applications system.

For both parties to the transaction this is not a very effective means of meeting inmates' needs. The probation officer is servicing a demand-led system (often led by the most demanding!) and the inmate has to learn to process all sorts of different needs through a unilinear and personality-dependent system. Whilst the probation officers are caught up in this welfare cycle (i.e. the better they are at dealing with applications the more they'll attract), they have no time left to do anything else. Inmates become dissatisfied with the lack of flexibility in such a system and probation officers operating as endless duty officers become demoralised. The other significant group in the welfare equation - prison officers - feels separated from the need to care for inmates (the probation 'do-gooders' do that for them) and concentrates on security and control; or, if the prison officer does care and has a relationship with an inmate, the probation officer takes away from that prison officer any opportunity to work with the inmate on the resolution of throughcare needs. Whatever the analysis, the result is a dysfunctional total institution with a lot of interdepartmental stresses.

A THROUGHCARE PROGRAMME

A throughcare programme shifts the emphasis completely. It does away with the notion of a unilinear, demand-led welfare system and replaces it with a needs-orientated, multi-linear system of throughcare services. To go needs-orientated a prison has to ask inmates directly what their needs are. At HMP Lindholme this was accomplished by means of a needs-profile questionnaire. The responses to the questionnaire revealed a range of needs which could roughly be divided into three types:

1. day-to-day needs created by imprisonment (e.g. maintaining contact with home, anxieties about a missed visit, no letter, etc.);
2. release and resettlement needs;
3. lifestyle and offending behaviour concerns (e.g. anger control, drug/alcohol misuse, etc.).

With these needs identified, the prison managers were in a better position to organise their throughcare resources to meet as wide a range of needs as possible. In practice this has meant that, since part of the prison officer staffing complement exists to deliver throughcare services, prison officers on the wings have taken over the welfare applications system (still necessary to resolve day-to-day problems) and probation officers have been redeployed to meet lifestyle and offending behaviour concerns as well as release and resettlement needs. Whilst day-to-day needs are often highly idiosyncratic, needs and concerns at the other end of the continuum are often more amenable to a groupwork approach, partly because groups can focus in on a specific theme but also because more inmates can have access to the service than can be dealt with by an individual applications system. Furthermore, far more control over the content and evaluation of the service is possible when it is provided in a groupwork format.

For these very sensible reasons they, the managers in the prison, opted to re-align radically their throughcare resources (mainly staff) in order to provide a wider range of services, including a number of groups.

THE PRINCIPLES OF GROUPWORK IN THE PRISON

Inmates

The groups which are available to inmates are based on needs revealed by the needs profile questionnaire. Inmates can choose to access all, some or none of these groups during the course of their sentence. Indeed, the principle of voluntarism extends into the groups to the extent that if the group turns out not to be what the inmate expected, he can leave and return to his workplace.

The groupwork modules are also designed to express anti-discriminatory principles, and staff and inmates are made aware that any racist, sexist or disablist remarks will be challenged. Positive action is taken whenever possible to include in groups inmates who are black, and two groups are run specifically for black members only, in an attempt to attend to the disadvantage of their being proportionately over-represented in the inmate population whilst simultaneously under-represented in the prison's staff groups.

Staff

The probation team's policy for staffing the groups has four main principles:

1. each group will have two group leaders;
2. staff will be trained in groupwork;
3. staffing groups will take precedence over other services;
4. all staff, during the course of their secondments, will have worked on each type of group offered.

The groups

The groups which have been set up to meet inmates' expressed needs number some eight different programmes and include: pre-release groups, induction, employment briefing, families group, drugs support, lifer support, alcohol education and parole information groups. The range of needs which can be met by groupwork is very wide indeed. In fact, the restrictions on the number of groups which the prison can provide are dictated more by factors such as staffing, and competing demands on inmates' time, than by a limited range of needs. Some subjects, of course, have a wider appeal than others.

For example, handling stress, anxiety and depression is highly scored as an issue while 'getting on with other inmates' is scored low. Both are amenable to a groupwork approach, although in practice, the first might run much more frequently than the other and the second would require a more subtle approach to recruitment. In this paper there is not sufficient space to deal with all the prison's groups in detail. Instead two suitably contrasting groups have been chosen for a more detailed description to afford some insight into how the groupwork element of the throughcare programme operates. The first of these - the Parole Information Group - is a straightforward information-giving group, while the second - The Families and Imprisonment Group - is concerned with the effects of imprisonment on family dynamics.

PAROLE INFORMATION GROUP

The Parole Information Group is a good example of how a groupwork approach to meeting a need is far more effective than a more traditional one-to-one approach.

When the prison first opened, inmates' parole applications were processed by the collection of reports to create a dossier for the Parole Review Committee to use when deciding whether to release an inmate on licence. Each staff member involved in report preparation found herself or himself having to spend some of the interview time explaining the parole process to the inmate. From the probation perspective it became obvious not only that precious interview time was being lost, but that it was impossible to control the quality of information each officer gave to inmates as this would depend on experience, training and the circumstances of the interview. Because most parole-eligible inmates identified a concern over parole in the needs profile, it was obvious that an information group would probably attract high take up. Also, by giving information about parole in a group setting, the probation teams gained control over the quality of the information given. The Parole Information Group was initially established by two probation officers who fully researched the facts about how the parole system works (visits to the Parole Board, Parole Unit, etc.) and then drew up the timetable for a one day group. This included some initial group formation exercises (names, outline of purpose of the day), plenty of structured space for 'burning questions' to be asked, brainstorms around elements of the review process and the persons involved, and the provision of detailed information about what is being looked for by members of the local review committee and the parole board, reasons for the refusal of parole, time-scales, etc. Evaluation was also built in.

With the information base and timetable of the group established, the next step in the logistics of running the group was to design a recruitment system. This was arranged through negotiation with the Discipline Office (which amongst other tasks issues parole applications to inmates) which agreed to attach a Parole Information Group application form to each parole form. A system was set up to collect and collate applications. A groupwork room was negotiated and booked on a regular basis (weekly) to meet demand, invitations distributed and then the groups were begun.

Inmate self-evaluation forms were designed to assess consumer response to the group, and details of attendance were collected on a regular basis to assess levels of uptake of the service. These statistics revealed a 70-80 per cent uptake and a 90 per cent satisfaction rating for those who attend the groups.

Certain features of the Parole Information Group are worth noting. Because of its information orientation the group does not require the disclosure of sensitive personal details in order to make it a success. There is also only a small mutual support element. This allows the group size to expand to meet what can be quite high weekly demands (sometimes up to 18). For other staff involved in parole interviews (Local Review Committee members, prison officers, governors, etc.) the advantages of the group are that inmates are well informed of the parole process and time for interviews can concentrate on the report rather than the process. Inmates meanwhile acquire information which helps them to make the best possible use of their part of the process (their own written representations and the interviews with report writers).

FAMILIES GROUP

The needs profile also revealed that many inmates are concerned about the effects imprisonment will have on their relationships with partners and children. The Probation Team designed a group to allow inmates the opportunity to support one another in examining how they would set about coping with the stress visited upon their families by their being inside. As the effectiveness of the group relies heavily on mutual support and trust elements, group members have to be confident to disclose sensitive information; consequently there has to be time for the group to form and the space has to be protected and confidentiality guaranteed. Prior interviewing of potential group members - in order to clarify their expectations - and limiting the size of the group to eight, are both part of the way in which this is achieved. The timetable is also far more personalised than is the case with the information-orientated Parole Group (see Figure 1).

Figure 1
The families and imprisonment group programme

* Introduction and warm-up exercise
* 'Me as I am' - inmate looks at himself and how he behaves inside as opposed to on the outside.
* Name game - to help group get to know one another.
* 'Who does what?' - looking at roles and responsibilities in the family and how these are altered by a prison sentence which removes a family member.
* 'Not in front of the children' - action maze in which inmates have to decide how to handle difficult issues relating to imprisonment of parent and subsequent dealing with children.
* 'Emotional wares' exercise to look at power of feelings distorted by imprisonment.
* Role play - of scenario from family life and prison created by group members.
* Problem solving exercises.
* 'They just don't think, do they' - video about prisoners' wives.
* What can you do? - session devoted to planning for the future.

Because of the subject matter involved, the Families Group has a far lower take up than the Parole Group (despite a high needs profile rating). Also because there is a small group size, and because the group runs over more than one day (in this case three days) it is subject to the exigencies of prison life and on occasions has not only been severely depleted but has also failed to run entirely. What the probation team has learnt from this is that getting the logistics of service delivery right are just as important as getting the content of the groupwork right!

CONCLUSION

Establishing a comprehensive groupwork service in prison is not easy. As just mentioned, there are inevitably logistical problems to overcome as well as the intangible culture of the Prison Service - which does not expect too much in the way of inmate groups - to deal with. But with the commitment of prison managers and the willingness of different staff groups to look at ways of developing an effective throughcare system, the conditions for groupwork can be found. More crucial, however, is a commitment and a willingness to find out from the inmates what their needs are and to endeavour to provide services which address these needs. Setting aside the induction group, which all prisoners entering Lindholme are required to attend, some 1500 inmates took up voluntary membership in the groups offered by the prison probation team in 1989, and also in 1990. While it is true that for many inmates the experience of custody is so demoralising and depressing that almost any group experience would do simply as a diversion from the routine, we believe that these figures reflect real need and are a measure of how valuable the groupwork element of the throughcare programme is to the inmates.

Mike Aske, Senior Probation Officer, West Yorkshire Probation Service.
This chapter is reprinted from Groupwork, *1991, 4(3)*

5

'Doing Something With Our Lives When We're Inside' Self-Directive Groupwork in a Youth Custody Centre

BILL BADHAM, BOB BLATCHFORD, STEPH MCARTNEY AND MALCOLM NICHOLAS.

BACKGROUND.

A number of factors lay behind the initiative to start groupwork with young men at Lowdham Grange Youth Custody Centre (as from October 1988 called Young Offender Institution). First, a voluntary sector youth project (Nottingham Youth Action) and two probation teams in Nottinghamshire had successfully undertaken groupwork in institutions for young men during the previous three to four years. Second, there was interest among a number of Probation teams in the city in developing the style of working adopted in these projects, to include all young men at Lowdham Grange who were from Nottingham.

Third, the senior probation officer (SPO) at Lowdham Grange was keen to improve probation worker contact. He told us that there were 22 probation officers involved with 27 young men from Nottingham, and that the service offered was variable and inconsistent, and that probation was often perceived as irrelevant or unhelpful by many of them.

Finally, statistics, published in June 1986, indicated that ten per cent of the probation service workload involved people in youth custody.

Prompted by these factors, an open meeting was called in February 1987. It was agreed there was a need for a better service to young prisoners, and one which they would see as useful and relevant. Groupwork could complement existing contact if it challenged the personal pathology emphasis of traditional casework by addressing the individual within the wider context of social and economic difficulties.

AIMS OF THE PROPOSED GROUPWORK.

Arising from the planning meeting, and informed by the previous groupwork experiences the worker team agreed a framework. A positive view of young people which recognised their understanding, ability and skill was seen as essential. In this context, they should be encouraged to define their own issues and take action on them. The workers' stand-point was that difficulties the young prisoners faced were not necessarily the result of 'personal inadequacies'. Social and economic factors, racism and sexism are major forces contributing to young people's problems. Practice should reflect this understanding.

Aims identified included:

1. to work with young people at Lowdham Grange on their concerns and issues in a group setting;
2. to be relevant, accessible, and consistent;
3. to develop critical awareness, challenge attitudes and help effect change, including developing anti-sexist and anti-racist practice;
4. to question the quality of current probation provision, and to propose improvement;
5. to include other agencies in the project, given that young people's concerns are not the monopoly of the probation service.

THE GROUPWORK APPROACH.

The way of working with the young men, arising from the above, was to be as follows:

1. to work with them in a group setting at their own pace, on the issues they identified as important to them;
2. to work in partnership with them, rather than being seen as 'experts' or 'provider' and doing things for/to them;
3. to draw on their experience and knowledge;
4. to encourage responsibility among them for actions and decisions taken, and to ensure that attendance was voluntary;
5. to develop anti-racist and anti-sexist practice, and to challenge racism and sexism among the worker team, the

group members and the agencies involved;
6. to reflect critically on the work being done, through regular planning sessions and occasional review meetings.

Starting the groupwork

The SPO arranged access to Lowdham Grange for the worker team, and probation management approved the work. The frequency of meetings and the style of groupwork were negotiated with the young men, and explained to prison staff. The first open meeting took place in October 1987, after eight months of planning.

All those from Nottingham at Lowdham Grange were invited by prior letter and a visit to the four separate 'houses' in the institution. This open access to the group allowed for renewing the links and contacts, in contrast to the usual strict segregation. Between 30 and 40 people came. There were six groupworkers, all white and from probation - two women and four men.

The worker team was explicit about certain constraints. For example, fortnightly meetings were agreed, though initially the young men wanted them to be weekly. Further, the worker group could not, except in emergencies, offer to follow up individual requests for help which would overlap with the field probation officer's role. However, individuals were encouraged to channel criticisms through the SPO. Given the principle of the participants working on their own concerns, the worker team established that it would not become the arbiter in disputes, or controller of resources. Thus, any complaints were fed back to the group as their issues, with which the worker team would offer support, but not take over.

It was established that racism and sexism were contrary to the way of working, and could not be allowed, even if the worker team sometimes felt it awkward of difficult to challenge such attitudes. The worker group resisted expectations of 'leadership', aware that their approach contrasted with the hierarchical structures of the institution. Emphasis was on the young men establishing their own agenda, with the team resourcing the work on the issues that resulted. This involved working together in small groups to arrive at some consensus, implying co-operation rather than competition. They adapted quickly, but were not always able to shed the habit of calling the workers 'Sir' and

'Miss'. Although sharing a common experience, the young men were not a natural group. Aged between 15 and 21, they were doing different terms of imprisonment and had different levels of confidence and expectations. This variation, combined with the turnover in the group, meant that momentum was sometimes slow. Yet it was recognised that the pace must always be dictated by the participants themselves.

How the process worked.
At the first meeting the young men identified important issues that they wanted to cover, and these were recorded on flip charts. Then a timetable for future meetings and topics was agreed. Being over 31 in number, they decided small groups would allow for greater confidence and sharing. They also decided outside speakers would be of use on occasions, but in order to share information rather than to deliver a lecture.

Through planning between sessions, the workers developed a framework for each meeting to help look at the area of concern identified. This was first checked with the participants and changed as necessary.

At the beginning, views about the reactions of prison staff and others within the institution were aired, so that ways of dealing with possible difficulties could be worked out (Occasionally, this led to meetings of the worker group and prison staff to overcome what were termed 'organisational difficulties'.) At the end of each session space was always given to allow individuals to seek support and advice from each other the and workers.

Some of the issues discussed.
At the young peoples suggestion, the third meeting included an outside speaker on welfare rights. The structure of this session set a precedent for the future. Questions to be put to the speaker were worked out in small groups before her arrival. In this way, group members kept a high investment in listening to what she had to say. Time was allowed after she left to check out how the session had gone and to plan for the next one.

Other issues looked at over the following months included housing, parole, legal rights and temporary release from Lowdham Grange. The sessions were dealt with similarly, using outside speakers. At a later stage the group returned to focus again on the areas of parole, housing and the benefit changes of April 1988. They worked out both what information they needed and how they thought this information could best be presented. Taking this forward, it was agreed to publish three booklets. Over the summer of 1988, the probation department's information officer and a Nottingham cartoonist (BRICK) helped some of the group to identify and undertake various tasks relating to the production of the booklets. These included editing the information, preparing illustrations and designing front covers. Through the young peoples involvement, it was hoped to increase the likelihood that the finished booklets would be in a style that would appeal and be read.

Though the young men tended to focus on worries that they had relating to their release, they also looked at concerns within the institution. While wanting to avoid workers in the group acting as an alternative complaints procedure, an assistant governor saw the value of this forum raising points to do with the functioning of the regime. The principal governor attended one meeting to talk with them directly and answer their questions. This they valued, though they questioned whether any concrete action would follow.

Issues of sexism and racism were often raised in group meetings as relevant to specific areas of discussion. For example, had the young men considered the effects on their female partners of their being in prison, and how did their attitude towards them affect their conduct when in the community? In what ways did the parole process discriminate against black people?

With the involvement of black workers from Spring 1988, the worker team was strengthened in its ability to offer support to black people in the group and ensure the maintaining of a black perspective. The group decided it wanted to look more closely at racism over three or four sessions. There was frank exchange and much honesty, with white people thinking through the effects of language and white education structures upon their own attitudes and outlook towards black people. Black members were prepared to share their own experience within this supportive context. All the group were concerned as to how to take this issue forward within an institution where a governor spoke of a few officers having an 'attitude problem', rather than acknowledging the existence of racism.

EVALUATION AND IMPLICATIONS

Reviewing the work with the young people.

Each session was reviewed at the end to ensure the group was running in a way that the members found most useful. At intervals of three months, a whole meeting was used to asses together the relevance of what was covered and how it had been covered. This was done in a variety of ways. For example, questionnaires were used. Twenty six young men were present, and all except one took completion of the questionnaire seriously. Comments were generally very positive. What almost all of them wanted from the group was information, advice and 'help'. They enjoyed the relaxed atmosphere where they were 'being listened to ', and responded to. The small groups were seen as a good way of sharing and gaining information. Comments about the role of the workers was favourable. They enjoyed 'being together as a group'. Continuing contact with their home probation officer was wanted, though some replies showed that they did not know who he or she was.

Review sessions also allowed workers to assess and feed back their impressions. These were generally very favourable, the manner of work was found stimulating, the motivation of the group members encouraging and the team work supportive. However, the work was acknowledged to be demanding, requiring a considerable degree of commitment to thorough preparation, and consistent practice, and some stubbornness in the face of occasional prison and probation intransigence.

At one review, the sexism experienced by women workers was confronted. The summing up of bad points about the group allowed the workers to be frank about the embarrassment and anger caused by certain looks and remarks, some most unpleasant. Quite a number of the young men approached the women workers later to apologise. They quickly entered into the discussion about sexism and showed sympathy and understanding for the difficult position of women working in an all male institution. This highlighted their willingness to listen and to enter whole-heartedly into what was being discussed.

A criticism voiced by some of the group members was that not all were prepared to get involved and contribute fully: small groups could be dominated by individuals, though this was seen as rare. There was criticism of the organisation of refreshments, which at one time became rather chaotic. The group wanted the workers to lay down laws and take control. Instead, they were asked to look at the issue themselves and work out their own agreed system. This was done by first brain-storming the question 'what is the current problem with refreshments?' In small groups they examined why the problems existed and how they could be resolved. Their findings were written on flip charts and the results drawn together in the large group to form the basis of a new system. There were no problems subsequently, and everyone stuck to the rules that they had made themselves.

Reviewing the work within the agencies.

There were four open review meetings, involving the groupworkers and other interested practitioners and management from Lowdham Grange, Nottingham Probation and more recently the Youth Service. It was through external publicity that Team Resources for Youth (a black youth work project with the Youth Service) became involved. These meetings, the circulation of the minutes, writing up the work, and going to probation field teams, were the means to encourage wider discussion of the issues raised by the groupwork practice, to ensure the group would continue through recruitment of new workers, and to avoid its isolation from mainstream probation and youth work.

These measures have had some success. For example, the inter-agency and anti-racist practices were developed through the partnership with Team Resources for Youth. Extending the worker team in this way helped to bring important different perspectives on issues raised and tackled.

It also allowed access to a local prison for a youth organisation that already had contact with some of the young men there. To enable the planning and preparation, an ex-groupworker agreed to act as consultant. Another undertook a development role, with the aim of promoting the work within the departments. However, these successful developments were somewhat undermined by the reluctance of some probation teams in Nottingham to look at the issues raised by the groupwork practice. Further, probation management seemed remote to the groupworkers, and more content to criticise from the sidelines than lend positive support. For example, when information was requested, and therefore sent, it was not acknowledged, or acted upon. This ambivalence raised questions about probation management's commitment to the inter-agency aspect and the development of anti-racist practice within the project. Team Resources for Youth and its management within the Youth Service were increasingly concerned that it was being 'used' by probation as a black resource to compensate for the lack of black probation workers, and the lack of a positive recruitment drive to appoint them.

For the probation field teams fully involved (about half of those in the city), the groupwork was seen to complement individual probation contact with individual young offenders at Lowdham Grange. Statutory responsibilities for throughcare were seen as needing both components. Yet, probation management spoke of duplication and questioned the use of resources (six workers for 30 young men). In turn, this undermined the position with prison staff. When there were significantly fewer young men at Lowdham Grange, there was pressure to fulfil workshop production quotas. Prison management then told probation what its job was: 'Your group still represents work in essence extra to the statutory probation links'. Probation management, without consulting Team Resources for Youth, commended and supported this view. The group was closed, though a stay of execution was granted for a fortnight on realising members of the Parole Board from London were due to attend the next session. After 18 months of fortnightly contact, the groupwork ended in January 1989, with little opposition from probation management, but much anxiety and regret from the young men.

Conclusion and way forward.

After 18 months of groupwork, it seemed that the initial aims, as set out in the beginning of this article, were being achieved. The response of the young men was encouraging. They showed great commitment in identifying their concerns, looking at why these existed, and how action could be taken. The worker team gained experience and developed a coherent practice, incorporating an inter-agency and anti-racist perspective. The groupwork revealed wide discrepancies amongst probation officers in the standard of their practice. It suggested self-directive groupwork should form a greater part of throughcare policy. It seemed to offer a model for Nottinghamshire and other probation departments to increase the quality and quantity of contact with young offenders making effective use of resources. It highlighted the need of all probation workers not to let prisoners out of sight be also out of mind. It underlined the need to be conscious of, and involved in, the broader concerns that go beyond individualised problems.

It is hoped the closure of the groupwork initiative is only

temporary. There is significant support from the Youth Service and Team Resources for Youth, as well as from many field probation workers and their seniors, for establishing self-directive groupwork as a central component of contact with prisoners. Many issues remain undecided. How would such a model transfer to prisoners on release? Should it not apply to other institutions? If so, how should this be resourced? What encouragement will be given to the active seeking of partnership between probation and local youth workers? Can such creative practice exist under the shadow of further punitive criminal justice legislation, threatening electronic surveillance, tagging and tracking of offenders. Whatever the unresolved issues, it is hoped that this inter-agency model of self-directive groupwork with prisoners will influence future policy and practice. The groupwork at Lowdham had demonstrated the group members' commitment and enthusiasm to this way of working. They showed the ability to take responsibility and control of their own group, to set their own limits and rules, to identify their concerns and work constructively at resolving them.

One young man said on leaving the group that it had helped 'us to be able to talk about ourselves as individuals; it made you feel as though you can do something with your life while you are inside'.

Acknowledgement
This article was informed by all the worker team, in consultation with the young men from Nottingham involved in the groupwork at Lowdham Grange Youth Custody Centre.

Bill Badham, Bob Blatchford, Steph Mcartney and Malcolm Nicholas, Nottingham Probation Service. This chpater is reprinted from Groupwork, *1989, 2(1)*

6

Inside Groupwork

KEN FISHER AND LIZ WATKINS

INTRODUCTION

Within the developing emphasis on challenging offending behaviour, the probation officers in the Main Prison probation team at HMP Wandsworth chose to allocate professional resources to a groupwork programme. The aim was to examine how prisoners got into trouble in the past with the intention of helping them identify when and where they might be at the greatest risk of reoffending, and how they could avoid such situations in the future. A further aim was to help them translate good intentions to stay out of trouble into concrete step-by-step plans for release.

In the majority of cases, particularly in a dispersal prison such as Wandsworth, probation officers do not have the resources or the time to develop casework relationships with all inmates. The reality is that many prisoners enter and leave this and other prisons without having had any contact with the Probation Department. Very few have had their offending behaviour challenged.

Simple observation of prison and prison life demonstrates the significance of peer group influence. Many commentators have chosen to use the term 'universities or schools for crime'. It would appear that within the prison culture criminal values and beliefs can be constructed and reinforced. It therefore seemed appropriate to use a peer group setting to explore and challenge some of the lessons being learnt.

Prompted by a Prison Inspector's internal report regarding the discharge and through-care of prisoners, a decision was made to target those prisoners who were within two months of their release. A further decision was made to direct efforts towards those prisoners who were due to be discharged on their EDR (earliest date of release), having either served a relatively short sentence or been considered unsuitable for release on parole. Our assumption was that this particular group was unlikely either to have established or maintained contacts with field work probation services and would have lengthy criminal records, including previous custodial sentences. As such, this group appeared to be at a high risk of reoffending and worthy of input by the probation service at the crucial point of release.

CREATING A PRODUCTIVE GROUP

Membership of the group was offered by letter to all those who were to be discharged from the prison on an EDR within the following six weeks. The letter made it clear that those attending had to be prepared to look at their offending behaviour. Resources did not permit an interview to be conducted with prisoners prior to their joining the group. This resulted in some members joining the group with a clear lack of motivation to change and on two occasions the leaders chose to exclude or have separate interviews with such members to resolve this difficulty and to reduce the discouraging influence on other group members.

Our choice of an open rather than a closed group was based upon a desire to offer the opportunity to as many men as possible and to lessen the consequences for the group if a member was re-allocated to another prison having just started the group. Although this was less likely to happen at this stage in their sentence it did happen from time to time and the open group structure enabled us to offer a place to another man with minimum disruption to the group.

We were concerned however that the open group structure and the short length of the group (four sessions in all) might militate against the development of trust between members. We therefore chose to aid the process of group formation by creating a degree of stability and a type of hierarchy within the membership. This had two main purposes: firstly to speed up the process of formation; secondly to reduce the time spent on the competition for leadership roles.

From the start we established a pattern whereby each week two members would leave the group (coinciding with their discharge from prison) and two or sometimes three would join it. This resulted in a weekly core membership, which assisted the group facilitators in the maintenance of the culture. Further, after ground rules concerning confidentiality and respect for other members' views had been negotiated with the group, these became the property of the group and entrusted to those members who had been in the group the longest. In effect they adopted the role of 'elders'. (As an exercise in itself, becoming an elder also provided the individual with the opportunity to have and hold responsibility and to gain confidence and self worth.)

We ended each group by focusing on those members who were leaving that week. The group considered the individual's release plans and offered constructive comments which, although candid, were nevertheless supportive. This meant that no matter at which point they had entered the programme, each member could be sure of some time in which to review their personal release plans with the group when release was imminent.

It was difficult to get the balance right and some members clearly felt a little intimidated by having the spotlight upon them; however others valued the encouragement. Plans which did not seem to be realistic were given the most criticism - in particular, where those previously addicted to drink or drugs were going out without any backup or professional help. Such challenges appeared to have more value coming from those who had similar experiences in the past than from us, the co-leaders.

On the whole, we found that the group culture did prevail and was warm and supportive. The weekly choice of the person whose turn it was to introduce the aims and the rules to newcomers was an important part of the group process, and most of those who took on the role showed an impressive grasp of and commitment to the ideals of the group.

THE PROCESS OF CHANGE AND THE PROGRAMME ITSELF

We devised a programme containing four sessions, each of which had a separate focus and was an entity in itself. Members could join this rolling programme at any point yet still find the content relevant. Each member had the opportunity to attend all four sessions prior to his date of release.

Changes in established patterns of behaviour clearly generate uncertainty. We therefore planned the introduction of exercises at strategic points so as to provide a framework within which members could evaluate their own plans and see how their attitudes were changing or developing as they examined different aspects of their lives. Of course for many in the group, change would mean giving up a whole way of life in which periods of imprisonment were not a particular stress and were even welcomed by some as an opportunity to withdraw from some

Table 1
Arguments for and against committing crimes and going straight

	Committing crimes	*Going straight*
Arguments for:	money; drugs; excitement; relieves boredom; because mates do it; good living	better life for your kids and family; no pressure from the Old Bill; better future; earn money legally; enjoy life
Arguments against:	prison; police; victims; record; upsets family; unstable future; can't lead normal life; lose respect; guilty conscience	unemployment; no money; hard to maintain standard of living; affects friendships; environment in which you are brought up

dangerously addictive behaviour or from the worries of basic subsistence living. We thus knew that change in the group would be limited but expected that the exercises would at least offer a reference point for the future and food for thought outside the sessions themselves. We also knew (and had occasions to observe) that the challenge which came from the other group members to accept responsibility for offending would be tougher, and all the more effective, because of the members having been in similar situations themselves.

The following session-by-session outline describes the programme and illustrates how the members made use of the exercises included in it.

SESSION 1: MOTIVATION FOR CHANGE

This session began with an exercise aimed at eliciting current attitudes and values concerning crime. Much has been written on the subject of attitudes and attitude change (Zimbardo et al., 1977) and this exercise was constructed to highlight the conflicting values which inform or influence attitudes.

The members were divided into two small groups, one of which was given the task of setting out its members' arguments for and against committing crimes, and the other the task of doing the same thing in relation to going straight. The two small

Figure 1 The cycle of change

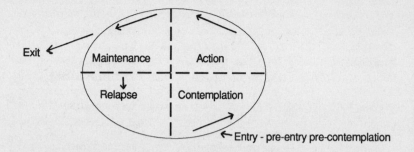

Exit

Maintenance

Action

Relapse

Contemplation

Entry - pre-entry pre-contemplation

groups were then asked to present their arguments to each other and Table 1 summarises the reasons provided by the various groups.

These demonstrated, as was expected, the members' real ambivalence between committing crimes and going straight and many commented that they had tried giving up on many occasions. This led neatly into the second element of this session, a discussion of the Cycle of Change (Prochaska and DiClemente, 1982), a model of which is depicted in Figure 1.

After describing the Cycle of Change model we asked the members of the group to use it as a way of reflecting on their experiences of trying to change their offending behaviour. What became very clear was that most members had attempted to give up crime at some stage and that they had all experienced breaking promises made to themselves and others. Using the model in this way was very productive, especially in enabling members to focus on the relapse stage and the overly-optimistic notion that, after relapse, one can move directly back, into the 'contemplation' or 'action' part of the cycle.

Each member was asked to write his name on a flip sheet diagram of the cycle, indicating his current position. Those claiming to be at the pre-contemplation stage were challenged by the other members on the basis that attendance at the group suggested some degree of contemplation and after reflection, a few returned to the flip chart and altered their position.

Overall, this exercise is probably most powerful for the member who is about to leave prison. When that person has arrived on an action plan, praise and support can be given. For those less committed to change, this fact is highlighted as is the risk of further offending and a further period of custody.

Stage 1

The number '609' refers to the designation of the form used to list a person's previous convictions and the first stage of this three stage exercise took just such a list - constructed however by the group's facilitators - as its starting point. The group members were presented with a list and encouraged to characterise the fictitious person to whom it applied (e.g. give personal, family and social attributes). The giving of life to this 609 character was generally light-hearted and John, as he was so often called, was also considered to be very close to that awful concept of the 'no hoper'.

Stage 2

The members were divided into smaller groups and given the task to list and prioritise the personal changes needed by John and to give suggestions as to how these could be brought about. This exercise had several advantages: those members most closely identified with John could listen to the group's conclusions and analysis and engage in a private process of self appraisal without the threat of exposure. Those with lesser criminal histories were provided with a picture of a possible future on which they could reflect. Finally the exercise gave experience in, and illustrated the value of, consulting with others to solve problems.

Stage 3

With the 609 exercise as background members were asked to identify something that they wanted to achieve - one change for the better. This was an individual exercise and each member was given a pictorial representation of a set of steps as a visual aid to highlight the step-by-step process necessary to achieve one's aims. Members were asked to write in their objective on the top step then work back, considering or calculating what had to be done to proceed to the objective. Individuals were provided with private attention and assistance by the facilitators throughout this exercise. Some members were encouraged to hold on to their notes for future reference. This exercise aimed at helping members to see possibilities for change and to target their efforts and set personal priorities.

SESSION 3: THE IMPACT OF IMPRISONMENT ON SELF

Given the negative and dehumanising affect of imprisonment it is difficult for many of us to understand why people make choices which result in them being returned to prison. One reason for this could be that individuals are damaged by the experience and are left even more vulnerable. The problem is then made more difficult if, because of this vulnerability, support or help from others is avoided.

To get at some of these issues we asked group members to brainstorm all the ways in which prison affected them. All manner of suggestions were given, ranging from bad food and bad conditions through to such emotional aspects as humiliation and frustration. To disentangle the massive amount of material presented the members were then asked to differentiate between those aspects that would end immediately on their release and those aspects which would remain with them, and to cross off all items referring to the former.

Crossing off bad things about prison life seemed to energise the group but what remained were aspects giving rise to feelings of hate, despair and anger which we discovered, in discussion, were rarely talked about with other people. We discussed this further, encouraging the view that if maintenance of change is to be successful then unresolved feelings of anger and blame must be addressed. As a follow-on, the members were asked to brainstorm a list of people to whom they could talk about such feelings. The list was generally a short one, concentrating upon partners, family members and friends but notably, rarely included probation officers or other professionals.

SESSION 4: WHO IS IN CONTROL ANYWAY?

Prisoners are often expected to have gained insight. Usually what this means is that they are expected to show remorse for what they have done or demonstrate a measure of guilt. But insight need not be viewed in this fashion and may instead be an appreciation of one's own behaviour and an awareness of the impact that such behaviour may have on other people.

However the notion of personal ownership of behaviour is complicated by social and group processes. Indeed certain groups in society, for instance black people, might almost be said to have been collectively criminalised. Not surprisingly, open ended group discussion with offenders about crime often leads to a discussion about victimisation and social conditions and structure.

Such discussions clearly have purpose but, from the point of view of an individual about to leave prison within a matter of weeks, it can be asked whether it is all that helpful to talk about changing the world. Arguably it is more important to concentrate on ways on enhancing immediate personal control.

We worked on the premise that if members are to change their behaviour or aspects of their world with which they are unhappy, they need first to feel a sense of control over their lives. In order to establish the degree to which members felt such control we used a questionnaire asking members to identify whether they had 'full', 'some' or 'no' control over a variety of aspects of their lives, e.g. getting a job, how others view them, getting into fights. Members then compared responses, which often provoked much debate between those who felt individuals were wholly responsible for their lives and those who felt that they were powerless to alter their circumstances in any way.

The main purpose of this exercise, usually achieved via the group discussion, was to reinforce the notion that each individual can have at least some impact upon his/her own situation given sufficient self-belief and a realistic attitude towards what can be achieved.

This discussion was then followed by the 'traffic lights' exercise. Each member was given a diagram of a traffic light with three large circles (red, amber, green). In the red circle they were asked to list all those behaviours they wished to avoid (in order to keep out of trouble in the future); in the amber circle what could be considered warning signs that they might be about to get back into trouble; in the green, behaviour that could positively help them keep out of trouble. Members seemed to pick up on this exercise readily. During discussions on offending we were often presented with pictures of good intentions going wrong due to a combination of factors and individuals describing a period prior to arrest when their lives gradually got more and more out of control, once described as like being on a rollercoaster. We hoped that by identifying (in the amber circle) the warning signs that this process might be about to start, each individual could be sensitised to the need to take preventive action. Often such signs did not seem to have an immediate connection with offending behaviour. For example, one member identified a lack of communication with his partner as an indication that things were beginning to go wrong. It did not surprise us that the amber section often proved difficult to complete nor that those with the least awareness of the reasons underlying their offending behaviour found it the most difficult. Members were encourage to take this exercise away both to add to as they gained greater insight into their behaviour and also as a reference point upon release.

ANTI-RACIST PRACTICE

Our aim was to run the group within the framework of Inner London Probation Service Equal Opportunities Policy. We were aware of the gross over-representation of black people in the criminal justice system and in HMP Wandsworth in particular. We were therefore keen to provide an equal service in terms of access to the groupwork programme and to be aware of the way in which racism could obstruct the process.

As a base line we decided to have more than one black member in each group. Our view was that the presence of more than one individual black person would be supportive and reduce the possible sense of isolation that one black member on his own might experience. But we were also concerned that if the black members in the group were in a minority they could feel less able to discuss issues from their perspective. Indeed our experience showed that when there was a majority of black members the impact of institutionalised racism and the criminalisation of certain sections of the black population (Ahmed, 1991) took on prominence in relation to individual offending behaviour as an explanation of causality.

In terms of the programme, racism was highlighted by the session on who is in control. Racism meant for many black members that they had less control over their lives than their white counterparts. They also felt that there were fewer opportunities open to them (e.g. in the job market) upon release. It was important therefore for the group to acknowledge this lack of equality before trying to assist black members identify where and how they could gain greater personal control. The positive experiences of other black members (again, for example, in the job market) was encouraging to those who doubted their chance of succeeding within a hostile system.

We were also aware of the imbalance caused by our being an all white staff group and our responsibility to confront racism. We did not witness overt racism from group members and indeed white members seemed to have a clear awareness of the disadvantage suffered by black people both within the prison itself and criminal justice system in general. However there was at times a marginalisation of black issues when black members were in a minority and we tried to redress this balance. We also had occasion to make members aware of racial stereotyping where 'John' in the 609 exercise was identified as black. It was our perception that we were more often asked to justify our positions within the power structures of the criminal justice system when there was a greater membership of black men in the group. This questioning of the very essence of our role in the prison highlighted our own ambivalence about this and our responses met with varying degrees of acceptance.

ANTI-SEXIST PRACTICE

The group membership was all male while two of the three workers were women. We made an effort to challenge sexist attitudes whenever expressed and it was particularly important that the male worker took a lead in this regard. Furthermore we made a conscious effort not to fulfil a traditional male/female role in our leadership and to show the female leaders taking an equal part (not surprisingly, though, we found that discussion tended to move into the area of relationships more readily when the group was led by the two female workers).

On the whole we felt that the members were sceptical of challenges that their behaviour was sexist or that this sexist behaviour had an impact upon their offending. At times we were told that we did not live in the real world. The men often saw it as their duty to protect and support "their" women and children, usually without any reference to the women and whether they wanted such protection or assistance. Paradoxically, the members paid little attention to the consequences of imprisonment and the impact that this may have had on the family as a whole. When challenged it was sometimes acknowledged that male pride had more to do with it (i.e. the offending) than did the supposedly altruistic notions first proffered).

CONCLUSION

The offending behaviour group ran for five months during 1990. Unfortunately, as members left the prison at the same time as leaving the group, there has been no opportunity to obtain a direct measure of its effectiveness. Our impression, however, is that the programme met its objectives. We were generally pleased with the content and found it could be adapted and improved quite easily. Members seemed to find the exercises relevant. The level of trust and depth of discussion often surprised us and we felt that our attempts to maintain a group culture to counteract the constant change of membership were successful. We believe that this model was time-effective in terms of staff resources as it involved little preparation time to maintain it once established.

The involvement of just three probation officers allowed us to develop good working relationships and helped us keep control of the changing nature of the group. The rolling programme and its content allowed us to provide a service to the majority of those who wanted it prior to their release and focused very clearly upon their offending and what they were going to do about it once they left the prison. At the very least it offered members the time and the opportunity to review their plans in a supportive yet challenging setting.

Ken Fisher and Liz Watkins, Inner London Probation Service

7

Culture Groups in Prison

GRAHAM TOWL

INTRODUCTION

There is clearly much untapped human potential within prison populations. However, informally one is often aware of a sense of fatalism amongst prisoners and an unquestioning acceptance of whatever values are conventional in their sub-cultural setting. This viewpoint is, we suspect, reinforced by prison regimes which emphasise passivity and compliance.

In our groupwork we set out to examine values, beliefs and relationships in their cultural context. The approach we took has at its roots a Canadian model of prison education which derives largely from the viewpoint of Moral Development Theory (e.g. Duguid, 1987). In his work Duguid emphasises the effect of poverty of experience in preventing cognitive and moral development. The basic enterprise of education is change, but for change to occur there must be freedom to question and debate as the individual makes judgements and evaluations (Marsh, 1976). Stephen Duguid's work in British Columbia involves the instrumental use of humanities texts as a tool in the development of 'cultural literacy' and 'critical thought' among prisoners. He uses brief extracts from literature as learning tools in explaining issues in terms of their relevance in everyday life. For example, he includes Berkman's (1912) Prison Memoirs of an Anarchist for a structured discussion on the general theme of the individual in society.

He acknowledges the awesome weight of cultural constraints on beliefs and behaviour:

> We are after all asking adults to reconsider a set of values they feel comfortable with and find supportive, to examine critically the lives they lead, to re-think familiar constructs (Duguid, 1986).

It is this re-thinking of the familiar, and exploration of unfamiliar cultural, social and personal constructs which is at the core of our approach.

It must be stressed at this point that we do not seek to inculcate prisoners with (white) middle-class values and beliefs. What we do seek to do is to develop the 'tools of self-reflection', to examine critically the accuracy and appropriateness of the ideas 'behind' beliefs without implying that ours are necessarily better or the only alternative. Unlike the Canadian prescription of 'neutral' facilitators, we openly discuss our own values and beliefs.

Thus we borrowed the idea of using humanities based materials (we included a film) and added some group exercises. The sessions were planned to introduce gradually and gently materials and exercises which invited a progressively personal input from prisoners. Heuristically, the course may be usefully conceptualised in two distinct, yet related parts. The first involves the impersonal. In practice this meant a fairly 'safe' consideration of culture 'out there' using humanities based materials. For example, in watching the film 'Educating Rita', course members were able to view and comment upon the influence of Frank and Rita's respective backgrounds on the portrayal of their characters in the film. The focus here was cultural influences on the values and beliefs we bring to relationships. The second part of our course involved an examination and personal exploration of how, despite powerful cultural influences, we may make decisions about our relationships in a rational way to help us realise self-directed goals. This aspect of the course was explored predominantly through a series of group exercises where course members' own values became directly available for examination. For example, in the 'Fathers and Sons' sessions, where group members generate ad discuss rules for such relationships, points are usually illustrated with personal accounts from childhood. The often moving nature of such accounts seems to bond and focus the group further in addressing personal issues within a supportive setting.

We claim no happy reconciliation between, on the one hand, the influences of culture or beliefs on behaviour and, on the other, on individual self-direction and understanding. We do however maintain that through discussion of values and beliefs in a structured and supportive setting we may increase self-understanding and cross-cultural tolerance.

Culture Groups in Prison

This a large training prison with a population of about 800 men. There is a significant measure of cultural diversity within this population and statistics indicate that about a third of the men are 'non-whites'.

TUTOR TRAINING

Two day training seminars were organised for prospective course facilitators from psychology, probation, education and uniformed staff.
These seminars involved:

1. an explanation of the history, approach and materials involved in the course.
2. trainee's experiential participation in some of the course exercises with subsequent discussion about key learning points.

TUTOR TEAMS

Teams of two are selected to facilitate the courses. Each 'team' consists of a teacher drawn from the Education Department and one person from either the Probation of Psychology Unit. Course facilitators are partly self-selected i.e. they express an interest and commitment to the groupwork, and partly selected on the basis of previous experience. Facilitators who are less experienced in the approach are paired with more experienced practitioners. Each team consists of either one man and one woman or two women.

COURSE CANDIDATE ALLOCATION

Offices were 'detailed' to recruit 12 interested prisoners each week. Earlier research indicated that more than half of 'inductees' (about 30 men are sent to he prison weekly) would express an interest in the courses. Selection thus involved an unstructured interview procedure as part of the usual 'induction' process.

COURSE CONTENT

What follows is a description of a small selection of sessions. Readers are welcome to contact us for further details of these and other exercises used in our work.

Day one: introductory exercise

The first morning session commences with welcome and the spelling out of the logistics and rules of the group. Logistics involved the timing, venue and refreshment arrangements. Group rules include an adherence to basic democratic principles of interaction within the group. Questions and comments are invited at this stage.

Next, we move on to our 'ice-breaking' exercise; the tea party. This involves each person speaking individually to each of the group members. Topics of discussion are provided in a booklet issued to each group member (e.g. my favourite television programme is ...). This exercise serves a dual function. Firstly, it provides a gentle introduction to others within the group in a general sense. Secondly, in terms of the model, the notion that individuals come from a broad range of individual backgrounds and cultures is usually indicated. Next we introduce the 'map exercise' whereby group members mark on the 'world map' where they were born and the furthest they have travelled. The morning session finishes with a brainstorming session on 'culture'.

The afternoon session starts with an exercise exploring nationality stereotypes. Handouts are distributed listing a number of nationalities with the adjectives. The results of this 'matching' are elicited and tallied on the board and a structured discussion follows.

Day two: 'Educating Rita'

Group members are reminded of some of the themes covered on the previous day particularly in relation to differing cultural backgrounds. This is used as a focal point and structure for the viewing of the film 'Educating Rita'. In the afternoon session the film is discussed and a number of questions are raised. How do the elements of Rita's culture differ from those of Frank's? Did Rita really break free from the constraints of her culture?

Day three: reflection and responses

For the survivors' session, the group is split into two subgroups. Each subgroup is asked to make rules for survival given that they are the only survivors after a natural disaster. (Subgroups work on this exercise for about half-an-hour in separate rooms.) The two subgroups are then brought back together and asked to recount to everyone else their rules for survival in their society. A structured discussion follows including questions such as: 'How did your values and beliefs contribute to the group decisions?

Day four: personal relevance
The 'Fathers and Sons' exercise involves the individual generation of rules for fathers and sons and vice versa. Also rules for fathers and daughters are sometimes explored to examine gender differences.

Day five: individual change
The final morning of the course begins with a consideration of the notion of 'life scripts' (an idea derived from Transactional Analysis). This is used to discuss how basic attitudes are 'programmed' by messages received in childhood. We discuss different roles people take in their lives and crucially why they take these roles. This leads to discussion about the extent to which we may 'edit' our scripts.

GROUP DYNAMICS: THEMES AND PROCESSES
The reader is reminded that the comments that follow refer to themes and processes common to 'culture' groups run weekly over the academic year.

The progressive cultural theme of the programme - from the impersonal to the personal - parallels the dynamics of the group. Initially there was some reticence about full involvement in the group. Indeed, one member pushed his seat physically outside the group and announced that he would 'wait, watch and see' whether or not he wanted to participate. He did not participate actively all day. In 'day two' he sat with everyone else watching 'Educating Rita'. He rejoined the group physically on the third day, but throughout the week, he said little about himself, preferring to comment on the contributions of others. The introductory sessions are crucial in setting the agenda for the group in terms of the basis of, or for, interaction within the group. The information exchange involved in the ice-breaking exercise provides, for some participants, a basis for further informal discussion and disclosure during the morning coffee-break.

The 'map exercise' provides the group with a geographical representation of cultural diversity. Although it must be acknowledged that on occasion this exercise has 'fallen flat' because all inmates have marked 'London' on the 'world map'!

However, this exercise, in combination with the 'cultural brainstorm' which follows, serves to focus the group's attention on the differing cultural backgrounds brought to the group.

The information collected in the brainstorming session is used as a framework for discussion in the 'nationality stereotypes' exercise. The ease with which group members are able to assign adjectives to particular nationalities in this exercise provides a salutary reminder of the potency of racial stereotypes. Such constructs are explored, examined and challenged. At this stage there is much 'checking out' with the rest of the group about the validity of particular views. Curiously, the notion of a 'stereotype' in terms of the consensus construct it implies is often reflected in the groups with attempts to involve all group members in giving their views and agreement with group norms. Attempts are also often made to help others clarify their ideas. However, at this early stage in the group's development some members remain 'outside' the group in much the same sense as the facilitators.

'Educating Rita' appears to have had an initial appeal largely because of the medium - a film. Watching a film together involves a fairly informal social setting. Informal settings beget informal interactions. In terms of the group's development over the week, such informal interaction sets the foundations for a greater spontaneity in contributions by group members and heightens the degree of self-disclosure. The increased trust and mutual acceptance at this stage are further developed and tested in the next major exercise.

The 'Survivors' exercise on day three usually marks a turning point in the group dynamics. The content of this exercise is such that two subgroups are given the opportunity to set their own agenda for survival and organisation of their society. The process involves their personal contribution to the task. Thus the theme switches from impersonal notions of culture to the personal.

Values and beliefs are illustrated in the generation of individual roles and collectives rules. There were many interesting aspects to this exercise (a favourite among participants). For us, the exercise provides a powerful illustration of just how quickly intergroup rivalry and intragroup affiliation can develop. The 'us and them' atmosphere characterised in this exercise by the respective groups makes for a useful analogy of how, for example, racial stereotyping may develop. We openly explored these aspects of the dynamics of the group (when reconvened) looking at the affective and cognitive concomitants of such rivalry.

The personal relevance of the course content is highlighted in the 'Fathers and Sons' session. The devising of father-son relationship rules leads into discussion of the balance between nurture and control; and usually it is at this point that course members start talking in earnest about themselves and the implications of their earlier relationships - in particular, attitudes towards authority. Two common and related difficulties are associated with this exercise:

1. First, the content is personal, and if the group processes have not sufficiently developed towards a supportive environment, tensions sometimes arise. On a number of occasions facilitators have felt it necessary to exercise their discretion and protect more vulnerable individuals from over-disclosure.
2. Second, the issues of attitudes towards authority is sometimes viewed as an invitation to make personal attacks on members of staff. Sometimes a great deal of anger is expressed about the iniquitous and corrupt nature of the legal system. As these themes and emotions develop, it becomes increasingly difficult to make the session beneficial and productive for group members. A sad and sour atmosphere of angry resignation can result.

Generally, however, the 'Fathers and Sons' session is popular amongst group members, particularly when a relatively high level of mutual trust and concern has grown within the group. Indeed the group usually appears reflective and thoroughly engaged in this exercise. The 'life script' exercise usually follows on fluently from the previous day's personal content. We place a great deal of emphasis on the need to develop the ability to 'edit' the 'script' as the next step. Of course, we openly acknowledge the problems and limitations of such editing. Participants often 'try out' ideas in this session - usually seeking approval, or at least acknowledgement, that their ideas about changes in their life make sense.

The final session involves an invitation to complete anonymous evaluation sheets. Generally comments are very favourable indeed.

The most important lesson learnt from the groupwork appears to be the paramount importance of communication between facilitators before and after sessions to discuss the development of group dynamics and the selection of appropriate materials and approaches in response to the individual group's needs.

REFLECTIONS

These courses ran for one academic year. About 40 per cent of men coming to the prison in 'term time' attended the courses.

A holistic approach - viewing prisoners and staff as whole people not restricted by their respective roles - underpins this work and thrives on the multidisciplinary and multicultural perspectives brought to the course. Regrettably, in prisons generally, groupwork is relatively uncommon and often sporadic largely because of institutional and resource constraints. Two of the institutional constraints are:

1. the ideological bias of 'measures of efficacy' of interventions in prisons in terms of institutional compliance and reconviction rates;
2. the imperviousness of prisons as institutions to outside agencies.

Our multidisciplinary approach is helpful in terms of the pooling of resources with resultant added institutional support. Working together provides an informal forum for the sharing of ideas and a common sense of purpose. The manifold indirect benefits of such multidisciplinary work include increased interdepartmental communication and cooperation.

In terms of the course itself, we have perhaps overemphasised the cultural constraints on behaviour possibly at the expense of the potential for self-change and understanding. Also the course concentrated on the re-thinking of attitudes, not the skills and environmental support needed to effect change.

Personal issues are sometimes brought up within the course which may require further intervention. There are very limited resources for such follow-up support for individuals. The institutional priority is to maintain course numbers, and the notion of voluntariness, fundamental to the approach is very much a secondary consideration. This is especially so given the practical constraints of a fluctuating 'reception rate' of new inmates.

The proactive approach involved in our courses means battling uphill against the ethos of a regime that emphasises passivity and compliance and often puts the smooth running of routines before individual concerns. Despite this, we see potential for course development in prisons, perhaps focusing more clearly on particular client groups. The approach may also have applicability outside the prison setting in adult education. It is our hope and belief that both prisoners and staff will continue to benefit from their increased understanding and acknowledgement of individuals as people in their cultural context.

Note
The views expressed are those of the author and do not necessarily represent those of the Prison Department or Home Office.

Graham Towl, Principal Psychologist, HM Prison Service. This chapter is reprinted from Groupwork, *1990, 3(3)*

8

Groupwork in the Luton Probation and Bail Hostel

CATHERINE MULVIE

Since its inauguration in 1979 the Luton Hostel has passed through various stages of development. Although groupwork has been practised there in the past, the style of work described here has evolved from the commitment of the present staff group to a set of principles popularly known as 'empowerment', getting in touch with feelings, and reality-based work, which I will describe in detail later. Perhaps the word 'evolutionary' best describes the dynamic approach we have adopted, since the hostel population of 21 residents is constantly changing and staff input is subject to the vicissitudes of a shift system and a host of other unpredictable factors. At the same time the twice weekly groups form an anchor point for residents, with a consistent, people-centred value base, which represents security for those who wish to take part. Our underlying belief is in the value of the individual, and that learning and discovery can take place best in the everyday situations of life

THE HOSTEL, ITS SETTING AND POPULATION

At the present time the hostel draws it clientele mainly from the whole of South East England. We are a bail resource for the courts and have a number of residents on bail assessment prior to a period of residence with us as a condition of a probation order. We also have probationers with a condition of residence who have been assessed as suitable and orders have been made. There are a small number of residents subject to parole licences. We view ourselves as an alterative to custody and therefore target 'up tariff' offenders. The hostel also prioritises places for black offenders, women, and the 17-21 age group. In the past year we have succeeded in maintaining a significant number of residents in the younger age group, and at the time of writing have seven females in residence but have had less success in attracting black offenders, not many of whom are referred to the hostel.

I believe that the composition of the total hostel population significantly affects the atmosphere within the hostel, and the groupwork programme. There is no attempt to segregate the different categories, all mix together to a greater or lesser extent and form their own natural groups. Sometimes these are related to outside factors, i.e. on remand together, but usually groupings within the hostel are ad hoc alliances based on shared values. A typical cross section of the hostel population would be as follows.

Age	17 - 21	10
	21 - 25	5
	25 - 35	5
	35+	1

Category	Bailees	10
	Bail assessment	4
	Probation	6
	Parole	1

By now it will have become apparent that this is a very fluid population. The greatest degree of movement is among the bailees who stay on average nine weeks. The bail assessment group usually have their eyes set on a condition of residence at the hostel and are particularly committed. Probationers and parolees form the more stable core, and parolees' interests usually lie in establishing a base outside the hostel.

A breakdown of the hostel population according to offence is also interesting but has less direct influence on the groupwork programme, since offending is not directly challenged. In the past year we received a high number of applications on behalf of men and women either charged with, or convicted of sexual offences. In one recent month four were in residence, three on bail including one female, and one on probation. Normally this resident group presents no special problems, and they either lie to the other residents about their offences or protest their innocence and claim victim status themselves (which is often true) or are simply accepted by the rest of the group in full knowledge of what they have done. Significantly within the younger age band we found at least five young people within the hostel at one time who had been victims of physical abuse or sexual abuse or both.

We have had some success in targeting 'high tariff' offenders. Some may be high tariff because of the frequency of reconviction, whilst others may have this status because of the seriousness of their offences. Add to this the additional factors of substance abuse, violence, and the occasional arsonist, and the reader will have some idea of the diversity of human problems to be found in the Luton hostel at any one time.

THE HOSTEL TEAM

The hostel staff team consists of senior probation officer, deputy warden, part-time liaison probation officer and four assistant wardens. We also have a cook, a maintenance person and a secretary. In the past year three student probation officers in training have made a significant contribution to the groupwork programme under the supervision of the liaison probation officer. The staff group meets formally every week to discuss policy and the progress of each resident. Although the hostel is a busy place during the day with the 'front office' being the home of the deputy warden and an assistant warden, and the hub of hostel life to which all requests are addressed, in the evening the ratio of staff to residents drops dramatically and only one assistant warden covers the sleeping-in duty. Usually the member of staff covering this shift will be kept busy in the evening, signing in new residents, conducting 'key worker' interviews with their own assigned group of residents, or playing the occasional game of Scrabble. After curfew at 11.30 the assistant warden retires to the sleeping-in room and usually obtains a reasonable night's sleep. However, this is sometimes broken by calls from the police, residents who have gone to the bathroom and locked themselves out, or more vulnerable residents seeking someone to talk to. The hostel wages a constant struggle with the resident group whose daily cycle of wakefulness bears no relationship to the normal working world. Since very few of our residents are successful in obtaining work they drift into late nights and late mornings. This can be particularly stressful for a member of staff taking part in the next morning's group activities.

HISTORY OF THE PROGRAMME

Our current groupwork programme is organised by the liaison probation officer who had some previous experience of groupwork in a residential setting. The programme developed a little like

'Topsy' using the resources of the members of staff available, usually the liaison probation officer plus an assistant warden from the rota. We started very hesitantly, aware of our limited resources but with a strong commitment on the part of those of us who were 'converted ' to groupwork. Since it would be unlikely that we would have the same two groupworkers involved in consecutive meetings we at least had the continuity of the liaison probation officer who planned the overall content of the sessions and participated in most. These sessions ran from 10-12 each Wednesday initially, and covered such areas as 'self', interpersonal issues, stress and loss, survival, personal aims and objectives, friends, relationships, and anger control. Despite the difficulties of the shift system and the 'moving' population, these groups worked well and great discoveries were made.

Halfway through the year we were asked to provide a practice-teaching opportunity for a student on her final placement who was especially interested in 'alternative' methods of working, so this provided us with the opportunity to expand from one weekly group to two. The second group was more structured and discussed issues such as alcohol abuse, health and hygiene, safe-sex, contraception, AIDS and related subjects. This group was run by two workers under the supervision of the liaison probation officer and was a popular addition to our weekly programme. At this stage we were joined for a three month period by two other students seeking experience in groupwork, and very committed to working with young people. They were absorbed into the programme as co-workers. One took over from the first student in the more structured group bringing his own expertise in interpersonal communication, and the other joined with the liaison probation officer in the Wednesday group. This increase in group leader continuity greatly benefited the way we developed. Both workers were very committed to a 'self-directed ' approach to groupwork and had sufficient confidence to allow this to work well, so that significant progress was made in helping some very disturbed young people to express their feelings. Inter-group support systems were developed and the resident group also felt able to challenge the staff appropriately. This became an additional means of dealing with hostel issues in a constructive way, which would not have been possible hitherto.

At the present time we are well occupied with two groups, with different leaders but co-ordinated by one person. The groupwork programme is at the heart of the hostel's proactive work with its residents and we look forward to developing a new phase in which new members of staff are absorbed into the training process, gaining confidence to run a group and gaining insight into the lives of the residents and the life of the hostel.

AIMS OF THE HOSTEL GROUPWORK

Although all of us would like to see ourselves as being clear about our aims from the outset, I would suggest this is very rarely the case. In our situation both the senior probation officer and the liaison probation officer had significant prior groupwork experience, but the high degree of convergence on the aims of the programme only emerged as we set about the process of discovery. The key aims of our programme are:

1. At the most basic level, to offer a groupwork programme which is constructive and relevant to the needs of the individual resident.
2. To help individuals to acknowledge their feelings. This involves articulating new thoughts and feelings through association with other group members.
3. To 'empower' individuals to 'deal with' their lives. To help them examine their offending behaviour where appropriate, and provide a check for reality through peer group feedback.
4. To impart a feeling of self-respect by giving space in which individuals can see themselves as being able to deal with their lives and with key issues. Allowing space in which residents not only experience realistic boundary setting from other group members but also receive affirmation from the group: a process of support and confrontation which stimulates personal change.
5. Finally, our aim is to hold these aims, and the values they contain, at the heart of our work in the hostel. It is critical that all members of staff (including students) acting as groupworkers subscribe to these values 'in the group'.

The value of our work to the individual resident lies in consistent application of these objectives and values across the board in all the other hostel systems: i.e. the one-to-one, resident/key-worker, resident/liaison probation officer relationships as well as in decisions about weekly management made by the hostel staff group.

METHODOLOGY AND TECHNIQUE

For the purpose of this discussion I have divided methodology into two subheadings; theory and practice, although they are inter-related in the hostel programme.

Theory

Four areas of theory have been found to be most helpful and relevant to our work. The first is Whitaker and Lieberman's (1964) 'group focal conflict theory', which described the intrinsic conflict of any group; between the process of sharing collective experience and the fear of the consequences of that sharing. This dynamic pervades the hostel as a whole, but is particularly noticeable within the small groups.

The second area of theory which has been most helpful is Tuckman's (1965) linear model of stages of group development. Again, this applies on a 'macro' scale to the hostel as a whole, but most usefully to the small groups. To be able to objectify and identify the various stages of forming, storming, norming, and performing, is particularly helpful to all of us, but especially to workers who are new to group process.

Thirdly, Bion's insight into the unconscious life of the group, and the extent to which the group's need to maintain itself is compatible with the group task, has also furthered our understanding of the dynamics of hostel work (Bion, 1961).

Finally, a 'systems' framework helps us to identify the relationships between the interlocking and overlapping parts of our establishment, the resident group, the staff group and the unit as a whole. Of continuing significance is the way in which what is happening in one group can be mirrored in another. Thus when residents are feeling angry and confused when events threaten the maintenance of their group, this is likely to be reflected within the staff group also.

These have been found to be the most helpful theoretical insights.

Practice

At a practical level the delineation of the 'self-directed' group by Mullender and Ward (1985; 1989) has helped us enormously. In their view self-directed groupwork starts from the person's own life experience, uses open groups and holds that the vast majority of people are emotionally sound, do not need treatment but lack power in their own lives. These individuals can be facilitated to greater power through questioning the attitudes of others towards themselves, and being more actively involved in decision-making. Although our hostel groups do not fit neatly into this model, the basic underlying values are those to which we would subscribe. We also note with interest their comments about the viability of self-directed practice where statutory requirements are in force:

> In our view, membership of a self-directed group is not precluded for those on such orders ... provided there is no actual or implied requirement that they will join the group (Mullender and Ward, 1989, p.23).

PROBLEM AREAS: ATTENDANCE VOLUNTARY?

Some passing mention has already been given to the question of attendance. Attendance within both of our groups is voluntary, although we ask probationers and bail assessment residents to make a particular effort to come. Mostly, this works out well for fairly obvious reasons. We hope that the content and process of our groups will encourage others to join and often this is the case. Many have confessed to an initial resistance to joining in, but have gone on to be our most enthusiastic regulars. Sometimes after a particular group in which disclosure has taken place residents are reluctant to leave and need special attention.

Most writers on the running of small groups stress the importance of planning. We feel that a comfortable balance can be drawn between being clear about the general area of focus, the expectations of the session and allowing the discussion to flow. Thus we have in our 'discovery' group a worker's agenda based on previous experience, but the group is encouraged to find its own point of entry using the issues of the moment and its own current life experience.

We have found that group size and structure affect the group process. Although all available residents are encouraged to attend, smaller numbers are usually present on Wednesday for the self-directed discovery group than on Thursday for the more structured group. The Thursday group contains more information-giving in its programme and is generally felt to be less threatening than the self-directed group. The latter, on the other hand, has its own strengths. It is largely self-selecting and democratic and contains within it the means for significant change, both for the hostel and the individual in the group. Being much smaller in number (average 6 or 7) this group has handled some very sensitive subjects, for instance, the shared experience of grief or loss, the experience of abuse within the family, and self-respect. Another feature emerging from this self-directed group is its desire to influence the hostel system as a whole. I believe that this is a necessary outcome of the successful enabling of residents to seek appropriate power within the immediate system. This also underlines the need for a common value base among hostel workers, which should inform the work at all levels and validate the work being done within the small groups. Some reference has already been made to the theoretical basis of hostel groupwork. We also try to make our sessions as practice-oriented as possible, using role-play and brainstorming, as well as warming up exercises and occasionally music and games. We have found the use of cartooning, collage and art therapy techniques especially useful in encouraging the participation of less verbal members of our groups.

Our very mobile population makes it difficult to plan ahead, or 'develop' the group over a period of time. Each session has to be capable of standing or falling on its own merits, and to be of immediate value to the members. Set against this 'fact of life' is the equally real desire for some predictability, especially from new members of staff and new residents.

In addition to the constraints of size and unpredictability a third potential area of difficulty lies with the intrinsic role conflict of members of staff who also act as group leaders. This factor cannot be ignored and requires two main comments. The first is that since reality is one of the main foundations of our work, groupworkers must be able, and willing to deal with it openly and comfortably, in a way which is compatible with the overall aims of the programme. This obviously means that groupworkers must be sufficiently confident of their own role to be able to handle this issue authentically and effectively. At another level, groupworkers must be sufficiently confident of themselves as people to be able to operate as people within the group and not be confused by the 'trappings' of their role.

SOME EXAMPLES

Three examples of our groupwork may serve to illustrate the variety of work attempted in the Hostel. The first is described by Veronica Mullen, a trainee probation officer, visiting the programme for a six week period, and co-working with the liaison probation officer. The group consists of: four members aged between 18 and 22 years (1 female) and two co-workers (both female). Members came into the group room with cups of coffee and the expectation that the workers would be 'leading' this group. What happened over the next two hours is an example of how the implicit needs of the group can be made explicit by using the worker's own store of agendas, and linking into what may emerge in the engaging phase of the group. After a few minutes of general banter, in which an atmosphere of trust was established, the group began to talk about Julie's boyfriend who had beaten her up, and her father's attitude to the beatings she had received. It was then the worker's decision to use the topic of violence, implicitly, although it would be the group members themselves who would later direct us to the specific area of child abuse. By responding at the members' level of acceptance of violence in their own lives, it enabled an unthreatening and non-judgemental atmosphere to continue. By not pushing members to reveal or share material before they felt comfortable, this also allowed the group to 'grow' as one by one each member felt able to share their experiences with the others. From the initial 'out-there' discussion of the violence in their lives, each began to give graphic detail of the personal experiences they had gone through.

At one point, one of the members, an aggressive, confronting, young man told his own story, claiming that he 'deserved all he got'. This was challenged by the worker with the words: 'No. No child deserves to be beaten'.

Work over the next two hours included the validation of each member and an attempt to reassess their belief system. Although it would not be considered unusual for members of a young offenders' group to have suffered physical abuse as children, each member had clearly not appreciated this and it appeared helpful to relate to each other at this level.

Towards the end of this session, all four were clearly in touch with what being beaten as children had meant for them, and the air was heavy with sadness. No one seemed to want to go. The last part of the group was spent retrieving the positives and giving reassurance.

The building of trust and the necessity for 'pacing' were the two most important elements of this session and the ownership of experiences and feelings would provide the basis for future individual work.

My second example is a more structured group session on 'communicating with people' which was part of a four monthly block co-led by student probation officer, Paul Jewitt.

The purpose was to explore the elements which make up communication skills and to show how we use them every day, to broaden our understanding of communication, and to make it more effective.

The method used was as follows:

1. Brief introduction about communication.
   Brainstorm - what do we mean by communication?
   What do we see and how much value do we put on each aspect of communication.
2. Visual game - comparison between heard list and seen items.
3. How do we learn? Who made the biggest impact and why?
   BREAK
4. The 'good friend' game - what happens when we rely on others to communicate for us (very lively).

Once the subject was expanded to the point at which new insights began to develop, the group determined its own pace and direction. This was an interesting presentation and a lively group which all members enjoyed and learned something from. The subject was broader and more relevant to everyday life than had at first been thought.

A third example concerns a group organised around the theme of anger control, a subject chosen by one member. There were eight in the group and two co-workers. There was considerable resistance to the task, which proceeded by way of completion of a personal inventory of 'the things that make me angry', and then a discussion of the results. The group became angry with the inventory, which summed up the attitudes of several very neatly. There was most common ground on 'I don't like people who don't like me', but there was great resistance to moving this into more positive territory. We assigned a task of preparing a role-play during the coffee break. They achieved this well enough, but again resisted any reference to anger or lack of control in their own experience, being determined to maintain the discussion in general terms. There were two important developments from this session which spilled over outside the group. The first was that the two least powerful members, who were both quite 'disturbed' buried the antipathy they had for each other and formed an alliance in the group which continued outside. The second point is that within hours of this discussion the pair described above were involved in a serious violent incident with other youths from a nearby housing estate outside the hostel, justified by the comment 'I hit him because he hit me!'.

Fortunately there have been few incidents like this, but we were left with many unanswered questions of our own.

No systematic approach has been adopted to obtain feedback about our groupwork programme. Although we are enthusiastic about it, there is a constant need to check things out, by observation and by discussion. Here are some of our resident's comments:

T. - (on probation with a condition of residence) said 'since I have been in the hostel, I have attended most of the activity group meetings. Some of the people who come are quiet around the hostel, but when they get in the group, they open up, which is good'.

J - (a young woman on bail hoping for a condition of residence) said 'the best thing about the groups is seeing how people operate. Everyone gives everybody else a chance, that way we get to know how people are. It's nice to come together to do something together. There's a lot of backstabbing here, so it's good to have a common topic. When I first came here, I didn't like the groups very much. If you're unsure of yourself then you'll be unsure in the group. Some people make a lot of noise and challenge why we are here, but the quiet ones know what's going on'.

J. - (a young man aged 17 on bail assessment) said the groups had helped him to 'pick myself up'. He said that there was more trust to deal with painful issues in the smaller groups. He also said 'the groupwork doesn't just make you want to do something while you're in there, you want to do it when you come out as well'. He enjoyed 'having a laugh, but working as well'. Before the group he often said to himself 'Bloody hell!, here we go again', but it changes when you come into the room. The group helps a lot of people. You can come in as grumpy as hell, but then you learn something new, someone always has something else to say, so no matter how many times you may have discussed a topic - there's always something to add.

The last comments in particular convey the excitement of sharing the commonplace experience, and discovering something new, which is at the heart of any groupwork programme.

RELATIONSHIP BETWEEN GROUPWORK AND THE HOSTEL AS A WHOLE

Mention has already been made of the relationship between the groupwork programme and the hostel group as a whole. On the part of staff there is an ongoing search for meaningful communication, experienced at the same time as continuing apprehension about its unpredictability and about our ability to cope. Where there is a lack of understanding there is also suspicion, and a cartoon illustration in the excellent workbook produced by the West Yorkshire Probation Service and Save the Children Fund (Ball et al., 1987) illustrates this with the caption 'You are in effect disturbing the equilibrium of your organisation and may risk cynicism and resentment from colleagues'. There is a permanent need for education and clarity of purpose within the organisation.

We have also found ourselves frustrated by a 'flight from the task' as each group of residents begins to become aware of the powerful forces at work within the group process. At such times there will be an effort to block or avoid the task in hand and, although the group frequently takes an unintended direction, sensitive management of the needs of the group ensures that the time it spends together always bears fruit. Anyone, therefore, approaching a more open style of groupwork with a very structured set of expectations will probably be disappointed.

Because of the way we are obliged to organise our groups, there are constant planning frustrations. We have found that we can only achieve the loosest form of programming, although each pair of workers needs to be in harmony. With this in place each group is free to achieve its creative potential.

CONCLUSION

One point which has emerged very clearly over the past year is the significance of the common purpose. Although we aim for this, it would be foolish to take it for granted in any team, but there is no doubt that this factor underlies the effectiveness with which a hostel staff group can engage with its residents. Our common purpose is based upon a belief in the individual, that offenders are 'worth the risk'. We are engaging in a process which is challenging and educative to residents and staff alike.

Secondly, we acknowledge that this is a costly process, in terms of preparation and planning. Writers agree that the preparation by the individual worker, his/her clarity of purpose, commitment to the task and self-awareness are an essential part of planning a group. It is costly also in terms of the power we are willing to 'give away' as we step out of role and become a member of a group.

Thirdly, we would stress to anyone venturing into the field of self-directed groupwork, that we have to be willing to 'pay up' at the end of the day if we are to give full weight to what we say we believe in. If we give with one hand and take back with another then we are simply compounding the problems we seek to address.

The final point I would wish to make is that helpful though the insights are, which we gain from theory and our own increasing experience, there will always be things which we cannot understand, which seem to be beyond our reach. For me, this only seems to underline the truth that the whole is always greater than the sum of the parts in groupwork practice.

Catherine Mulvie, Hertfordshire Probation Service. This chapter is reprinted from Groupwork, *1991, 4(3)*

9

Groups and Groupings
in a Probation Hostel

CAROL SAPSED

INTRODUCTION

Probation and bail hostels were introduced by the Home Office
and voluntary agencies approximately 45 years ago, but the
majority stem from the 1960s and 1970s. There are national
guidelines regarding their governance but considerable local
variations in style and composition. This chapter is concerned
with living and working in a probation and bail hostel in Bristol.

My underlying belief is that offending behaviour is produced
by inappropriate responses to circumstances, often beyond the
clients' developed sphere of influence and understanding. Many
offenders nurture the expectation that they can, and would,
cease to offend if the circumstances were propitious. I think my
task as a probation officer is to enable clients to develop resources
either personal or political to have greater control over their
offences. Before describing the various groups and groupings of
the hostel, I want to describe the hostel, its environment, the
hostel residents and it programme, to create the backcloth against
which staff and residents work, live and interact.

THE HOSTEL AND ITS SETTING

The hostel was inaugurated 10 years ago to provide a south-west
resource for adult offenders on bail or probation. The aims of the
hostel are to offer the courts and offenders a viable alternative to
a custodial sentence and to offer the courts a residential facility
for people on bail. The objectives are to assist and to prepare
them to leave the hostel at the end of their period of residence in
a planned and purposeful manner.

Initially the hostel consisted of two terraced houses with

residential accommodation for staff and residents. The similarity between the renowned Topsy and the hostel is obvious. The hostel now occupies five houses. It has a staff group of seven social work staff, one clerical officer, one cook/housekeeper, one assistant cook and two part-time cleaners - and twenty nine residents. The house is divided into 19 beds for male probationers aged 21 and over, two bail beds for women, and eight beds for male bailees aged 17 and over. The problems of the building and its development are obvious to visitors; the buildings were incorporated as the opportunity arose, there are odd cupboards, narrow corridors and an excessive number of front doors (five). The bail and probation beds are at opposite ends of the terrace with a secure office and staff accommodation wedged between. Thus physical communication between various sections of the hostel is restricted, indeed the easiest route between the main office and the bail wing may be by going through one front door down the road to another. The physical separation of the two groups can reinforce the feelings of 'them' and 'us' between probationers and bailees. This affects inter-group behaviour, and on occasion disparaging remarks are made by individuals to each other. House meetings, held on separate evenings for the two groups, may include a discussion on the various iniquities of the other group. The staff have to be aware of this tension and to utilise their understanding of how to overcome its when working with the total group - for example, on a hostel expedition.

The hostel is situated on the edge of a deprived inner city area. Formal contact between the community and the hostel is mainly limited to links with local agencies. Informally, there are some links with the local residents, on a basis of mutual acceptance. The location of the hostel in that particular situation does result in the residents' excesses of behaviour passing unchallenged by local residents as the area is busy with a plethora of inner-city activity. This is in contrast to some other hostels which frequently face active public criticism from their neighbours.

Within the work of the probation section of the hostel there has always been a commitment to a programme whereby residents can engage in the complex issue of reducing the risk of further offending. Initially the programme focused upon improving residents' prospects for employment, use of the well-equipped workshop being an integral component. It was based upon the theory and available evidence that the risk of further offences was reduced if a man was in work. Much of the programme was undertaken corporately by the whole hostel group. Today, however, where the prospect for full employment for all is extremely remote, and where the evidence is that before a man can consider work other issues need to be examined, residents and staff create individual packages comprising some corporate hostel activities, using outside specialist resources, for example, drug and alcohol centres, and employment specialists. Individual residents still believe that work will reduce their offending and frequently the problem for staff is to encourage men to examine the issues around their offending behaviour before trying to obtain work. These issues can include personal areas such as addiction, sexual abuse, and physical or verbal aggression.

Referrals for the probation section come from probation officers. The criteria for referral are that the man should be at risk of a custodial sentence and should be prepared to agree to the conditions and rules of the hostel. Prospective probationers are placed at the hostel for one month's assessment period following conviction. This allows time for both staff and resident to assess what needs to be done to reduce the risk of further offending. A court report is prepared by the individual 'key worker' detailing the work to be undertaken and the methods used, for example, referral to employment resources, counselling techniques. Whilst it may be argued that many residents do not have a choice regarding the probation order - or prison - it is important that all parties concerned think that the probation order is viable. The order can be made for a period of up to three years, the most usual being a two year probation order with a six month condition of residence.

Daily life

How does a person pass his day at the hostel? Breakfast is available on a 'help yourself' basis from 7.30-8.15am; staff officially ask residents to be up and about by 9.30am when the hostel is cleared so that cleaning, repairs (endless), and individual work can be completed. A resident may be seeing his key worker, or visiting the Department of Health and Social Security, a frequent event given vagaries of both the postal system and the social security. He may be joining in an activity such as hostel football or outdoor pursuits organised by Fairbridge Drake. He may stay in the hostel to help paint a room, dig the garden, or repair something. From 12.30 pm onwards he prepares his own lunch - bacon saved from breakfast being the usual dish. In the afternoon, the procedure may be the same, returning to the hostel for a cooked tea at 5.45 pm. TV, snooker, darts, seeing the key worker or visiting the local hostelry may be the evening format. At 10.45 pm for bailees, 11.00 pm for probationers - the timing spaced to allow staff to cover the five houses - the building is locked up. Many residents watch TV, cook more bacon - or, hopefully retire to bed.

On certain days groups are run in the hostel by staff: a group for bailees to discuss their feelings about being on bail, for residents to explore issues of self-help, or to hear speakers from outside agencies (e.g. on health matters). The subject of hostel programmes is a wide one and I can only hope to touch upon how one hostel tries both to meet individual needs and to manage a total group.

Staff have to complete formal tasks, such as mealtimes, handing out post, seeing individuals, taking bail referrals, inducting new bailees, and packing up departed residents' belongings. Then there are the tasks defined in job descriptions as 'any other duties' such as showing a workman how to find Room 4, House 12, in order that he may mend a broken basin, unpacking vast amounts of frozen food, helping a resident dig the vegetable patch, and answering the front door to unexpected callers ranging from the police for a cup of tea, to a person looking for accommodation.

Bail referrals are taken on a daily basis by telephone, on average ten people arrive each month. The criteria for acceptance are extremely wide, the most usual reason for refusal being lack of a spare bed. Bailees arrive at the hostel any-time following their release from the court or prison. They are frequently anxious, uncertain as to why they are at the hostel and unsure of themselves. Staff may have to counsel people with very little knowledge of their history or the circumstances of the charges. Once the initial settling in process has occurred, bailees will pursue a similar routine to those on probation.

Hostel rules

Hostels are empowered to devise their own rules; there are significant variations between hostels, although the majority impose a night curfew. The reasons for abiding by them can be accepted as a commitment by the resident to the hostel as an alternative to custody, and they do afford some security for those whose lives are not circumscribed by internal controls. In addition to a curfew, the rules include no alcohol or unprescribed drugs on the premises, payment of weekly rent, and no violence against residents/staff. Interestingly, one exercise used in the formal group requires members to plan a hostel programme and rules. The devised rules are usually extremely stringent.

Infringements of the hostel rules by bailees can result in staff taking breach action, the offender can be asked to leave the hostel immediately, returned to court via police custody, and either rebailed to another address or remanded in custody. Thus departures can be precipitate and unplanned. Probationers are subject to the same hostel rules but for them the outcome may be more protracted; breach hearings currently taking up to three weeks to be heard by the court. During this period staff and residents may, or may not, be able to construct a further working agreement to put before the court. The subject of rule making and breaking is an enormous one; the hostel tries to apply them in a flexibly consistent manner.

To summarise, it can be seen that the hostel is a complex organism/system; it has a boundary which is penetrated both by individuals and organisations. It is a self-determining body within a constellation of external systems mutually dependent, sometimes in conflict, sometimes in agreement. It is fuelled by external sources such as the courts and resourced financially entirely by the Home Office. It has to comply with conflicting demands and maintain an uneasy balance between various bodies. Within its physical boundary there are further groups between which there are tensions, alliances, and fusions. Viewed objectively from outside, a total of forty one people form the hostel. This large grouping is separated formally into a staff group and a residents' group.

RESIDENTS AND STAFF GROUPS

The residents' group

The residential group can be subdivided into long-term (which can include bailees) and short-term; some people place themselves within these groups, others are defined as members by those around them. Further, an unofficial sub-division of the residents' group could be an openly delinquent group and a conforming group; the former displaying to the world around it manifestations of its delinquency, e.g. people driving cars to the hostel whilst disqualified, abusing themselves by either drinking, taking drugs, or gambling to the edge of disaster. The latter group appears to be (and the hostel staff devoutly hope it is) conforming to the hostel's expectations; it is relatively pliable, and acquiescent.

Again the group's membership may be self-defined or externally attributed. Residents may define themselves as members of a particular group; this can be in order to gain advantages for themselves, for example, peer group status.

Often, to the staff cost, membership of the conforming group may abruptly change to the delinquent, leaving staff perplexed as to the cause. However, this type of change from the conforming to the delinquent group can in part be attributed to pressure from the delinquent group. In addition, it may appear that the delinquent group is achieving more in terms of subcultural goals, for example, power, attention, or prestige.

Many of the residents will have considerable experience of institutions and have strategies for coping with their pressure. However, institutions are powerful organisms which do not easily accommodate individuals needs. Nowhere is this more evident than when black residents, who form a small percentage of referrals, are placed at the hostel. It is imperative that the hostel continues to develop, monitor, and evaluate positive action against institutional racism.

Further analysis of the hostel residents group is necessary before we can discuss the various groups as a medium for work. There are the two statutorily defined groups of bailees and probationers. The former is a small group of ten, eight men and two women, rather isolated from the main hostel by physical segregation. The latter is a larger group of twelve men which may contain some overspill bailees, and one or more parolees; and it has easy physical access to staff via one main office door. A further sub-group comprises seven self-catering probationers and parolees, housed in three self-contained units. Their physical movements are discreet and they can avoid contact with the staff and other residents for long periods.

Across the sub-groups further groupings will occur, those of friendship, various but loyal, perhaps having been forged in the context of a shared prison cell or wing, or made by arriving at the hostel from the same court, or through sharing one of the six shared bedrooms (still surprisingly popular amongst residents). There are groups formed by staff for specific purposes; an offending (induction) group, parole group, activities (usually sporting), repair and maintenance groups. There may be groups set up for a 'one-off' particular purpose, such as video filming, visiting the cinema, or coping with a difficult resident. These groupings can include a mix of bailees, probationers, and parolees in varying numbers.

The staff group

The staff group is organised into a formally designated social work group and a support group, the latter being sub-divided into catering and clerical, full and part-time. There are other 'divisions' according to age, race and gender, work role and hierarchical position. Other sub-groups of staff are formed by the staff group itself for specific tasks such as planning an event, reviewing procedures and training sessions. Notwithstanding these various differences, all staff are engaged to a greater or lesser degree in the social work task of negotiating with, supporting, and confronting hostel clients. Shared experience of crisis events can create sub-groupings across formal boundaries as, for example, when three colleagues on duty one morning, a part-time cleaner, relief worker, and social worker, had the shared experience of coping with a serious suicide attempt by a resident.

Within the staff group there may be discreet sub-groups sharing a commonality which can delay or enhance the overall group process. Decisions to be taken regarding residents are often debated by staff using different theoretical and value bases. For example, men who continually abuse alcohol form a large section of the residents. How we work with them and if, or when, we return them to court for failure to abide by the rules is a constant topic of debate. Within the hostel, staff have to work closely together, trust and understand each other; the process of achieving this takes place partially within the context of the staff meetings and can prove both painful and enlightening. Evidence of racism and sexism is not unknown and the team's development is not always even or uneventful. The staff may wish, because of issues of control, to present a united front to the hostel residents regarding decisions, hostel activities, etc.

The practice of upholding other staff may be indicative of the extremely powerful maxim 'united we stand, divided we fall'; the fear of being overwhelmed by the resident group taking precedence over other responses. The danger of this maxim is that the implementation of rules and the decision-making process can become excessively rigid. It is necessary for staff to monitor this and try to maintain a 'flexible consistent' attitude towards the application of rules.

I have a special interest in groupwork and, whilst I understand and occasionally apply a number of different groupwork theories, I consistently apply the Group Focal Conflict Theory (Whitaker and Lieberman, 1964) which states that groups have two processes continually at work within them. One process is the sharing of collective experience; whilst the other is a fear of the consequences of that sharing. Thus, within the hostel a collection of individuals may be united in their stated aim to achieve intimacy, but individuals voice their fear of ridicule if they do so.

The other theory I find particularly helpful is Tuckman's linear model of stages of group development (Tuckman, 1965) which is outlined in another chapter. By applying both theoretical models I can consider the total hostel group or certain sections of it, and try to understand what is happening in terms of group process. To claim that my understanding and perspective of the process is objective is to ignore the fact that I am a component of the total group, have membership of a number of sub-groups or groupings, and have the most powerful formal position. I can, by commenting upon what I perceive, try to increase my personal skills and raise other people's consciousness; however, to claim that I have an objective overview is an assumption that should be, and frequently is, challenged by others. Furthermore, my view of the hostel will enable others to articulate their own view so that together we may compose a picture, jigsaw or mosaic of the whole. Any one of us would like to claim a uniqueness of perspective, uncontaminated by our personal beliefs and values. This, I believe, is not possible - my chosen area of residential work says as much about me as any other facet of myself, and recognition of this gives my work a peculiarity of its own.

It may be that my enjoyment of working and 'quasi living' with a group of people, within the confines of hostel life, affords me experiences of both security and risks. I doubt that any social work can be 'value free'. I cannot claim that working with offenders is purely altruistic, enabling others to change; theory and experience tells me that I will be influenced by those whom I seek to influence and this will deepen and inform my work. One theory suggests that we empathise most closely with our chosen client group. We may choose to work with offenders because we acknowledge those parts of ourselves which could be offenders and, by working with others on their offences, clarify our own offending behaviour. In the formal groups the staff participate in many of the exercises; thus diminishing the boundary of 'us' and 'them'. This may assist considerably in the process of group development, for example the 'forming' and 'norming' stages as defined by Tuckman. However, boundary crossing will undoubtedly reduce the leaders' objective views of the group process, and possibly diminish their ability of influence it. An awareness of these factors can assist us all in our work.

Formal groups
In the total mosaic of the hostel life some groups emerge as having an apparently greater importance than others; these would appear to be those that have the label of 'groupwork': in particular the induction or offending group. The hostel tends to attribute to it qualities that it does not possess; the leaders may be seen as omnipotent, highly skilled, and its contents can be wrapped in mystery. It is a relatively high status group, possibly because it forms the major initial intervention for a probation client, because its programme is predefined and because membership also includes residents from a neighbouring probation hostel.

'Induction groups' have been used in the probation service for approximately ten years. Initially they were closed groups for probationers at the commencement of their orders. They were designed to overcome the potentially collusive nature of 'one-to-one' supervision and reduce the power base of the probation officer by using group dynamics and peer processes to focus upon ways of reducing the possibility of further offences. Their use remains highly popular, particularly in fieldwork.

The fieldwork induction group model used at the hostel has undergone a number of evolutionary changes since the introduction a few years ago by the then Warden and Deputy. This model, which was a closed one, used two leaders and was designed to include all new probationers. The task of the group was to consider and discuss four questions:

Why do people commit offences?
Why do I (the client) commit offences?
What can I personally do to stop committing offences?
Do I want to stop committing offences?

Clients would complete the group having defined a number of areas that they wished to continue to examine with their individual key workers, specialised agencies etc.

It was realised that application of the model in its closed form was not possible, there rarely being sufficient residents on bail assessment to form a core group, and that therefore an open group model would have to be used. In practice this meant that clients joined the group when they arrived on bail assessment and left it after six weeks. Obviously this required that the original four questions needed to be adapted.

The present format which consists of six topics such as relationships, addiction, self-and-others, uses a variety of exercises, games, and discussion.

One advantage of running a formal open group is sharing group leadership between the two hostels. This is both exciting and challenging: at present all staff have the opportunity to lead an induction group; the set six-session programme reduces the anxieties of inexperienced leaders to a manageable level; and it is sufficiently flexible to allow individuals a chance, within the programme, to 'try out' different skills, games, etc. Second, residents join the group on arrival at the hostel. The impetus achieved by beginning soon after the court's decision for a four-week assessment period gives the man a forum for focused work. Third, a formal group allows leaders to practise different skills and develop expertise.

Inevitably, there are difficulties. No rota system known to the residential world allows for two workers from different hostels always to be available at the same time every week, shifts have to be changed and, on occasions, continuity of leadership has to be abandoned with staff coming in to replace one or other of the leaders. The current practise is for each worker to undertake a total of twelve session of the programme to assist continuity.

Initially one leader does only six weeks, then leaves, being replaced by a worker from the same hostel. The remaining leader completes a further six weeks, then is replaced, and so on. This allows for the development of skills and its intended to increase feelings of competence among staff. It is noticeable that by the end of the 12 weeks staff demonstrate considerable confidence in their group skills. However, given the physical and rota constraints, leaders do have difficulty in having time to discuss and review the group. All groupwork writers emphasise the need for time to prepare and review the group, and rightly so; but this may have to be reduced to telephone discussions and mean loss of time off-duty. It is frequently observed that a leader will have accrued considerable 'lieu' hours when she/he completes a series of groups.

In addition to the prepared material, groups leaders have to learn to manage a number of confusing issues. Gender issues are an important dynamic; a female leader may find that she is marginalised by a male-dominated group discussing relationships. For example, one session focusing upon a 'What I need to go straight' brainstorm exercise, produced 'a woman to look after me', a statement which I felt had to be confronted when we were examining the contents of the brainstorm. Unwisely perhaps, I questioned the assumption that a woman's role was to act as a mother and I was roundly dismissed as being bound to say that - as a woman. When a similar example occurred in a later group, my male co-leader confronted the group to better effect in that individuals acknowledged that their lack of confidence led them to believe a woman would be both a prize and support for their own uncertainties. Furthermore the group members, to manage their inadequacies, may project upon the female leader qualities she may or may not possess; strengths and more commonly weaknesses are perceived and commented upon; 'just like a woman' is a phrase frequently used as I have struggled with recalcitrant 'Blutak' - 'cannot put up a sheet of paper without us to help you'. Preparation for such issues is essential, and both leaders need to acknowledge their position on gender issues.

Leaders need to be aware also of their own attitudes to racism. The hostel group is predominantly white, and black residents can find themselves severely disadvantaged if leaders do not confront white residents regarding their racist remarks. It is important for leaders to challenge racist remarks in context; there is no doubt that this can be demanding particularly if a leader is struggling to articulate anti-racist views. The group member who stated that black people received positive discrimination by housing associations because black people made a fuss was confronted, first in his use of language and second on the evidence and reasons behind his remarks. On reflection I consider that I should have ignored the language and tackled the statement, but anxiety and 'gut reaction' had encouraged me to intervene upon the emotive words first.

Many groupwork writers advocate encouraging a group to define its own values and this can prove a minefield regarding the relative merits or otherwise of various offences. Leaders have to struggle with a desire to get a 'correct' answer, for example, assaulting someone is more reprehensible than stealing dog food, and avoid imposing their own values.

I would like now to explore issues of group dynamics, particularly those of a group composed entirely of male members aged between 21 and 60. At this point an understanding of group focal conflict theory which states that individuals will fear a loss of personal identity in a group is particularly useful. Our residents, being predominantly in the older age group, do experience difficulties in working in a group composed partly, as they see it, of 'youngsters'. To enable themselves to maintain their individuality they may adopt the 'elder statesman' role, issuing portentous utterances which can be extremely useful; an insider's view of a maximum-security prison when those around him have yet to enter the custodial system by the lowly portals of a detention centre, gives a member prestige and status. However, this may be of mixed benefit to leaders trying to focus the group's attention upon personal strengths and weaknesses.

In contrast to the fieldwork model which is usually held at a probation office, the residential group takes place at a hostel with the influence of the members' own territory affecting its process. Individuals will know quite a lot about each others idiosyncrasies, and the group is potentially an extremely powerful agent for confrontation and catharsis.

However, one of the benefits of residential formal group work is that the process of forming may have occurred within each hostel sub-group; residents and staff will have met in groupings; joint hostel activities will have facilitated the process. The three probation hostels in Bristol are developing a practice of joint activities, for example, competitive 'sports days' which are usually very arduous for our residents (30-year-old plus bodies abused by alcohol/nicotine being no match for 20-year-olds). All this aids the group settling into work; but difficulties can arise when the group moves to 'norming'. Here, 'hostel relationships' between leaders and group members can lead to a situation where ideas are not explored and collusions between members allow possibilities for important discussions to pass by.

However, this permeable boundary between the 'formal' group and groupings can be useful. A hostel event can be used directly by group leaders to assist the group in its task. Group members are able to confront each other based upon directly observed incidents; two men who shared a room were able to examine their perceptions of personal hygiene based upon reality.

Endings of individual sessions or formal groups can be less painful than those of fieldwork groups, although difficult to utilise fully. Members know that they will be in contact with each other on a daily basis. Sadly, sometimes the context may be different; a confrontation between staff and residents regarding behaviour being one example.

The interaction between the two groups, clients/residents and staff is a fascinating arena. It is obviously the hope and expectation that the staff group will positively effect change (and covertly establish compliance and conformity) within the resident group. Evaluation of change in behaviour is still speculative and residents may have learned that verbal protestations of reformation satisfy staff, who equally accept such protestations as evidence of a change. We need to retain the client's stated aims of how he wishes to conduct his life and measure it against observed behaviour recorded by both the man and others. Only then can we conclude that the group experience may have been in part responsible for progress.

The practice of review meetings is used in the hostel so that keyworker, group leader, and client can evaluate the group and agree subjects for future work.

The exploration of group process and dynamics by the leaders is assisted if consultancy is available. A full discussion of the use of consultancy lies outside the scope of this chapter. However, in the hostel where leaders and members frequently meet informally as well as formally, the opportunity to discuss the group either in a staff meeting or with an individual in order to disentangle the various elements is found to be of considerable benefit to the leaders.

To conclude this section, formal groups have a place and a function within the total hostel programme but they need to be adaptable to fit the circumstances and to be congruous with the hostel ethos, not enshrined on tablets of stone.

INFORMAL GROUPS/GROUPINGS

There are a number of opportunities, some natural, others developed, for informal groupwork in the hostel. The most obvious natural ones are shared mealtimes which can offer a useful context. I do not wish to conjure up a picture of cosy domesticity, an enlarged, distorted image of an extended nuclear family with blue-ringed china, honey and a striking church clock, but they do present staff and residents with an opportunity, which can be grasped to discuss issues informally. The dining rooms at the hostel are furnished with small tables and the policy is for one staff member to sit in each of the two rooms. An unfortunate factor, not easily overcome, is for food to be eaten as if in readiness for the starter's gun; meals - three course ones including washing up - can be completed in under twenty minutes. So staff and residents have to utilise time available effectively. However, time spent after a meal can be expanded into informal discussion. Staff can use the time to discuss hostel life, individual issues, sharing of the good as well as the bad events. The need for individuals to feel nurtured and supported is evident when one knows that hostel life with its impersonal physical features and rules and regulations frequently denies individuality. Residents are often prepared to support each other when staff model a caring approach. The physical restrictions of communal living can produce individual or group anger and overt violence, and staff have to be aware of the potential for this; and to be prepared to intervene, support or challenge the group whilst retaining an understanding of their own role. Food, so symbolic of caring and needs, is a constant focus of hostel life and there is a tendency to become resistant to the complaints of residents.

The evening shift, ending as it does with the hostel being locked up and residents signing in, is notable for residents seeking staff for discussion, advice, or company. It is unfortunate that on occasion they are somewhat intoxicated and staff have to be sensitive in their approach. Abrupt termination of contact may actually prolong the end of their shift; whilst a short discussion regarding the meaning of life may be quicker in the long run. A resident announced at 11.15pm that he intended leaving the hostel 'right now and you're not to stop me'. 'Of course not, I wouldn't want to try - would you like a cup of tea before you go?' Half an hour later all retired to bed, including the resident who had threatened departure.

As mentioned earlier, groups/groupings can form following particular events; a commonality of experience following a night of internal or external disturbances is not uncommon. Staff can utilise this unity actively to facilitate change, using the experience to illustrate for residents the shared desire of hoped for change.

There are house meetings held every week allowing residents a forum to discuss house affairs. Viewed negatively they are an opportunity for residents to complain about those minor and major irritations of institutional life - food, bath water, noise, lack of adequate corporate cleaning, etc. I have observed a tendency for the hostel group to focus upon one issue - e.g. the allocation of food - for several weeks, with staff attempting in vain to deal with the problem when suddenly, one week, as unexpectedly as it arose, it subsides into the sea again. The management of the house groups which are not compulsory, rests upon staff on duty, and minutes are taken and distributed.

It is difficult for the leaders not to adopt a defensive posture when complaints are voiced, and it requires diplomacy of high order to ensure that the group has aired an issue which may not have a practical solution. One 'textbook' approach is to attempt to unveil the pressures and irritations that lie behind the issues in a manner that is not challenging and derogatory. Bearing in mind group theories, I am aware that the group may remain in a 'forming' stage for considerable periods of time due in part to the group being an open one particularly the bail section of the hostel where arrivals and departures of individuals are unplanned. Commitment by both staff and residents also affects the group process; it is not easy even with a well-developed understanding of group process to facilitate a group when staff have been confronting individuals concerning their behaviour in another context. The sense of the house meetings being stuck can be overwhelming to all members including staff, and the need to reflect upon this in both group and staff meetings is essential. The blurring of the boundary between staff and resident is easy to envisage when everyone has suffered from the ravages of institutional food. The mood of the resident group be it sad, energetic, angry or impatient will affect staff. Staff can use the feelings aroused in them by the resident group to enable discussion of the pleasures - and irritations - of hostel life. For example the demands on staff by residents following the new social security act and rent increases resulted in staff feeling defensive and becoming increasingly authoritarian in their manner. Initial discussion at the house meeting produced a defensive response 'who - us' from the residents, and a very quick change of subject. It was only weeks later that all parties could discuss their behaviour and responses in a more productive manner.

GENDER AND RACE

The hostel is predominantly male, and white; its rules and regulations reflect the assumed norms of society and make it a testing environment for those people defined otherwise by gender or race. Nowhere are these differences more explicit than regarding the preparation and production of food. Whether this is unique to offenders or a common human trait is open to question, but the exploration of alternative food is certainly seen by residents as a risky business. Equally staff, unless encouraged to consider the implications of white British food for black residents, will remain complacent and regard those who wish for a selection of food including Italian and Caribbean to be 'difficult'. It requires group vigilance if we are not to perpetuate stereotypes of imperialism.

Readers will have noted that there are only two female bail beds. Unfortunately, despite apparent evidence to the contrary, demand remains sparse and erratic and there is no acceptable argument in the current climate of high occupancy demands to increase the number to a more viable female group. Women offenders in the hostel have to cope with an overt sexism which defines them as 'available and willing'. The very fact that they have appeared before the courts renders them in male offenders' eyes as suitable for further exploitation. Equally problematic for staff is the evidence that many female bailees have developed a number of strategies for coping based upon their life experience, which can have included physical and mental abuse. It is not easy to retain a positive anti-sexist strategy when those one seeks to allow privacy and security apparently do not consider them to be worthwhile. Gender issues are not the prerogative of the residents; female staff members do experience them also, and are subjected to sexism both overt and covert. Within a group context this will manifest itself, often subtly, in a range of issues regarding attributed qualities of the sexes. Socialisation about domesticity is still largely based upon gender, and behind the hotly contested issue of washing up will lie the implication that 'it' is women's work. Female staff find that residents have expectations of them - from being a mother, to girlfriend - which will test their skills to the limit. Infatuation and excessive dependency by residents is not uncommon and the staff group has been the forum for explorations of how best to manage these issues professionally. This is not always easy when male staff may deny their reality and indeed may collude with residents in their attitudes. The watching of 'soft porn' video films by residents was the subject of much debate, the women staff feeling that it was condoning and colluding with residents' attitudes, the opposing argument being that it was entirely natural and indeed preferable to being away from the hostel in possibly nefarious pursuits.

Despite an open-door policy for all referrals, and the development of anti-racist publicity, the fact remains that black clients form a barely perceptible percentage of the hostel residents. With increasing evidence that black offenders are remanded in custody unnecessarily, the residential sector and others have to work to challenge the institutionalised racism of the criminal justice system, to redress these injustices. Whilst the hostel considers its own racist practices and seeks to change them, this will be unavailing if alterations do not occur in other sections of the system; Avon Probation Service as a whole has a commitment to anti-racist strategies and this is a positive step. The current system of monitoring social enquiry reports should encourage the service to consider its practice more thoroughly. The hostel needs to be alert to its own behaviour and to ensure that a black perspective is visible. Limited changes are evident, but monitoring and evaluation show that for many black offenders the hostel remains a hostile environment. Written information by the hostel can help to dispel some of this, but it requires strenuous effort by all sections of the service if we are to offer black offenders an acceptable alternative to custody.

Within the setting of the hostel, discrimination by residents can be problematic. Not only women and black people suffer, but those whose offences are defined as abnormal. The hostel accepts men charged with, and those convicted of, sexual offences. The task of working with these men can be very stressful in its own right; in addition, staff have to challenge attitudes expressed by other residents in regard to sexual offenders. Perhaps challenge has connotations of confrontation which is not always the best approach.

Staff have to question the triple assumption of white, male, heterosexual superiority. When a resident requested that women friends should be allowed to stay overnight the answer, that this made an assumption of universal heterosexuality and that some men would feel pressure because of this, produced a discussion at the house meeting. The group tentatively explored sexual attitudes and concluded that the rule of no guests overnight was a useful one.

Residential living provides opportunities for staff and residents to explore the strength of groupwork, and the pleasures of groupings, as well as their disadvantages. Because of the nature of their period at the hostels, the element of compulsion and the boundaries imposed, many residents feel unable to separate the process from the content of their experience. We can enable this reflection by allowing time to discuss, to evaluate, to consider and to prompt by 'do you remember when we were all talking about...?'

Carol Sapsed, Assistant Chief Probation Officer, Avon Probation Service. This chapter was first published in Brown, A. and Clough, R. (eds.) (1989) Groups and Groupings: Life and Work in Day and Residential Centres. *London: Routledge.*

10

Evolution and Accountability: Ten Years of Groups in a Day Centre for Offenders

JUDITH EARNSHAW

HISTORICAL ORIGINS

The Alternative Probation Project (APP) Day Centre was founded in 1976, the brainchild of a Farnham Probation Officer, Jeananne Medd. It was a pioneer programme, started when neither day centres nor groupwork were popular in the Probation Service. The APP Centre was also an early example of statutory and voluntary co-operation in a multi-disciplinary setting. With its keenly felt idealism, its therapeutic community model (see Jones, 1953), and its urge toward integration - both within the programme itself and with the local community - it was a product of the liberal, yet 'home-grown' thinking of the early 1970s. Its professed aims included preventing the loss to offenders and others caused by separating them from society, looking at patterns of offending behaviour, and developing and widening the offenders' frames of reference (APP Archives, Original Objectives, 1976-91).

Although Jeananne Medd was seconded by the Probation Service and had their full backing, it was left to her to find members of the local community to form into a support group for the project. Eventually they became a management committee with the tasks of raising funds from charities, employing support staff, and providing resources essential to the running of the Day Centre. Until Richard Cook joined in 1978 there had been several changes in co-worker, making it difficult to sustain the intended familial, caring milieu. Numbers and referrals were often low, and there was a persistent struggle to justify the continuation of the project. Until 1984 members did not attend as a requirement of the court, but because persistent offending, employment problems, lack of social skills or emotional difficulties indicated a need for extra attention. The supervising Probation Officer normally referred the offender, but if they failed to attend, or arrived late or inconsistently, there were few sanctions that could be applied other than group pressure and suspension. It says something for what the early Centre had to offer that, in the first two years, 31 stayed for more than three days, and 19 for over a month 'on a wholly voluntary basis' (First APP Annual Report, 1976-78).

CURRENT POSITION

The Day Centre now operates as a community supervision programme for the highest risk offenders (80% upwards on the Cambridge Risk of Custody Scale, see Bale, 1987; HMSO, 1989) who would be considered for a probation order. Almost all now attend for 60 days on Schedule 11 4(b) day centre requirements of the Courts (Criminal Justice Act, Home Office, 1982).

PERSISTENT THEMES

From the beginning the modified therapeutic community model has been central to the atmosphere of the Day Centre (see Burney, 1982). Members and staff have lived, worked, cooked and cleaned together, and all transactions between them have been available for feedback. In this context of day-long exposure, the modelling and example of staff has always been seen as important, although the emphasis remains on helping offenders to take responsibility for themselves and others, and to make choices (one of the initial aims and objectives).

The programme continues to offer a combination of group and individual work; to emphasise and teach constructive leisure pursuits; to foster team-work and co-operation within the group; and to undertake reparative work within the local community (see Cook, 1988).

DISTINCTIONS

Perhaps the main differences between the current and the original orientation is the sense of whom the Centre serves. From primarily offering a service to offenders who joined the group voluntarily in order to enhance their social development, it now sees itself as providing resocialisation to members whose group participation is a consequence of pressures from the court and from society (Garvin, 1987). Inevitably, members do not identify with all the goals which the Day Centre has targeted in the programme.

The Probation Service has, since its inception, aimed to offer probationers a wholesome blend of 'care and control'. However, in our work with increasingly high risk offenders, the control aspect has become more dominant over the years. There has been some loss in members' sense of commonality as a result, and a diminishing of trust and altruism. There is far more emphasis on boundaries, and we strongly discourage association between members outside the programme. Contagion regarding offending is not our only consideration in making this policy: an average of 90 per cent of our members are frequent or habitual drug users, even though we do not take opiate addicts. In the 1970s about 20 per cent were drug users.

Breach - a return to court for disciplinary proceedings, occasioned by absence, lateness, or failure to co-operate with the programme - and re-sentencing are now available sanctions at the Centre, approached through a verbal and written warning system. Although the need to confront offending behaviour was always present, it now forms the core of a much more structured groupwork programme, and the emphasis, which used to fall upon the self-destructiveness of offending, now falls on the destructiveness to others. Representatives of the local Victim Support Scheme regularly attend the programme to present the victim's point of view; direct mediation has been undertaken when the victim has been willing; and group members are now often asked to speak from the point of view of those they have injured.

Another early objective was to 'give opportunities for members to say as well as to act out their feelings' (APP Archives, 1976-91). Now we place a stronger emphasis on cognitive processes and thinking errors (see Yochelson and Samenow, 1985). We believe that much criminal behaviour is the acting out of faulty belief systems which the offender needs to revise. Typical beliefs include the perception of self, rather than society, as the victim; a belief that the offender's strong feelings cannot be controlled; and a belief that power over others is a primary objective in life. We draw out the presence of these erroneous beliefs underlying the offender's day-to-day behaviour, and counter them. We also offer coping strategies for 'survival' situations, and deterrent strategies to be used when there is a temptation to offend or act out. Ways in which we do this include improvised role-plays of difficult situations, with the action being frozen at points where the protagonist needs to re-think, or discuss, his next move; and the preparation of 'aversion scenarios' - the worst possible consequences of a typical offence. The whole group uses its imagination to concoct the scenario, and it is typed up on a card which the offender carries in his wallet. The orientation of the work is more confrontational and less supportive.

AGENCY STANDARDS AND MONITORING

The Centre has now been more fully adopted by the Probation Service, and we no longer work in isolation but as part of a projects team. There is a high consciousness of working within an agency to agency standards. In the past five years, this has involved an even stronger emphasis on objective evaluation and quantifiability of work, on the identification of shared key areas of activity, and on the agreed action plans to achieve goals within these. We keep monthly statistics monitoring attendance and reconviction rates, and estimated risk to the community from current members. We also track former members for two years after completion of a day centre order, for reconviction, employment record, and evidence of lasting implementation of change. There is also more accountability to the courts, and we are conscious of this in our day-to-day supervision of offenders. There is a rigorously implemented 'breach' policy. Recommendation reports to the court include action plans for work with the offender, and we are frequently called upon to explain or justify these in our Court attendances. Reports on response to the programme are also available to the courts when a member completes, and we now have frequent contact with the judges, the magistracy, and the police.

GAINS AND LOSSES

The Centre's much greater acceptance by Surrey Probation Service and the strong commitment from the APP Management Committee have led to more resources and support being available from both. There is a continuous flow of referrals to the programme and it has a good reputation with the courts and other agencies and organisations working on behalf of society's interests. We no longer have to spend time justifying our existence.

There are better recording systems, regularly assessed statistics, more clarity about the work undertaken, and support in determining areas of change and development.

There has been an inevitable loss of the pioneering energy and vision both with the passage of time and the loss of the charismatic leader. Jeananne's total dedication to the Centre led her to work extraordinary hours. Early records indicate that some offenders recognised and responded to this investment in them. Elizabeth Burney (1980) quotes early members as saying:

> I just feel so grateful. Not over-grateful - I just know I made a start. I didn't enjoy what I put into being at the centre, but I so enjoyed what I got out of it.

> I thought it's really making me feel fresh and light again.

These statements are reinforced by the fact that members from the earliest period have remained in voluntary contact with the Centre for seven and ten years.

The original emphasis seems to have been on encouraging attitudes or aspects of behaviour seen as positive by the workers. A basically negative self-image was assumed amongst the offenders, and there were efforts to improve this through education, social skills teaching, and reinforcement of positive behaviour.

There was a greater emphasis on the family as a source of emotional conflict. Workers encouraged the free expression of feeling, and saw discharges of feeling as an achievement. They attempted to work with the regressed child in the offender by offering a re-parenting model via the male/female group leadership (see Heap, 1977). Yet at the same time, there was always a concurrent strand in the model which urged members to take responsibility for themselves and their actions, and encouraged them to engage positively in determining the rules and content of the programme.

The current, tougher approach to offenders means that we are not fooled so easily, but we may not be conveying to them as much of our faith in their goodness and potential altruism. The early approach did not engage, or succeed in changing everybody (nor does the current one), but those who were affected retained a long-term loyalty to the Centre, continuing to visit for years after they had left.

CHANGING APPROCHES OF THE CURRENT WORKERS

Both of the current group leaders, who have now worked together for ten years, came from psychotherapy backgrounds, and had experience of working with neurotic non-offenders. Like those who started the programme, we were accustomed to methods that aimed to decrease fear, guilt and anxiety, to encourage the open expression of feelings, and to improve self-esteem.

Now, with ten years of working with offenders, we tend to see the experiencing of fear, guilt, and shame as potential spurs toward responsible citizenship. These feelings are normally 'cut off' during the offending process. We are more apt to encourage control of feelings rather than their free expression, seeing most offences as overly disinhibited. We advocate that members 'think before they speak' about the likely impact of their words, and we place emphasis on careful listening, and monitor that this is taking place. We no longer attempt to 'improve the self-image' of offenders; we encourage the offenders to dislike themselves as they are, and to begin to be motivated to change. We find this hard to do, since many offenders hear selectively only those items of feedback which build them up.

Current work does not favour working with the regressed child in the client, but with encouraging the thinking and reasoning adult. We spend time examining in detail the thinking processes through which offences are devised and justified, and in exposing the errors and gaps in this thinking. The activities programme, which involves risky activities such as climbing, abseiling and canoeing, demands adult, co-operative behaviour and team-work; irresponsibility increases the risk and cannot be condoned. The offender group also work twice a week with groups of people with moderate and severe learning difficulties teaching them, in a supervised context, the physical skills they themselves have been learning. The work with these groups is seen as requiring adult and parental behaviour from the offenders.

However, these emphases on adult responses are partly undermined in the current model by the fact that members no longer exercise as much responsibility or 'own' the Centre to the degree they used to. They no longer determine the rules or the programme; the staff do, and impose sanctions and breach when the expectations are not met. This removes the risk of exploitation of privileges, which did occur in the early days, but some of the personal identification with the Centre and its positive values are also lost.

The sources of these changes stem quite largely from the White Paper *Punishment, Crime and the Community* (Home Office, 1988a) and its associated Action Plan (Home Office, 1988b), although our movement in this direction antedated the publication of these proposals. It is hard to say whether we were at first responding to the lessons of our own experience with offenders, or to a sensed change in the political climate which crystallised in the White Paper (see National Association of Probation Officers, 1988). Five years ago we integrated a community service element into the offending behaviour-focused groupwork programme, and added victim awareness sessions and mediation work. We have also matched Audit Commission Review guidelines in identifying target work areas and action plans for challenging criminal thinking (Audit Commission, 1989). A visit last year to the Day Centre from John Patten, Minister of State, confirmed the Home Office's commitment to strongly confrontational groupwork (Patten, 1990).

We studied the work of two American psychiatrists, Samuel Yochelson and Stanton Samenow (1976), on the criminal personality, and have adapted our groupwork as a result. It was their emphasis on the cognitive approach: eliciting the thinking processes that underpin criminal actions, and recognising and countering faulty belief systems, that helped us to develop a new core programme. This demands rigorous reporting of daily activities and thinking, with diaries being kept during the short breaks in the programme.

EVALUATION OF THE CHANGES

It remains uncertain how much of the learning that appears to occur at the Day Centre is lip-service, and how much offenders' lives outside the Centre are affected and changed by their learning within it. Even where there are no reconvictions, it is impossible for us to know whether offenders are really living more responsibly and, if they seem to be, whether this is due to the Day Centre's influence, or other factors. It is possible that the loose boundaries and greater accessibility of staff out of hours in the early model meant that more learning was 'transferred out'.

During the first two years, out of 31 offenders who spent more than three days in the programme, 15 re-offended within that two year period - almost 50 per cent (First APP Annual Report).

In 1988-89, out of a throughput of 35 offenders whose average stay was 29 days, 16 were either breached, suspended from the programme or re-offended - about 46 per cent (APP Annual Report, 1988-89).

In 1989-90, out of a throughput of 28 offenders with an average stay of 29 days, 10 were either breached, suspended or re-offended - about 35 per cent (APP Annual Report, 1990).

The figures are not entirely comparable, since we are now working with larger groups of higher risk offenders, and because a member who is breached or suspended has not necessarily been re-convicted. Nonetheless it is a gauge of continuing irresponsible behaviour. There was a period of two consecutive years in the mid-1980s when our non-reconviction rate was 60 per cent and 75 per cent respectively, two years after the completion of the programme. We believe that this was because we had introduced a more structured 'offending behaviour based' programme, but were not yet targeting the highest risk offenders.

In the earlier recorded groups a more intimate and accepting atmosphere is perceptible. It looks as though, despite the fact that some offending and irresponsible behaviour was missed, this may have led to a more caring group atmosphere in which members showed more concern for one another's authentic well-being. A loss inherent in the current regime may be that members have a tendency to band together to oppose the staff's higher authority profile. Also, there is not the same model of acceptance from the staff on which members can base acceptance and help towards one another.

Overall, our impression is that there is rather more quantifiable success in the current regime, but that it is possible that the quality of the success with those who were affected by the early model may have been higher - the change more personally felt.

Judith Earnshaw, Psychologist, Hampshire. This chapter is reprinted from Groupwork, *1991, 4(3)*

11

Opening Doors with Offenders:
Groupwork in a Probation Day Centre

JAN HILL, SUE THOMAS AND MAURICE VANSTONE

The group sessions described in this paper take place in the
Pontypridd Day Centre and need to be understood within the
context of its fifteen year developmental history of groupwork.
The Centre was opened in 1973 as one of the original Day
Training Centres set up experimentally as alternatives to custody
for persistent offenders. Apart from the first two years during
which there was a focus on practical life skills some form of
groupwork has been a consistent feature of the programme.
Early groups in the centre were little more than loosely structured
discussion groups and it was not until the influence of the social
skills and personal problem solving approach promulgated by
Priestley and McGuire (1978) that a clearer rationale and
structure for the groups began to emerge.

It was at this point that a closed group intake system was first
introduced. The principal reasons for this were that it was
believed that the management of a small group whose members
started and finished the programme together was likely to be
more coherent and that the experience for the group members
was likely to be more potent and beneficial (Douglas, 1976;
Preston-Shoot, 1988). Also underpinning this decision was a
belief that the closed group afforded an increased opportunity for
collaborative self help and change. As Brown states:

> Attitudes, feelings and behaviour may be changed in a group
> situation. This can occur through social interaction, including
> role-modelling, re-inforcement, feedback and a range of ideas
> available to each member (Brown, 1979).

The social skills and personal problem solving approach which
predominated in the Centre for approximately seven years,
involved the use of a wide range of methods which included group

discussion, direct teaching, video, role play, simulations, films, talks and pencil and paper exercises. Group members were encouraged to share the responsibility for assessment, the setting of objectives and the work undertaken to achieve those objectives. A particular emphasis was put on the involvement of group members in the evaluation of the attempt at change. In order to formalise the spontaneous, direct and sometimes unsolicited evaluations that were made by group members, direct written comments on their experience of the programme, as well as 'before and after' measures, were gathered as often as possible. The use of that material significantly contributed to incremental change in the programme (Vanstone, 1986). During that phase of the groupwork history of the Centre the programme was structured around a series of compulsory group sessions which focused both on people's offending and on an assessment of the problems related to that offending. These were then followed by a variety of groups - each dealing with different problem areas - which were offered to group members who, in the choices they made, tailored their own programme.

During the past few years transactional analysis theory has influenced the direction of the programme. Indeed it has always been the case that changes in the programme have occurred not only because of evaluation but also because of changes in group workers who have brought with them new skills, knowledge and training experience. Nevertheless, the influence of the values and framework of the Priestley and McGuire model remain pervasive and can be discerned in the current programme which we now describe.

The focus of the current sessions remains primarily the same and they are, therefore, designed and structured to facilitate change across a broad spectrum of problems and particularly that of offending. A direct attempt is made to influence and enable the group members to change their anti-social behaviour to prosocial behaviour. In doing this the group leaders rely on three basic categories of influence. Firstly, normative influence which induces people to act, think and feel in ways which fit the pattern of the norms of the group. Secondly, informational influence which emanates from the process of looking for information and thirdly, interpersonal influence which includes persuasion, bargains, promises and, possibly, threat of rejection (Forsyth, 1990). A critical part of this change effort involves teaching the group members a model for understanding their thinking, feeling and behaviour. (This model is based largely on transactional analysis theory and will be expanded on later in this paper.) Additionally, by creating a challenging but supportive environment the group leaders encourage group member autonomy and not only teach new thinking and interpersonal skills but provide the opportunity for members to practise and test them out. They recognise that many of the problems faced by people who attend the Centre are structural and to a greater or lesser extent beyond their sphere of control (e.g. structural unemployment, endemic poverty and government benefit regulations). However, the group leaders do not ignore these but rather work at helping the group members to identify those problems which fall within their sphere of control and then concentrate on the behaviour and decision-making necessary to cope more effectively with these problems.

The groups run for a period of ten weeks during which time the group members attend the Centre between 10 am. and 3 pm. The group is closed and ranges in size from eight to twelve people. There are three group sessions in a week and each group lasts for two hours. A co-leadership model is used because of the complexities of tasks facing the leaders in this kind of group, the level of support required and the richness brought to the group by the different skills, styles and personalities of the leaders. Both male/female and female/female pairings are used. The latter often leads to more overt and aggressive sexist behaviour and language from group members and heightens the need for a strong co-leadership alliance. All sessions are filmed with the knowledge of the group members and there is a video link to a consultant in an adjoining room. This is a modified version of a technique used in family therapy. Occasionally the leaders will take time out but consultation occurs primarily after the completion of each session. It is seen as an invaluable part of the leadership process and makes a very significant contribution to staff development and improved performance. Direct and specific feedback is an essential element (Ainley and Kingston, 1981). The group members are themselves encouraged to watch the video in order to consolidate and reinforce learning that has taken place. This is seen as a particularly powerful experience.

The group sessions themselves do not take place in isolation and they are an integral part of a general weekly programme. It is not within the scope of this paper to describe the other activities in the Centre but it is important to appreciate that efforts are made by the staff to use the group's 'living in' experience to reinforce the learning within the groupwork sessions. Indeed the day to day life of the Centre creates an important context within which a very significant degree of relationship building takes place.

Particular attention is paid to the imperative of working from a clearly defined value base. Therefore, the rules of the group are made very explicit and whilst each group is encouraged to develop its own norms, some clear boundaries particularly in relation to anti-discrimination and violence are prescribed. The group leaders recognise that because of their own experience, skills and role they have a significant contribution to make to the group sessions and some definite responsibilities. Within this context an attempt is made to develop open and collaborative relationships with the group members, based on agreements. In so doing they pay heed to the dangers of producing agreements that are rendered meaningless because no account has been taken of the power imbalance between group leader and group member (Rojek and Collins, 1987; Corden and Preston-Shoot, 1987). The relationships are purposefully challenging and based on a fundamental respect for people (not necessarily their behaviour) and a basic optimism about the possibilities of change. In transactional analysis terms the reference point for the relationship between the group workers and members is 'I am OK, you're OK'. It follows, therefore, that power is a critically important issue. It threads its way through a complex maze of relationship combinations - leader/leader; leader/group member; male/female and group member/group member. This particular client group will have both abused power and been the victims of such abuse. It is vital, therefore, that the group leaders construct a different power model which incorporates the sharing of power. Accordingly they strive to achieve 'referent power' (French and Raven, 1959). Where this exists in a group, members critically compare their own values and standards with those of the group because they identify with those values and standards. Similarly where a group leader has referent power, group members will aspire to be like her.

The notion of sharing power implies a particular style of leadership. The group leaders accept that groups have at least two basic objectives - task completion and maintenance of collaboration between members - and adopt a distributed-actions model which 'emphasises that certain functions need to be filled if a group is to meet these objectives' (Johnson and Johnson, 1991). This model also incorporates the idea that any member of the group can become leader if they assist the group in task or maintenance functions. The leaders are, therefore, striving to achieve a situation in the sessions in which members are empowered and the leadership function passes appropriately around the group.

The men who attend the groups fall into a category commonly characterised as high risk offenders. The Mid Glamorgan Probation Service uses a risk of custody scale based on the Cambridgeshire model and the group members all score above 80 on that scale. They are, therefore, at considerable risk of a custodial sentence when their orders are made and invariably have a history of numerous previous convictions and several custodial sentences. It would be a reasonable generalisation to say that they are all socially and economically disadvantaged and primarily from large urban estates or from former mining communities in the Welsh Valleys. Eighty per cent admit to having been emotionally or physically abused and approximately eighty per cent are products of both the care and prison systems; all are unemployed and tend to be unskilled and educationally disadvantaged. Over a period of time, common needs have been identified which cluster around cognitive and behavioural skill deficiencies, relationship difficulties, problems relating to boundary-setting, poor modelling, unemployment, accommodation problems and general life instability.

The group leaders' theoretical position is shaped by transactional analysis (Berne, 1961) but also quite significantly by open door theory as expounded by Paul Ware (Ware, 1983). This theory is formed around the proposition that people have need with regard to feelings, thinking and behaviour and, in relation to these, different open, trap or target doors depending on their particular characteristics or personality. The doors are points of potential contact for worker and client. So the open door is for making contact, the trap door is to be avoided and the target door points the way for desired change. For instance, a person who has unrealistic self expectations and rigid thinking patterns might be offered the following hypothesis. Their open door is thinking which is predominantly negative; their trap door is resultant behaviour which leads to offending; and their target door is feeling more positive about themselves and others. It would, therefore, be the worker's task to help the individual towards the target door. Whilst the group leaders are conscious of the danger of pathologising the group members by using this framework and are only too aware that their offending is inextricably linked to social and economic disadvantage, it is the group leaders' experience that offences often result from poor coping skills and the making of anti-social, albeit constrained choices. A significant number have learnt to shut down on feelings and demonstrate thinking patterns which lead them into trouble. Such thinking characteristically tends to be survival based, manipulative and often contains errors induced by inadequate information.

The group leaders resist engaging with the group members' negative self-talk and instead encourage and reward clear thinking around alternative ideas. Many of the group members repeat patterns of behaviour and thinking even when they have a limited range of alternatives. As a starting point, therefore, the leaders challenge belief and value systems, particularly as they relate to negative, pessimistic and poor functioning positions. Once beliefs and values have been challenged and successfully negotiated, the group begins to work and is encouraged to examine thinking patterns. During this process family messages are examined and reframed, the leaders at this point acting as consultants and giving new positions and providing new information. Family messages often will have been transmitted through either physical or emotional abuse in childhood and the leaders, therefore, lay heavy emphasis on positive strokes for risk-taking and exploratory work.

The leaders do not arrive at the group sessions with a prescribed programme of activities. A range of methods and materials are used depending on the needs and responses of the group and particular attention is paid to the group process. The leaders' thinking is influenced by Tuckman's work on stages of group process (Tuckman, 1965) and in particular Petruska Clarkson who, in her analysis of the stages of group process, argues that:

> A theoretical understanding of these stages can help the group psychotherapist conceptualise occasionally baffling phenomena, aid discriminating selection of techniques and interventions and find support in drawing on the experience of pioneers in the field who faced similar moments of anxiety, despair, pleasure and pain (Clarkson, 1988).

They accordingly adjust their behaviour and responses to match the particular stage of the group. Thus during Tuckman's 'storming stage':

> ...the leadership task is to survive with the leadership boundaries and the group task intact at the same time as allowing individual members of the group maximum opportunity to test. The leader needs to survive verbal attacks from the group without punishing or collapsing, neither becoming

punitive nor apologetic' (Clarkson, 1988; see also Corey and Corey, 1987).

Each group session and programme is unique but over the two year period during which this model has been in use, a familiar pattern has emerged. In order to illustrate this a generalised description is now given.

WEEKS 1-2

The concerns of the group members at this stage are getting to know each other, beginning to share some of the anxieties and fears about involvement in the group and negotiating a value base. Cohesiveness is dependent on the setting of boundaries during this period and in this respect the leaders play a crucial role as models. From the onset it is established that the group exists to examine both offending and offence-related behaviour. The group leaders at this stage pay heed to pace and gently encourage people to share information about themselves. They adopt a much more active role during this period than in later weeks and increase the use of exercises and method such as warm ups, trust games, brainstorm, exercises around listening skills, pencil and paper exercises, hot seat exercises and moral dilemma games such as Scruples. Significantly the group leaders constantly attempt to model appropriate relationship behaviour and consistently challenge any negative, destructive behaviour which reinforces unhelpful belief or value systems. It is considered vitally important that group members are given clear information about what is and what is not acceptable behaviour within the group. This will include such norms as avoiding cross talk and giving everyone the opportunity and space to contribute.

WEEKS 3-4

This is normally the period which members often express their ambivalence about being in the group and their uncertainty about how the leaders react to such ambivalence. Understandably they frequently anticipate rejection because of previous life experiences in which adults have both rejected, deserted and punished them when they have broken 'rules'. The primary concern of the group leaders at this stage is to keep the group together and to maintain boundaries which are usually being tested to the full. During this period group members will often behave in ways characterised by Tuckman's storming phase.

Their natural inclination is to resist tasks either by withdrawing or becoming passive or alternatively becoming antagonistic and verbally abusive. When this happens it is important that the group leaders distinguish between inappropriate behaviour based on anxiety and comparisons with previous experiences, and appropriate reactions which represent reasonable criticism of the behaviour of the leaders or the content of the group sessions. Moreover, the group leaders must avoid stifling resistance through their own rigidity or by resorting to prescription through the inappropriate use of prepared materials and methods. It is deemed to be more apposite to pay attention to the process that is occurring, to work with the resistance whilst at the same time creating an optimum level of security for it to run its course. The leaders at this stage typically resist threats and attempts at emotional blackmail, for example - 'I won't come back to this group if I can't smoke'. They will be concerned instead to validate people's choices, their rights to their feelings and thoughts, options and concerns but without giving up on the established focus. Negotiation often takes place between group members and between group members and leaders, but the leaders avoid getting hooked into unproductive and diversionary arguments. It is a salutary realisation that group members have usually learned the survival technique of manipulation and can apply it far more effectively than the leaders!

WEEKS 5-6

This is often a period in which the members seem more willing to work and are ready to explore other areas of their lives. They are assisted in this by the use of family trees, a technique borrowed from family therapy. The leaders also work at enhancing group cohesiveness, encourage group members to set personal objectives for the remainder of the group and, at this stage, provide group members with a framework for thinking about themselves and their lives by teaching some basic transactional analysis theory. This is done didactically with the use of a flip chart. Firstly they are introduced to Berne's ego state theory (Parent, Adult and Child). This quite specifically enables the group members to recognise how they communicate with each other and also offers a potential framework within which they can change their own behaviour. At the forefront of the leaders' mind at this point is the fact that group members are disadvantaged in a number of ways and they are concerned with increasing their coping and interpersonal skills. Particularly relevant here is the teaching of how to give and receive positive strokes. Generally they have been used to living in a climate dominated by the giving and receiving of negative strokes. A consistent theme throughout the group therefore, is to intervene in their stroke pattern with the specific aim of helping them to change their thinking and behaviour in this respect. In particular they are taught the accruing advantage of using their adult ego state in their transactions with other people. They are also taught games theory at this stage in an attempt to help them identify the games which permeate their relationships with the people close to them. This is a precursor to the task of identifying ways of discarding those particular games which they assess as unhelpful. This didactic phase is then used as a backdrop to consistent and active encouragement of the practice and implementation of the learning throughout the remaining life of the group.

WEEKS 7-8

This is a period in which group members are encouraged to apply their newly acquired theoretical knowledge and skills to those problematical aspects of their lives which they consider to be important. Often at this stage the group functions effectively and performs purposefully on the agreed tasks. There is frequently a discernment of change in thinking patterns and interpersonal behaviour and a commitment to problem solving. It is critical at this particular point that the group members work with issues important to them so that it is their agenda and not that of the leaders. There are, of course, still difficult emotional issues to grapple with and not everyone's behaviour is constructive, but there is usually a distinct sense of the development of a culture within the group in which everybody is struggling not only with their own learning but also the learning of others. The leaders concentrate on maintenance tasks by offering praise, giving positive strokes, exercising minimal control, encouraging autonomy, spontaneity and fun but also managing the boundaries of the group in order to ensure safety.

Trust levels are particularly high and members often bring personal problems which continue to be dealt with from within a behavioural and cognitive framework. It is what they think and do about the issues in the here and now which are considered important. 'Two chair' work borrowed from gestalt therapy (Perls, 1971) and role play will be used frequently at this point and other methods are used that the leaders deem appropriate for the particular individual and the specific problem.

However, people are not coerced into work and leadership characteristics of flexibility, adaptability and creativity are applied to the goal of attempting to meet the needs of the group members. The primary purpose here is to help people to make new decisions and to apply newly acquired behavioural and cognitive responses, which free them from old and unhelpful strategies to problem situations. The three key principles underpinning leadership behaviour here are permission, potency and protection.

WEEKS 9-10

The aim now is to help the group end in a positive way and to facilitate an ending which the group can use as a learning experience for future endings. The leaders increase their presence here and encourage a review of the group work experience, highlighting funny moments, low spots, high spots, achievements and lost members. Clarkson's guidelines are particularly useful at this time in helping the leaders to avoid defensive reactions to some of the responses of the group. Paradoxically, people who have worked at some depth in the sessions and have acknowledged a variety of achievements can become quite negative. The focus here is one in which each person is given an envelope and asked to write a positive comment about every group member and then put it in that group member's envelope. They each take their envelope with them when they leave.

Group members are also encouraged to evaluate the programme. However, currently there is no attempt to systematically measure change and the group leaders acknowledge this as a significant gap. This gap is to be filled shortly by a research programme which will focus on the whole of the Day Centre programme. For the moment, therefore, for an indication of the impact of the group experience, we have to rely on the observations of the group leaders and the group members themselves.

The leaders are striving to achieve Henry Maier's 'model C' in which the leaders' potency comes from 'practice capacity earned by competency to deal with the situation at hand' (Brown and Caddick, 1986). Within this model they are aiming to enable people to think differently; to recognise that they have choices (albeit constrained); to help them change aspects of their behaviour; and to understand and deal more effectively with some of their emotions. Within the short period of the group's life the leaders observe different patterns of thinking and behaviour and this is confirmed to some extent by the comments of those who complete the programme. There is a drop out rate but the reasons for this are no doubt complex and will form part of the focus of the research; therein might lie an interesting story. The comments of those who stay illustrate different kinds of impact. Some have learnt new ways of thinking:

> I remember looking at the stuff on the wall, particularly my family tree and thinking that's my life but it doesn't have to be like that...

For others it gave different ways of responding to problematical situations and a clearer understanding of their choices:

> It made me see that I could do things differently - without using my fists...(and)

> It made me realise that I could act differently, that I had more choices than I thought.

Another group member had moved to a different perspective on himself and his personal history:

> It's like having an outsider's view of your life. The way I was beaten as a kid wasn't right.

Victims figure strongly in the comments of one group member:

> The sentencing exercise made me think about victims. I remember I felt rotten when they all had a go. I've never done a house burglary since. I've done other things like shoplifting and handling but never a burglary in two years.

Finally, the aim of the group leaders to establish a group culture based on openness and mutual respect is at least confirmed by the observations of two group members:

> I thought, God, she's straight and that made me want to listen...(and)

> I've never in my life been spoken to (with respect) like I was by the staff at the centre and I'm 36.

The group sessions described in this paper need the full evaluation that will result from the research and there will be lessons to be learnt. On the basis of their experience so far, however, the group leaders are convinced that a very important aspect of effective work is a confident and flexible approach to leadership. They are also excited by the potential of teaching theory to group members and humbled by the quality of their response.

Jan Hill, Sue Thomas and Maurice Vanstone, Mid-Glamorgan Probation Service

12

Offending Behaviour
or Better Adjusted Criminals?

PETER MARK

THE SETTING

The Day Training Centre is a large centralised resource taking adult clients from the entire Inner London Probation area. The work mixes intense closed morning groups with afternoon 'practical' workshops where clients choose specific skills they want to learn, such as computer skills, music, etc., or adult education courses they wish to pursue.

CLIENT

The type of clients referred to our Centre experience a range of difficulties, including problems making relationships, sexual confusions, guilt relating to past relationships and society's view of them, traumatic memories of childhood, anger all too evidently close to the surface or deeply buried, envy often manifesting itself in compulsion to steal from others, and usually a loss of contact with, or denial of, reality. All this is amplified by the social pressures of unemployment, inadequate housing, and discrimination.

Most of the offenders we see have a very low view of themselves, do not really consider themselves worthy of attention, often look for it in manipulative ways, often act in an irrational and immature way that belies their years, and generally lack confidence. Crime has become a habit and/or a compulsion in their lives which perpetuates their view of themselves as losers doomed to go in and out of prison for the rest of their lives. The resultant institutionalisation further reinforces these perceptions and takes away any sense of responsibility. It is this very lack of self-responsibility that we tackle directly in our 12-week programme, with its concentration on the core closed group experience of 125 hours in a room together with about ten peers and two probation officer group leaders.

The group is an intense, closed experience for 2.5 hours on every morning that the clients attend the Centre; it focuses on how the members relate to each other and emphasises the giving and receiving of 'feedback'. The leaders attend particularly to the group process as the instrument of change and movement within the group, avoiding thematic leadership but encouraging the group as a whole to take responsibility for the content of the sessions and how they use their time together. The leaders stimulate and activate the process by commenting on what they see as the process within the group and encouraging members to be as open and honest in their communication with each other as possible. The group situation can be seen as a laboratory offering choices and the possibility of change. The starting point is always the assumption that members will relate to each other in the group in ways that reflect their relationship in the outside world. The group leaders act as mediators between the client's internal world and his/her environment.

The group develops as a safe place for members to observe their own and others' communication, to test ideas and begin the process of change if they choose to do so. The emphasis is very much on the internal view of self and how this affects their relationships with others. Any agent of change lies in the relationships with peers and with the leaders, and it is often feedback from peers which is more effective in the long run than any input from the group leaders. This is a particularly social and democratic approach to change, with the power focused within each individual as part of a larger network of peers.

The here and now communication is probably the only truly relevant and real part of the probation officers relationship with the client at the Centre. Past material, of course, does come up and it is significant mainly in how it affects the way the client is seen in the group. The other crucial strand is making the link between the client in the group and how he is outside the group - connecting the group behaviour to the social behaviour and the offending behaviour.

LEADERSHIP

The probation officers' role requires a great deal of skill and patience with a very professional check kept on the need for self-gratification. The initial refusal to parent the group through structures and exercises often leads to anger in the clients and refusal to take responsibility for themselves. Regression usually follows and with it transference, placing the leaders in the frustrating parental role. This transference is invariably negative or defensively idealised. I believe that handling this well is one of the most skilful and complex tasks that any social worker has to learn. To be confident enough within oneself to separate out angry feelings directly dumped, but not belonging to the workers, requires a mature sense of containment. As social workers we are often much more comfortable seeing ourselves as allies and befrienders and it can be traumatic to find oneself actually impotent, manipulated and exploited. Yet, however difficult, I believe this way of working allows honest and real feelings to emerge. It is not possible to avoid this negative transference by adopting overly supportive collusive relationships. Instead of being openly hated, the worker is instead more subtly denigrated in more structured groups.

By allowing the anger expression, the clients take responsibility for their own group and begin working on filling the gaps left by their previous experience of relationships and authority. Here the probation officers provide consistency of treatment by strictly holding to the boundaries.

The Centre itself provides the sense of community and clients do the significant work with each other aiming towards an opening up of choices in that client's life. This is not achieved by the leaders' clever interpretations, but by the clients learning about themselves, particularly the parts they deny which the group reflects. The process of reflection helps a more realistic sense of themselves to emerge. When verbalised, this change gets expressed as care and concern for each other.

RESISTANCE

The whole 12-week experience is often one of working through some tortuous resistances towards on experience of resolution and growth, and 80 per cent of the work here could be said to be dealing with resistance. However, it is often the most resistant clients, the ones who challenge the boundaries endlessly and express the most anger throughout who come back to visit months later with quite dramatic changes in their lives to report. The penny sometimes takes quite a while to drop. The microcosmic reality of the group provides the boundaries for the clients to test and accept the realities of each others' experience, as well as differences of race, culture and class, and modify their attitudes and stereotypes, making it clear to them what can and cannot be changed.

The rationalisations for not changing are consistently challenged and the members' previous experiences can be re-assessed in a new light. The characteristic low self-esteem which often results in rejection and self-fulfilling failure as a means to defend against fear of loss is gradually modified and a new confidence allows them to recover some lost ground and begin to trust.

I suppose the ultimate aim in this 12-week programme is to enable the clients to realise what their own responsibility is and do away with the rationalising and excuses they are so often fed by society and even by other social work interventions. There is certainly much more recognition in the clients leaving the Centre that to a degree they make their own worlds and carry them inside. They are much more aware of their choices and positions even in a depressed society. This has been true of most members in every group I have experience of at the Centre.

AIMS AND REALITY

Before attempting to answer whether or not these groups meet the needs of tackling offending behaviour, I want to look at what I believe is realistically achieved during the three months.

Personal responsibility and widening of choice

As I have already said, one of the most important aims of our programme is to instil a feeling of more personal power in the individual offender to counteract the feeling of being blown by circumstances so characteristic of an institutionalised person. Like so much of what we do this is a feeling related to experience - increasing self-esteem cannot be picked up from lectures or discussions. T.S. Eliot said that the 'happy necessity of this human existence is for men to find things out for themselves'. For me, this refers to the clients' need to create some order in chaotic lives, to develop self-identity in clarifying who they are, establishing a sense of belonging, and building on a mutual trust and respect of peers in the group. Most clients achieve this in the context of the community boundaries with the emphasis on making their own decisions, and negotiating sharing in the group through the development of mutual trust.

Importance of individual curiosity about self and others
Little can be achieved until clients get to the point where they are able to ask questions and empathise with others. There must be a willingness to test out ideas in both the group and practical side of the programme. Individuals need to question for themselves how the group can help them increase their choices and give them the option for change. They will be encouraged by the group leaders to question old and practise new behaviour, and ask why they believe what they do about themselves. An important point needs to be made that the staff can only validly ask the clients to face the truth about themselves and to discuss their fantasies, fears and anxieties about each other because they are also open to doing the same in the weekly support group crucial to this type of work.

Movement towards honest expression of feeling
The group reaches a performing stage when the members can express their feelings openly and receive genuine and direct responses. The process works towards gradually confronting and removing the barriers to real communication. Most of our groups begin with defensive or selfishly manipulative behaviour which gradually opens up to more honest communication, with members gaining the confidence to confront as well as support others in an emotionally genuine way. Before reaching this stage however there lies a minefield of resistance for the leaders and group to struggle through.

Freedom from role
Initial group norms and roles will reflect each member's previous experience of relationships and role behaviour outside. As the group develops these roles are challenged and there is an opportunity for spontaneously trying out new behaviour and reinforcing it if appropriate. Many clients begin the group in fixed roles they choose or the group chooses for them e.g. joker, talker, helper, victim, etc., and the leaders, by commenting on this, offer the possibility of the client trying out new behaviour, and enlisting the support of the group in this endeavour. This may be resisted in an early phase of the group because of the void

it may leave if, for example, the joker restrains himself from filling the anxious moment.

Collaborative leadership

It is not the leaders' role to set tasks for the group, but to use their authority in a collaborative manner to develop the ground rules for group development. Holding the boundaries of the group whilst encouraging self-responsibility and inter-dependence involves shifting leadership within that framework. Any member facilitating the needs of the group is performing a leadership function. I believe it is only a strict emphasis on self-control and self-motivation which can effectively counter the effects of the institutionalisation our clients will have gone through prior to coming to the DTC. All this, of course, must be done within the boundaries set by the rules of the Centre and held by the authority of the professional staff. Constantly we see institutionalised, manipulative clients asking to be told how to be and what to say and think. Refusing to give them this leads to much petty acting out more akin to childhood behaviour, but out of this comes the seeds of responsibility for themselves and by the end of the three months, the penny has begun to drop with varying degrees of understanding.

EXPANDING CHOICES

Given that our programme is only three months, some of these aims can only begin to be effective when the programme ends, so I personally believe it is much more accurate to talk about expanding the choices for clients rather than changing them. I believe change is the clients' privilege, but choice is something for the staff leaders to emphasise. Change may come out of accepting a less deterministic view of the self and the awareness of expanding choices comes out of the relationships formed at the Centre, both with the leaders and with the peer group. In stating that choice is something for the leaders to emphasise, I believe there must be limits to a non-directive approach. It may be necessary, for example, for the leaders to sometimes quite doggedly insist on feedback to be given and received as a group experience so that members can have that experience and then have some basis for choice in their behaviour afterwards.

I strongly believe it is this experience at a feeling level which deeply influences and modifies behaviour although again the choice stays with the client - presumably it can be no other way in a non-totalitarian society. In my experience many people say to probation officers that they want to change, but what they are actually saying is 'I want to stay the same, but please make me feel better about it'. I think we effectively confront this at the Centre and do not give people rationalisations for their behaviour. As an example, I quote from a final assessment on one of our more disturbed and difficult clients at the point of completing the programme:

> In writing this summary I haven't wanted to sugar the pill for A. He's far too bright to be fobbed off with yet another social work assessment which provides him with excuses or ammunition for going on with what he does very effectively, which is to say 'you can't catch me'. I believe his contract is a genuine one - I think. A. is lonely and isolated, adrift and gambling with his life, and unmotivated to try anything different since a more conventional existence doesn't provide enough of a buzz to keep him on his toes. He is a talented young man, but he has learned to use his excellent brain to keep his feelings well boxed-in, though they are still bubbling away wherever they are. It is not surprising that he has so little respect for others if he cannot find any respect for himself, and it is a great shame that he couldn't use the group to start being with people as himself rather than as a performer. We believe it is possible for A. to be, rather than to perform, and we hope he will have enough faith himself in this possibility to start finding out how else to live rather than just recuperating between bouts. It may be much riskier and harder work than doing what he is doing now, but it's a gradually opening door rather than a rapidly slamming one, and it's not too late.

The cause and effect remains within individual responsibility. This, of course, means resisting the social worker's desire for self-gratification, to be liked and to do things for people. This needs to be contained and professionalised and related to doing enough and no more to empower clients to own the experiences which belong to them.

OFFENDING BEHAVIOUR

The most anybody can do with offenders therapeutically is to increase the choices and control they have over their lives. This, of course, means that they may well change the type of offending they do or even become 'better adjusted criminals'. However, the type of problems exhibited by the clients on arrival here strongly suggests that their internalised view of themselves contributes significantly to their offending. Low self-esteem, envy, anger and other ultimately self-destructive behaviours are evident in almost all. A depressingly high percentage has experienced severe rejection by one or both parents.

In dealing directly with the whole person the group widens the choices available and gives other options than the client mindlessly returning to the same type of habitual compulsive behaviour which leads to prison. Our experience at the Centre in empowering institutionalised clients to take that responsibility and to work on those personality defects is that this approach is more effective that input-style social skills leadership directed at the head and intelligence of the client rather than the gut and feelings where real potential change is stirred. An old French proverb states 'Everything a child is taught at school he forgets, but the education remains'. We cannot ignore the meaning the client gives to being sent to the Centre and the early resentment towards authority and inevitable anger and storming the group must go through is essential if any of our aims are to be achieved.

In my experience, structured task groups for offenders which minimise this dimension have limited value, and the clients often spend most of the time avoiding the leader input and manipulating in ways which disrupt the group. This is the same resistance, only there is no chance that the real issues underlying it will be dealt with. Initially all groups of clients tend to rationalise their reasons for offending along the lines of needing money, the influence of mates, etc. It is only in the context of the developing group, with individuals' behaviour fed back to them by their peers and through skilful handling of the feelings they have towards the group leaders, that we begin to get near the important inner meanings that their offending behaviour has for them.

If we give offenders questionnaires and ask them why they offend, most will comfortably answer 'money', 'boredom', etc., rather than 'anger', 'fear', 'fear of forming trusting relationships', etc. We are not trained to work with the unconscious, but I believe understanding transference issues and working in a skilful and questioning way, helping members to reflect on the meaning of their behaviour which may often not be immediately evident to them, is a really effective way to help open up choices in their lives and ultimately make decisions for change. The meanings should come from the interpretation of the worker, however insightful.

So we can talk for hours on end to compulsive thieves about

other (rational) ways of getting money and be surprised that they simply start stealing again as soon as they leave our workplace. But work with them on issues of envy, guilt, greed, what they feel when they steal, who they choose to steal from, and perhaps more important, how they feel about the you, and you begin to work on the very defences that they set up to protect them from influences and change. The Centre programme does deal with the initial problems the clients bring, but it uses the intensity of the group to go deeper into motivation and personal meaning, using the material of how the client relates in the intensive group (and also in the afternoon practicals) to develop an overall picture to reflect back to the client.

SUCCESS RATES

It is not surprising to me that there will be an effect on offending behaviour when, as never before, a person receives peer feedback on how he behaves in a group, reflects on the connection with offending behaviour, looks at his responsibilities in relationships, works on personal factors behind addictions, improves self esteem and develops a sense of being good at something for the first time. But how easily this effect can be measured remains another question. Working with the whole person beyond their rationalisations of their behaviour creates change that may be impossible to quantify.

This does not mean that this method of working is not open to statistical analysis and providing the figures necessary to show effectiveness on re-offending rates. However, I reserve some scepticism as to what these figures are actually telling us. If the Centre's method is open to the charge of producing better adjusted criminals, then any method which attempts to change behaviour will be open to similar accusations, as a change in any direction has a paradoxical built-in tendency to opposite effects. (For instance, Youth Custody's emphasis on changing people by extreme physical fitness programmes produced much fitter criminals - better able to evade police capture; and social work groups which emphasise leader input and discussions on causes of crime can provide clients with greater rationalisations for not honestly confronting their own behaviour).

We have no doubt that our method of working considerably increases the choices that clients can make about their future behaviour and lifestyle. It leads them towards a 'gradually opening door'. Most importantly it looks at the whole person in the 'laboratory' of the closed small group. Certainly clients are constantly being confronted by their deviant behaviour whilst here and connections are made with crime outside. However, I feel it is not usually helpful to make offending behaviour the sole focus and separate this from all the other manifestations of the client's personality. To use the example of A: His not typical approach to life was so all consumingly self-destructive that it would have been hopeless to see his offending behaviour as somehow unconnected with that. His whole life was offending behaviour, largely against himself, but occasionally against others when he would end up back in court.

IN CONCLUSION

Psychodynamic groupwork emphasising 'here and now' communication and member responsibility has been used with numerous sets of people (including probation officers). There is no reason to believe that it is unsuitable for our clients, who often adapt to the emphasis on honesty of expression of feeling much more quickly than many intellectually defended 'professionals'. The art and skills of facilitating the positive force of such an approach remains the probation task at the Centre.

Peter Mark, Senior Probation Officer, Inner London Probation Service.
This is a revised version of a paper which first appeared in Probation Journal *(1986), 33(4), pp.127-131.*

Part Three

Groups in Field Settings

13

The Newcastle Intensive Probation Programme: A Centralised Approach to Groupwork

JANE MACKINTOSH

THE EXPERIMENT AND ITS RATIONALE

The Newcastle Intensive Probation Programme (IPP) is now in its second year. It began in April 1990 and is one of ten Home Office[1] Pilot Projects, which are initially funded for two years, and whose stated aim is to confront offending behaviour and divert young offenders from custody.

The Newcastle Division of the Northumbria Probation Service had already recognised the value of groupwork in dealing with young offenders and, as part of its Action Plan[2], had begun to develop a centralised groupwork programme which operated across the team boundaries of the six probation field teams within the Division. It thus seemed logical that the proposed Northumbria Probation Service IPP should be located in Newcastle and build upon the work already begun in the existing programme.

The Home Office set three general objectives which the Intensive Probation Programmes were to meet:

1. to reduce offending during and after the period of supervision;
2. to improve the offender's attitude, skills and way of life;
3. to reduce the proportion of young adult offenders convicted of less serious offences who receive custodial sentences.

Within these three basic objectives, four 'core' elements were to be included:

1. a personal action plan for the offender setting out goals and targets for improving his/her behaviour;
2. frequent contact between Intensive Probation staff and the offender(s) involved;

3. work which focused on offending behaviour;
4. attendance to be enforced, by the court, through the attachment of an additional condition to a Probation Order.

Other suggested elements included work on specific areas of offending behaviour, for example motor crime, partnerships with the voluntary sector, reparation (i.e. the offender making recompense to the victim or community), work focused on employment and training, drug or alcohol misuse, and the use of a signed contract with the offender.

It will soon become clear that the Newcastle IPP does incorporate the majority of the elements mentioned above. However, there are three notable exceptions: it is not involved in any reparation scheme; we do not ask the offender to sign a contract: and participation is on a voluntary basis rather than as a result of any specific condition imposed by the court.

THE PRINCIPLE OF 'VOLUNTARISM'

It has to be said that most sentencers would prefer attendance to be on the basis of an additional condition attached to a Probation Order. This is seen as providing some kind of assurance that the offender will attend. However, the voluntary attendance of offenders at groupwork sessions in Newcastle had recently been agreed with the courts for the Action Plan so it made sense to develop this further once the IPP began. An approach in which offenders attend these 'courses' by choice rather than as a result of a direction, or condition, from the court is preferred. Whilst we acknowledge that individuals will have personal reasons for attending a certain group, and these may include a forthcoming court appearance, the understanding within the group that no-one has been forced to attend helps to create a motivated and positive atmosphere in which participants feel it is safe to admit to having made mistakes and to a desire to change. Northumbria Probation Service showed courage in pressing this point to the Home Office in the early negotiations to set up an IPP and despite the present climate of the Home Office demanding more punitive schemes, in the case of Newcastle it agreed to relax this 'core' element of Intensive Probation.

Over the past 12 months the Newcastle Intensive Probation Unit (hereafter referred to as 'the Unit') has seen an increasing number of offenders becoming involved in the Programme, and a consistent attendance rate of 80-90 per cent over a full year would suggest that additional conditions are not necessary. The achievements of the first year, particularly in terms of attendance rates, seem to have helped allay some of the initial fears that offenders are not motivated to attend the groups on a voluntary basis.

THE PROGRAMME: WHAT IS OFFERED

The Newcastle IPP is essentially a centralised programme of groupwork, which focuses on offending and factors which contribute to offending. It is a modular programme which offers a series of short but intensive courses lasting for three or four days and involves small groups of offenders in highly focused work relating to their offending. The Programme is non-discriminatory and, as a result, has developed a number of successful initiatives for women only.

Course titles include:

'Staying out of bother'
'Keeping your head'
'Motor crime'
'Drug problems'
'Alcohol awareness'
'How to assert yourself'
'Employment and training opportunities'

These courses are offered at regular intervals throughout the year and it was planned to provide a minimum of 18 groups during 1991. It is hoped that by raising the participants awareness about their offending, and highlighting the options which were available at the time, the offender will become more confident and in a better position to make informed choices about his or her life. As the Programme is a modular one, offenders (in consultation with their probation officers) can choose to attend as many or as few modules as they wish from the wide range of options. This flexibility means that a programme can be tailored to meet individual needs. The Unit also administers an outdoor activity programme throughout the year. Various opportunities are made available to offenders living in the city through the partnerships we have developed with agencies such as The Fairbridge Drake Society and The Ocean Youth Club.

RESOURCING THE PROGRAMME

The Unit is staffed by two probation officers and one probation ancillary. The three workers share a room in one of the field team offices (Byker) and the senior probation officer of that team also carries managerial responsibility for the Unit, which includes two part-time secretaries.

From its inception the IPP has had its own budget which in our opinion has enabled the project to provide good quality course materials, effective publicity including a high quality annual report, and a good standard of accommodation for the groups. In addition, we are able to reimburse clients with travelling costs and to supply group members free of charge with refreshments, buffet lunches and creche or child-minding facilities.

From the beginning the Unit decided to adopt a corporate image and our publicity, including information sheets for sentencers and posters advertising forthcoming courses which are displayed on probation office waiting room walls, is copied on blue paper. This distinguishes it from the mass of other papers colleagues have to deal with. At the beginning of this year (1991) we produced a good quality calendar highlighting the forthcoming year's programme. This was distributed to all staff working in Newcastle and enabled colleagues to 'forward plan' their work with clients in terms of any proposed involvement with the IPP. It has also helped to keep this resource in people's minds.

The development and success of the IPP has in part been due to the good relations that have been forged by the Unit with probation officers in the field. The existence of a steering group, made up of Unit staff and representatives from each of the six probation offices in Newcastle City, also provides an essential link between the project and the field. This close involvement of colleagues is essential if sufficient confidence is to be gained which will result in a significant number of clients being referred to the Programme.

The courses which focus upon offending, e.g. 'Staying out of bother', 'Keeping your head' and 'Motor crime' are led by the Unit staff and interested probation officers from the six teams. These groups take place at the Newcastle Probation Day Centre. The modules are usually run with three leaders and a mixed gender leadership is preferred for a number of reasons, not least the opportunity this provides for challenging stereotyped responses. The exceptions are those modules designed for women only groups which are led by female staff. Usually we aim for a high ratio of staff to course participants - 1:3 or 1:4 - however, we have found that a group where there are more than 10-12 participants can result in a greater drop-out rate as members do not receive the individual attention which is often needed. A high staff/client ratio allows us to accommodate various levels of literacy including the occasional person who is unable to read or write at all.

Other courses such as 'Drug problems', 'Alcohol awareness', 'How to assert yourself' and 'Employment and training opportunities' have been developed and are run by the Unit in partnership with other statutory and voluntary agencies in the community. These groups usually take place in the other organisations' premises. Such partnerships reflect the philosophy of the Unit that offenders should be encouraged to make contact with, and make use of, community resources where appropriate. We have found that other organisations are very keen to become involved in joint work with the Probation Service. Participants have also said that they enjoyed the mixed probation/non-probation leadership and have welcomed the input from those whom they regard as 'specialists' in a particular field.

EXAMPLES OF THREE OF THE COURSES

Example 1: The 'Staying out of bother' course

The 'Staying out of bother' course is a three day group focusing on offending behaviour. The Unit offers a separate and different module which runs over four shorter days for women only groups. The programme involves participants in an assessment of their offending. The idea is that this assessment can then be used as a focus for future supervision and also to identify the need and potential for follow-on courses, referral to outside agencies, etc.

From the outset participants are asked to think about their offending rather than their criminal record, having established that the latter is not necessarily a true reflection of the former. We have found that participants are generally willing to be very honest about this. At the beginning they are asked to assess how likely they are to offend again by selecting one of four categories ranging from 'definitely won't' to 'definitely will'. This exercise is repeated at the end of the course in an attempt to measure change, particularly attitude change. Invariably we have found that change does take place over the three or four days even if it is not in the obviously required direction. On occasions a participant has started the group feeling very much in control of his/her offending. However, as the programme has proceeded they have become more aware about their offending, and the risks they may be taking, and realise that further offending is more probable than they initially thought. More usually though, the change is in the direction of increased determination and confidence in 'going straight'.

Much of the 'Staying out of bother' course centres around the premise that offences do not just happen, rather they are a result of decisions taken, consciously or not. Participants choose an example of their offending to look at in more detail. They are asked to identify six stages in the commission of their offence and draw these on a flipchart. The group then looks at how each individual's offence occurred and together the members highlight the options the offender had during each of the stages, i.e. what s/he could have done in order to prevent the offence taking place. This concept of stages and 'options out' is illustrated further by a Unit video, made by offenders, showing the commission of a burglary in its various stages. Again the participants are asked to identify the options available to those in the video and then to see the process through, by enacting a court room scene during which the burglars are sentenced.

The final day involves participants making plans for their future. They are asked to identify the things in their life they want to change and then to decide specifically how they can change these things. There is an opportunity for individuals to practice dealing with difficult situations which may result in offending, and this usually results in some excellent role-plays.

A copy of the action plan, together with a brief evaluation on the participant, is sent to his/her probation officer. Participants leave the course with a better understanding of their offending and with clear ideas about what they will need to do if they are to 'go straight'. At this stage individuals may opt to pursue other modules of the Intensive Probation Programme, and many do.

This particular course, for mixed gender groups, has been offered four times, at three monthly intervals, during the first 12 months of the Programme. The similar course for women-only groups has been offered twice.

Example 2: The 'Keeping your head' course
The 'Keeping your head' course is a four day group programme focusing on violence and management of aggression. It is intended for people who have some degree of awareness that their aggressive and/or violent behaviour is causing problems in their

life. Its aims are: to provide some understanding about the nature of violence; to increase participants' awareness of what may lead them to commit acts of violence; to consider the consequences and effects of violent acts; and to help participants develop strategies and skills for coping with potentially violent situations without resorting to violence itself.

The establishment of basic ground rules is important in any groupwork. During the 'Keeping your head' course people learn by their participation in a number of exercises. Because this will involve them in re-enacting situations which will have previously upset them and perhaps resulted in violence, it needs to be very clear that any actual violence during the group will not be tolerated. To date we have not experienced a situation which has become out of control, nevertheless the potential for violence is clearly present and group leaders have to be very aware of what might happen.

This module is based on a conceptual framework of five stages involving loss of self-control, violence and its aftermath (Smith, P. mentioned in Kaplan and Wheeler, 1983)

1. The trigger

Everyone has their own 'baseline' level of inner tension, relaxation or anxiety. The 'triggering' stage is our first move away from it and we give off warning signals which need to be recognised by ourselves and others. For example:

> *Trigger* - a remark from someone, say in a pub, or the mere sight of someone you dislike or fear; or in a discussion you feel out of your depth or embarrassed - you would prefer to leave but you can not - and your baseline tension increases.
> *Signals* - you might gulp your drink; fidget in your seat; go silent or noisy; in fact any kind of behaviour which might not be typical of you at other times.

2. On the escalator

Imagine an escalator moving you quickly upwards. The danger signals become obvious to those around you. Your chances of being sidetracked in a sensible direction decrease, but you are not beyond control at this stage. You can get off, as it were, at a lower floor.

For example, you may suddenly stand up, break a glass, knock over a chair. Friends may be anxiously trying to calm you down. You can half hear them doing it, but you also hear yourself getting angrier. Your body's adrenaline is beginning to pump around - a natural reaction, to give you extra strength to cope in a difficult situation - and you may find it hard to think clearly. You are dangerously close to the next stage, but you are still in the relax and count to ten stage.

3. The crisis

Direct verbal or physical violence. You are a danger to yourself as well as to others nearby.

4. Recovery

Stage two all over again. You are now at the beginning of a gradual return to baseline behaviour, but still on the verge of lack of control. The 'firework' could go off again, as adrenalin stays in your blood for 90 minutes after the crisis. You need to be reassured of your own safety and calmed down, preferably away from the scene to avoid other triggers.

5. Depression

Mental and/or physical exhaustion or tiredness. Your behaviour drops below baseline behaviour.

For example, there are often tears and remorse, you may feel ashamed. Because of guilt, you may need to make it up, directly or indirectly, to the victim.

To illustrate this process the Unit has produced a video which shows someone moving through the five stages, the trigger in this case being the failure of a social security payment to arrive as expected. The process can also be shown in the diagram above.

Group members have said that they find this framework very useful in understanding their anger. I quote a typical remark from a participant's evaluation form:

The first day with the diagram and video showing trigger to escalator to crisis and recovery really set me up for the rest of the Course (R.R.).

Initially the course helps participants to identify why it is they lose their temper. It then moves on to introduce various skills and strategies that help a person to stay in control and prevent things from getting to the point where a crisis seems inevitable. There are opportunities for group members to practice such skills, for example: how to negotiate; act assertively; keep yourself calm; cope with criticism; and different relaxation techniques.

As with the other Intensive Probation courses participants are given a folder in which they can keep the exercises and

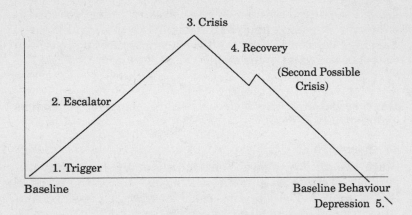

handouts which will accumulate over the four days. This serves both as a source for future reference and helps to encourage group members to share their work with their probation officer. The 'Keeping your head' course is seen very much as an introduction to work on anger management and emphasis is placed on participants continuing to practice the skills learnt once the course has finished. A brief evaluation form is sent to each person's supervising officer and after this particular course, a three-way meeting between a group leader/participant/ probation officer often takes place.

During the first year of the IPP the 'Keeping your head' course has been offered at six monthly intervals. Experience has shown that it may be inappropriate for women to participate in a group where the majority are men, some of whom have been violent towards women.

Example 3: The 'Drug problems' course

The 'drug problems' course is a three day group programme focusing on the implications of illicit drug use for offenders who have some awareness themselves that the use of drugs causes problems in their lives. This course aims to raise participants' awareness about the role drugs play in their lives; to consider the legal aspects and long term consequences of drug use; to look at the benefits and costs of taking drugs; to explore the options available; and to develop an action plan for the future to enable the participants to achieve their set goals.

The 'Drug problems' course is one of a number of modules which the Unit has developed and runs in partnership with other agencies. In this particular module the Unit works with social workers from the local authority Alcohol and Drug Problem Service. The course is held on the latter's premises, in the hope that participants may feel more able to use this community resource once the group has finished.

The programme begins by looking at drug use in general. Participants' knowledge about drugs is considered and time is spent exploring the essential question, why do people use drugs? During the second day members are encouraged to examine their own personal use of drugs; to identify situations which can trigger drug use; and to consider the alternatives in such situations. The final day moves on to look at the problems associated with making the transition to a drug free life and ways to divert participants from their risky situations into safer ones. This final day includes sessions on harm reduction, relapse management and its prevention. There is an input on the facilities available in the community.

The 'Drugs problems' course is one of the more recent additions to the Programme. During the first year it was offered on only one occasion, to a mixed male/female group. The Unit intends to offer this group at six monthly intervals during its second year.

EVALUATING THE PROGRAMME

Each course is fully evaluated and written-up in detail. Consequently, if any client is unable to cope with the groupwork setting, the course material is available to colleagues in the field for use on an individual basis. Participants assist in the process of evaluation and complete forms both at the end of each day and when the group is finished. Invariably their comments have been positive and many express interest in attending other modules. The following are just a few comments taken from their evaluation forms:

> At first I thought the course ('Staying out of bother') was going to be a waste of time and I had second thoughts about going but I really wanted to stay out of trouble so I went and I am glad I did. It made me look at what I did and why I did it and how I could stop it happening again (Darren).

> In my opinion the part of the course that really brought home how stupid I had been was when we remembered a crime we had committed and worked our way through it in stages noting

where we could have stopped and done something else and not actually committed the offence (Fiona).

If you really want to stay out of trouble and away from prison I can highly recommend this course and it is for your own benefit (Alan).

I've learnt that it is possible to change your life even if it is going to be hard (Steve).

The course had its funny moments as well as its serious ones - it's a shame it was only for four days (Mark).

Within a 12 month period the IPP has gained credibility amongst probation officers working in the field. Many have supported the idea of a centralised group programme and the fact that every officer, minus one, working in Newcastle city has referred to the Programme seems to indicate that it has become established as part of the fabric in which we work in Newcastle.

Management have watched the development of the Unit with much interest over the last year. The onset of the Programme has been timely in terms of the current debate about extending the work of probation day centres in the hope of offering a more flexible service both to the offender and the court. So often it feels as if groupwork in the probation service is done on a shoe-string with little or no workload relief for those involved. The fact that the Unit has been properly resourced, both in terms of staffing levels and having its own budget, is an indication that management is committed to this programme and really does want to see it work well. Considering the number of clients already involved in these groups, there seems to be general agreement that the Unit's costs represent money well spent.

An analysis of participation

During the early discussions between the Home Office and the Probation Service regarding the proposed IPP, it was suggested that each scheme should achieve a throughput target of 50 offenders in the first year. Of these it was felt that most should be 'young offenders' (17-25 years) deemed to be at 'some risk of custody'. The Newcastle Programme has more than achieved these targets and the statistics for the past 12 months, shows a total of 102 participants, many of whom have attended more than one module (see Table 1).

Table 1
Number of participants and courses attended

Number of courses attended:	
One	82
Two	14
Three	5
Four	1
Total number of participants	102

Women constitute 17 per cent of the overall number of clients who have attended at least one module (see Table 2). This figure compares favourably with the current proportion of statutory female clients in Newcastle which in February 1991 was 13 per cent. The evidence suggests that this successful targeting of women has been made possible by offering separate modules for women only, with creche facilities.

To date, all the participants have classed themselves as 'white'. The absence of referrals from people from other ethnic backgrounds is a cause for concern and this issue is currently being discussed both within the Unit and in the field. Compared to other urban areas in England, Newcastle has a particularly small proportion of people from ethnic minority backgrounds. This is reflected in the Newcastle Division's caseload; in December 1990 only 1.2 per cent had classified themselves as being 'black' or 'other than white'.

Almost 75 per cent of participants have been in the target age group of 17-25 years (see Table 2). Over 65 per cent of participants have been convicted on three or more separate occasions and of these a significant proportion have a considerable number of convictions, i.e. seven or more (see Table 3). This suggests that the Programme is attracting many clients who are likely to have been at risk of receiving a custodial sentence which in itself is evidence of success in gaining credibility with the courts. The data also indicates that many of these participants have substantial experiences of imprisonment and that 52 per cent have previously received either a custodial sentence (29%) or a high tariff disposal such as a community service order or probation order with day centre conditions (23%) (see Table 4).

Our data shows that of those who begin each course the vast majority complete it. Attendance/completion rates have remained consistently high during the first year and after fifteen separate

Table 2
Participants by age and sex

	17-20 years %	21-25 years %	26 plus years %	Total %
men	38	26	19	83
women	4	6	7	17

groups the average rate is approximately 85 per cent. The question is not so much one of whether a person will stay but rather whether they will arrive on the first day. In an attempt to encourage offenders to attend we request that their probation officer brings them to the group on the first morning. Without a doubt this helps to secure attendance and once the offender has arrived we have shown that he/she will usually stay. This, along with the formal evaluations which are completed by group members, would seem to confirm the value of our approach.

Table 3
Number of previous convictions   n=102

	%
10 or more	21
7-9	12
3-6	32
0-2	29
Not known	6

Table 4
Most serious previous disposal   n=102

	%
Custody	29
Suspended sentence/Community service order/Probation order and additional conditions attached	23
Probation order	20
Fines/Conditional discharges/ Attendance centre orders/ No previous convictions	22
Not known	6

THE FUTURE

The Unit is now in its second year. Whilst the intention this year is to consolidate the groupwork programme there are a few new developments under way, most notably an extension of areas of the programme designed specifically for women, and a motoring project. The Unit is also involved in supporting a new project called SCOPE, which is a partnership between the National Association for the Care and Resettlement of Offenders (NACRO) and the Northumbria Probation Service whose aim is to divert young offenders from offending into constructive activities. This project provides an excellent opportunity for those who have been involved in the Unit's courses to follow up certain interests which they have identified in their personal action plan.

As yet it is too early to present evidence that our work has had an impact on re-conviction rates, the custodial population or indeed attitude change in the long term. Research into these areas will be a priority during the next few months and an independent study/evaluation of the work of the Unit has been proposed by a research unit at Newcastle University. In the meantime, all ten Intensive Probation Programmes are being monitored to varying degrees by the Home Office. This is in addition to our own systems of monitoring and evaluation which are seen as an integral component of our work.

CONCLUSION

The intention of centralising groupwork provision was not to replace or prevent any initiatives within teams but rather to enhance and supplement the current work of the Northumbria Probation Service. It was felt that by centralising some provision, the Newcastle Division could ensure that certain groupwork opportunities would be made available to clients on a regular basis both for their intrinsic value and in an attempt to divert them from custody when they appear in court. Offenders seem able to relate to the focused approach used in the various modules and certainly by the end of each course they feel a definite sense of achievement which is not always so apparent in other, more traditional, methods of work.

Not only is the IPP a resource to benefit probation clients, and probation officers in their work with them, it is also a means of enabling more colleagues to become involved in groupwork.

Whilst this example of a centralised programme is clearly only one way of approaching the groupwork task, it is proving to be an extremely effective way of organising and implementing a comprehensive groupwork programme in the context of the Probation Service.

Notes
1. The Home Office is the central government department responsible for the Probation Service in England and Wales.
2. The Northumbria Action Plan (1989) is a policy document which was a response to the Home Office request that each probation area should develop a policy strategy of how they work with young offenders in an attempt to divert them from custody.

Jane Mackintosh, Northumbria Probation Service, This chapter is reprinted from Groupwork, *1991, 4(3)*

14

Establishing a Feminist Model of Groupwork in the Probation Service

TARA MISTRY

TARA MISTRY

WOMEN AND THE PROBATION SERVICE

Women are proportionately more likely to be placed on a probation order than men. In 1985, 7 per cent of male offenders received probation compared to 17 per cent of women (HMSO, 1986). Despite this, provision for women on probation has been limited mostly to a 'one-to-one' individualised response which is often based on a notion of 'women needing help'. Because women form a relatively small percentage of the probation caseload, they have been continuously marginalised, reflecting both their position in society and the dominant power position of men in the criminal justice system - particularly the probation service hierarchy.

In many social service organisations, the attitude of the service to the female client can be easily understood when observing that service's treatment of women workers. There is undoubtedly a correlation. The probation service is predominantly run by men with most of the female workforce concentrated at the main grade level. This reflects an attitude which permeates the treatment of women clients by managers and, subsequently, by main grade practitioners who 'absorb' the culture of the agency - initially during practice placements while on training courses, and later as employees.

Historically, women clients have been 'social worked' and pathologised by social workers and probation officers on the basis of whether they were good wives, mothers, daughters, sisters and so on. If they failed to fit the gender specified role, both male and female workers would undertake to supervise them individually in order to 'support, guide or prepare' them more usefully for the feminine role. Women who offended had after all stepped out of their natural place. When groupwork began to make an impact in the probation service, some women's groups were organised, but these often took the form of *ad-hoc* arrangements with poor facilities for childcare; using inexperienced workers to run creches without proper toys; and with everyone huddled together in one room. Discussion and activities often focused on good grooming, cooking and sewing, and suffered from the 'coffee morning syndrome'. These types of groups perpetuated the image that women could make do with poor provision, and they also reinforced the role stereotype of women needing to prepare to fit into their 'rightful' feminine role, for example, learning to budget effectively in order to stay out of trouble. Unfortunately, women probation officers running groups of this kind were not offering women clients any different avenues for enhancement of their lives. I would argue that in many ways these groups were no more than an extension of individually focused work.

It seemed from my own experience as a worker supervising women on probation and observing colleagues' work, that social workers and probation officers, and those in other state institutions, colluded with the view that women are subordinates, and were slow to respond to the challenge of feminist thinking in their social work practice. It was against this background that our desire to empower women offenders, albeit under a probation order, resulted in the establishment of the women's group in the Easton probation office.

THE CASE FOR A WOMEN CENTRED GROUP

Questions have regularly been posed by practitioners and magistrates as to why there needs to be a separate group for women. Apart from the points raised above, there were a number of other reasons. Some of these were based on our own assumptions informed by our feminist perspective, and some on the experiences of women clients who had been in mixed, voluntary and compulsory groups.

As the potential co-leaders of the pilot women's group, Gwen Booth (a student on placement) and I made certain assumptions that women working together would naturally develop a support system. In this way they would enable each other, through discussions and activities, to establish a different method of coping from that which developed in the more structured group model. Our experience also indicated that the degree of emotional and practical support derived from an all women group would be more constructive, relevant and practical than in a one-to-one client/worker relationship. This assumption was based on our own experiences as women living in a patriarchal society who found support in formal and informal women's group settings (either in the workplace, such as Women in the National Association of Probation Officers, or outside the work context in a variety of women's groups).

From our observation of women's participation in the mixed sex 'induction group' model (Brown and Seymour, 1983), it seemed that the combination of the structured framework and the proportionally small number of women in any one group (usually two women to eight to ten men), women's needs were 'submerged'. Women often enabled, accommodated and assisted the male members to understand their society, women clients were often forced to nurture and support the men (and often the leaders), their own needs getting lost in the process (Garvin and Reed, 1983). In effect they helped 'service' the group without getting much for themselves. Almost all the male and female probation officers in the team thought that the women were getting a poor deal in a mixed group for these reasons.

In my discussions with women clients over the years, it was also evident that a structured group such as the induction model did not help to pin-point their offending behaviour, not did it show them a way forward to stop offending. This was because the focus often shifted to the men's reasons for offending. Writers such as Pat Carlen (1988) have illustrated why women offend less than men. The main reason highlighted by Carlen is that women are 'controlled' to conform by informal family systems and societal disapproval, whereas men are controlled to conform by formal agency systems such as the criminal justice system. It follows that even though the nature of women's offending has changed in recent years due to changes in socio-economic conditions , for example the rise in the number of households headed by single women, women's offending behaviour mostly has a different basis to that of men. This explains why it is difficult to have a structured package of equal relevance to both men and women.

We were also unhappy about using breach (of probation) proceedings and the courts as a 'stick' for non-attenders, as we thought that this ran counter to feminist philosophy and would not create an alternative model for the women. Although the group had to be a credible option for the courts and the probation officers, we felt that women had to have a choice as to whether or not they attended the group. It could not however be regarded as a totally voluntary group, because it was part of probation supervision and they had to give a commitment to attend for a certain number of weeks on a basis negotiated between themselves and their respective probation officers. If women chose not to continue coming after the minimum negotiated time, then the supervising officer would explore other avenues. Many people argue that this principle does not apply only to the feminist group model but should apply equally to all groups. However, I think that many male colleagues found the lack of clearly defined boundaries difficult to accept, which may say more about the nature of the probation service and its relationship with the courts than it does about an attitude typical of male probation officers!

In summary, we described our model of groupwork as having a feminist perspective because:

1. the group is run for women by women only;
2. it has a value base that does not assume women are subordinates or fit the stereotype of 'feminine' women;
3. it seeks actively to promote women taking control of their lives by methods devised through collective discussion (and action, where appropriate);
4. it views the offending behaviour of women within their socio-economic position in a patriarchal society;
5. it starts from the point where women (in the group) choose to start and seeks to build on that rather than adopt a 'baseline' which the group leaders define as the 'norm'.

ESTABLISHING THE GROUP

In 1983, the Easton probation office had a variety of client groups, but all were of determinate lengths, were office based, and offered 'structured packages' for the courts with a promise to return anyone to court at the first sign of non-attendance. Most colleagues found the launch of our women's group difficult to accept, and some were slow to refer women because of the feminist perspective and the lack of traditional sanctions for possible non-attenders. Initially, many male colleagues also felt threatened by the nature of women only groups, but despite this resistance the group was launched in March 1983 as a six week pilot scheme with seven referrals. Before the start of the pilot, we had produced, discussed and debated with colleagues a planning paper which outlined the group's aims, objectives and methods.

Aims and objectives

1. Increasing awareness of strengths and weaknesses; understanding potential and increasing confidence.
2. Getting in touch with, and discussing, feelings and emotions.
3. Examining specific problems that women encounter, e.g. sexual harassment, domestic violence, powerlessness in a patriarchal society, racism and its effect on black women.
4. Providing a forum for exploring interests and increasing knowledge, e.g. resources in the community, education and information.
5. Recognising that offending is closely related to socio-economic factors, changing roles of women in society, personal history and poverty, and exploring offending patterns within that context, e.g. prostitution, isolated single mothers breaking the law as a pattern of survival.

Organisation and method

1. Negotiating the agreement at the social inquiry report stage with the probation officer and the client, initially outlining a possible timescale of attendance at the group.
2. Assessment to be negotiated regularly between the client, the group leaders and the referring officer:
   - for entry into the group;
   - for exit from the group;
   - to maintain group cohesion;
   - to maintain continuity of client contact.
   The frequency of assessment would be at least three-monthly, but could be varied by any party.
3. An open weekly group with creche facilities and help with transport.
4. Most sessions to be discussion based with occasional outside speakers, e.g. from the Workers Education Association, Well-Woman Clinic, Shelter, Women's Aid, housing department, welfare rights units, Rape Crisis etc.
5. The group meetings to be mainly unstructured with the group deciding the level at which the discussion would be pitched.
6. Activities/trips to be integrated in the group programme as appropriate.
7. The sessions to be during school hours in the afternoon.

Venue

The group was held at Barton Hill Community Centre which is

situated in an area of high-rise flats and older council dwellings, half a mile from the probation office. The community centre venue enabled us to use the creche facilities staffed by qualified nursery nurses, and gave the group access to local courses, education, literary classes, welfare rights, and most importantly other groups in the centre. It was the first step to linking the women with the resources in their neighbourhood.

The pilot

The six sessions in the 'pilot' were a real 'success' with the women feeling that they had begun to trust each other. Most of these working class women had never met in this type of forum before and were astonished that it was a valid activity to sit and discuss personal and wider issues as well as share each other's troubles. For many it was the first time that they had realised that they all shared similar problems. This illustrated that some of their problems had social bases outside their immediate control, and were not always due to their individual paranoia or inadequacy, but were a reflection of their position as black and white working class women. The group had facilitated this process of 'conscientisation' (Donnelly, 1986).

Establishing the group with the central team

After the pilot period, in discussion with out consultant, Hilary Burgess, we decided that the group should be properly established as the need had been clearly demonstrated. We wanted to open up the resource to the neighbouring 'Central' team, which worked in a similar way to Easton, as this would sustain an adequate number of referrals and provide a co-worker to help run the group. In addition it would provide cost-effective and meaningful 'supervision' for women from two inner city teams. One major problem, which had no easy solution, was that for women from another part of the city the community centre did not cover their own neighbourhood, as it did for the Easton women.

It was essential that my co-worker shared a feminist perspective, and in May 1983, the group became a two team venture with Carol Sapsed from the other team as the co-worker.

Funding

As well as having to develop a rapport and style for co-leading a fairly unstructured group, Carol and I had various battles to right on the way, including seeking funding from our agency for the room, creche, transport and consultancy. We were determined that as the courts were using the group as a facility for women offenders, it should be funded properly, especially the child care arrangement. Unfortunately, despite our belief that the group should not be marginalised by the absence of agency funds, we had to run it for two years without official funding. We started with a £50 donation from a local solicitor; lobbied local magistrates (some of whom donated money); wrote begging letters to charities; organised a summer fayre: and approached The Prince of Wales Trust, which granted £400 for a group activity. These funds paid for the running costs, occasional speaker, visual aids and, most importantly, transport for the group members. Initially, we were collecting women from our respective 'ends' of the city, running the group, taking them all home, and then meeting to evaluate the sessions. Not surprisingly, we were often exhausted by the end of Tuesday afternoon. The financial struggle was finally resolved in 1985 when the agency granted funds for the group, thus giving it full recognition as a valid way of supervising women offenders.

THE GROUP

The group was 'open' with the exit and entrance of members phased. For the first two years it ran every week throughout the year except for statutory holidays. After that, it ran only in school term time as the creche was not available in school holidays. Also, as workers, we needed to reappraise our aims and objectives frequently and spend some time away from the group to evaluate and develop our own styles and skills.

Content

The main recurring themes of discussion were motherhood, childcare, relationships, sexuality, health, poverty, status, class, welfare rights, racism, sexism, family, criminal justice system, offending, coping alone, domestic violence, portrayal of women, stereotyping and power. The discussion gave rise to various dynamics within the group. In the early days the leaders played an active role in getting the women to address and challenge each other. As each particular group membership cohered and developed its own momentum, we had a correspondingly reduced role in directing the group. The programme of discussion and activities was always negotiated with the group, but sometimes the direction would move away from the original plan if the group dynamics needed exploring or external problems encroaching on the women members' lives arose, e.g. problems with the children, relationships, violence as home, an outstanding court case, or possible risk of re-offending. Ironically, in view of earlier criticism, this flexibility made the group both demanding and stimulating for the leaders and the members.

On one occasion, when £400 was granted for an activity, the women wanted to use the money for a three day residential trip to a Butlin's Holiday Camp. This was demanding for me as my co-worker could not attend, but it proved to be a most rewarding experience. Nine women and six children went on the trip, and events over the three days revealed that despite the positives we felt about the group, the issues of discrimination, lack of status, rivalry for men and resources, racism and lack of money had not been addressed in a manner which was pertinent to their lives. One evening, I attended a dance with other women in the group and we were set upon by white women holidaymakers. I was terrified, but the other black women (having always been on the receiving end of this type of behaviour) dealt with it in the most skilful way possible. It demonstrated to the white women in our group how racism worked against the black women, and reminded me as a middle class black woman how I had been protected from this in recent years since the change in my status. There were occasional rivalries between the younger women over men, and much of this shared experience formed an important focus for group discussion in the next twelve months in the group. This trip also provided a useful lesson for me about the importance of probation officers being in touch with the experiences of women who become clients.

EVALUATION OF THE GROUP

The process of the group bore out our initial assumption that women would naturally draw together and develop their own support system. They were generally prepared to talk about themselves and their families once they had had adequate time to get to know each other. There was often a sharing of intimate personal details, particularly with reference to relationships with men and motherhood. These two factors often caused stress and worries which were alleviated by the offer of active practical support from other women within the group, e.g. volunteering to baby-sit, inviting isolated women to their homes, and, on occasions, providing accommodation in the event of physical abuse from male partners. There was ample evidence of physical and emotional support both inside and, more importantly, outside the group. This went beyond the hopes and expectations we had expressed when we originally set up the group.

Some women learned to use their skills of listening, understanding and counselling with each other, and were able to extend their support beyond the boundaries experienced by us as co-workers and probation officers. One problem which can and sometimes did arise was that this type of supportive relationship makes it difficult for group members to challenge each other. When this happened the group leaders had to take up their responsibilities, and use their skills and position to direct the group to challenge in a constructive manner. As in any group, the co-workers also had to be sensitive to general groupwork processes, e.g. dealing with scapegoating, engaging the quiet member, controlling the more dominant member.

Overall, in making a process evaluation of the group, we can say with confidence that the women's group had portrayed levels of self-disclosure, nurturing, and emotional and practical support of a quality which we had not experienced as workers in other mixed groups or in individual work with women.

Eighteen months after the group started, a student from Bristol University undertook an independent consumer study of women who had been through the group. Her findings confirmed our own positive views. They showed that the women had felt safe to talk about themselves and did not feel judged. They felt more supported than in one-to-one settings with their probation officers, and welcomed the regular meetings with other women in the community setting. For some, it was nice to just get out of the house for an hour and a half while their children were being looked after! It may be worth repeating this monitoring of consumer feedback with a larger sample now that the group has been in existence for six years and more than 120 women have been through it (by January 1989).

DEMANDS ON THE CO-WORKERS

For us as workers, this type of group made tremendous demands on 'self' because it was not possible to maintain a distant, 'professional' stance. As women we all shared common experiences, and as a black woman I had the specific experience of racism which could be shared with other black group members. However, it has to be acknowledged that as probation officers we were often in a more privileged position, and there was a clear power imbalance (although not as marked as the one-to-one client/worker relationship) because we 'ran' the group.

Carol and I felt that it was important to acknowledge our differing positions, but utilise our skills and knowledge to facilitate the group where and when it was needed (especially at the early stage of a new term). However, at certain stages of group development the boundaries between 'worker' and 'client' were often blurred, especially if certain shared experiences were being discussed, i.e. the role of mother, daughter, girlfriend, lover, etc. Sometimes Carol and the other white women would be discussing the experiences of racism as expressed by myself and other black women. One of the clear recollections I have of this is black women (in the majority at that session) challenging and then explaining that stereotypes of 'dirty black people' were ill-founded and not based on facts but on distortions. I am sure that the white too remember the collective voice of the black women from that session! For many working class white women, this was the first time that their stereotypes of black people had been challenged by their black friends.

In our co-working relationship, Carol and I spent a lot of energy developing a strong partnership in order to work effectively together as black and white co-workers. We also had different class backgrounds and sometimes we clashed due to the differing positions of black and white feminists on certain issues. We felt however that this was a healthy sign which acknowledged that having a feminist perspective is not enough. As workers we had to be open and responsive to our own history and the needs of the group.

This qualitative evaluation of the outcome makes it clear that most of the aims and objectives of the group have been met, and the arguments for establishing a women centred resource have been validated by the effectiveness of the group. A further positive indicator is that regular attendance was never a problem: in fact persuading women to leave the group proved to be the difficulty!

GROUP DATA

Summarised below are some of the group data from an analysis undertaken in July 1987:

Size and turnover

From 1983 to July 1987, 90 women went through the group

(average 18 per year). At any one time there were seven to eight women attending and, because of the staggered entry and 'rolling programme', the throughput rate varied. Referrals were generally steady with occasional peaks and troughs. Easton's referrals were higher at first, mainly because the project was initiated there and was discussed regularly at team meetings. Carol had to continue to 'sell' the project as a shared resource. We became much more confident about the project ourselves, not least because it had proved itself quantitatively to be a resourceful and relevant way of working with women.

Age and racial composition
The age range was 18 to 65, but most of the time the composition was predominantly of young women aged 18 to 25. The racial composition was half black and half white with black women being referred mainly from the Easton team due to the demography of black settlement. There was a period between 1985 and 1987 when the proportion of white women was greater than black due to a reduction in the proportion of black women placed on probation. A speculative explanation is that a more rigorous anti-racist approach to social inquiry reports may have been a contributory factor.

Socio-economic position
Group referrals from 1983-1987 indicated that:

1. 65 per cent of women were single parents;
2. 90 per cent lived in council or housing association property;
3. 97 per cent were on state benefits;
4. 94 per cent left school without any formal qualifications.

Analysis by offence
Sixty per cent of the women had two or more previous convictions (one woman had 30, another 18; both had served significant periods in custody). The type of offences are summarised below in decreasing order of frequency:

1. theft;
2. deception;
3. drugs/prostitution;
4. assault;
5. taking and driving away;
6. criminal damage.

It is clear from our sample that most women were caught in a poverty trap (Becker, 1989), and much of their offending was related to their poor socio-economic status and survival on subsistence levels of state benefits. The last two categories of offences were committed by women in the youngest age group who had offended in situations of dare, revenge or as a result of peer-group pressures.

It must be of interest to the probation service that whereas the national figure for completing probation orders without further convictions is 80 per cent, we estimate that the comparable figure for women in this group is about 90 per cent.

A VOLUNTARY 'MOVE-ON' GROUP

Ideally, we wanted a group of women from this statutory group to set up their own voluntary self-help group which would provide continuing support enabling the women to move out into their own group allowing them total control without probation officer involvement. This aim was achieved in autumn 1987 by another student undertaking the work as part of her placement, in consultation with some women in the statutory group who were ready to move on. When I left in December 1987, this self-group was in its early stages with a core membership of six committed women. It was held on the same day as the statutory group at the same community centre, and initial funding was secured by a grant from Bristol City Council's Women's Committee.

When I checked the progress of the voluntary group in January 1989, I discovered that it was no longer meeting. It needed more agency support to help it become re-established, but the current climate in the probation service is geared more to putting resources into alternatives to custody rather than any investment in preventative work. With the forthcoming implementation of the Government's proposals in the Green Paper *Punishment, Custody and the Community* (HMSO, 1988), it seems unlikely that projects such as these will be high on the agenda. This is unfortunate, since, in the long term, these types of self-help groups would provide a useful resource for women ex-offenders, with the potential to prevent them from re-offending at times of pressure.

OTHER ISSUES

Whilst we had no doubts that the women's group was a worthwhile project, we recognised that there were some shortcomings. Even though black women were getting a better service in an all women group, my own growing awareness led me to believe that their needs could be met more specifically, for example, through the establishment of an all black women's group. Most of the black women I spoke to felt uneasy about this, but, like the issue of black and white co-workers, this issue needs another article which could explore the race dimension and the contradictions that the feminist model throws up for black women leaders and members in a racially mixed group.

Another limitation was that people referred from the Central team were not meeting within their own community setting, although this did not seem to worry the women unduly, preferring sometimes not to be in their own neighbourhood. Our original wish to help them move on to community based groups or projects did not materialise and the voluntary 'move-on' group seemed a better alternative.

CONCLUSION

The most significant learning points were that, given the opportunity, a women's group consisting mainly of working class black and white women who had been caught up in the criminal justice system and placed on a probation order, could develop members' self-confidence and increase their self-esteem. Self-disclosure and the sharing of personal, social and economic problems in a safe comfortable community setting with adequate childcare facilities, and sensitivity to a feminist philosophy, allowed the women to explore their own positions within society. This inevitably helped the group to achieve a framework of practical, physical and emotional support. Although I personally have reservations about the term 'empowerment' there is no doubt in my mind (having run groups of various types over the last eight years) that we did see women helping each other to take control of their lives in a manner I had not witnessed in other probation group settings. For myself as a worker, this piece of practice was the most stimulating and personally fulfilling of all.

For the courts and the probation service, the scheme proved that an all women's group is successful, not only in terms of the low re-offending rate, but also because it demonstrated that attendance does not have to be a problem if the needs of clients are being met in a constructive way which is relevant and pertinent to their lives. The feminist model with flexibility for women to explore the concept by reference to the effects of offending on their lives was the key to this group's existence. The fact that after six years the group is still running with regular referrals and commitment from probation teams is evidence that collective single sex groups within the structure of the probation order are a viable method of supervising women offenders.

Since the Easton/Central group was legitimately funded and established, a number of other women's groups based on this model have been set up in Avon by women probation officers. This has to be seen as a positive move, although, as with all groups, workers must always be clear about whose needs they are meeting.

In the climate of *Punishment, Custody and the Community* (*HMSO*, 1988) and greater 'packaging' of probation orders, it will be very interesting to see whether the group can continue to survive without controls imposed by the courts. It augurs well that despite the change in the political climate of the probation service, a group based on a feminist ideology has so far succeeded in keeping to its principles and diverting more women away from further offending. It continues to provide a relevant and useful facility where women are not seen to be consistently in need of help but where they can understand why they have been caught up in the criminal justice system, and seek to find their own short and long term solutions, even if they are not in a position to challenge the whole structure of a patriarchal society.

Tara Mistry, Bristol University. This chapter is reprinted from Groupwork, *1989, 2(2)*

15

The Miskin Model of Groupwork with Women Offenders

MARION JONES, MARY MORDECAI, FRANCES RUTTER AND LINDA THOMAS

BACKGROUND

Miskin is the name of a magistrates court area comprising the Rhondda Valleys and the district of Taff Ely. It lies within the county of Mid Glamorgan in South Wales and is serviced by two teams of probation officers based in Porth and Pontypridd. Most of the area is made up of traditional Welsh valley communities which have, for a sustained period, experienced social and environmental problems associated with the decline of coal and related industries. Life in the valleys is close-knit. It tends to be a male dominated society with traditional family and 'working class' values ingrained in its political, sociological and economic structure. The roles of men and women in most households are well prescribed. Generally the female role centres around domestic concerns, caring for parents and children and ensuring "'that the world turns a little more smoothly for men' (Buckley and Wilson, 1989, p.165). The men are expected to be the material providers. Women who deviate from the expectations of their role are not readily tolerated or accepted.

The Mid Glamorgan Probation Service has, since 1985, been reviewing its work and developing strategies to provide more effective supervision for offenders in the community. This reappraisal has emphasised the limited provision for women offenders and highlighted the reality that Probation Service supervision structures have been developed to meet the needs of the predominantly male offender group.

This shows in several ways:

1. Local courts, whilst seeking advice about how to deal with women offenders, are sometimes inclined to make probation

orders on welfare rather than offending grounds. For example, Mid Glamorgan Probation Service statistics show that 22 per cent of the women on whom a social inquiry report was prepared during 1990 had no previous convictions, compared with only 9 per cent of men.

2. It is arguable that women offenders are being assessed and treated inappropriately by probation officers. They are being worked with on the fringes of mainstream probation intervention; usually on the basis of needs perceived by others rather than defined by themselves, and with a welfare rather than offending focus. This state of affairs does little to encourage self-awareness, assist them to change their offending behaviour, or view themselves as individuals in their own right with dignity and worth.

3. The responses of these women offenders range from refusing to comply, being elusive, fearful or suspicious, being excessively demanding in regard to welfare issues, or merely paying perfunctory lip-service to the existence of the probation order. For example, Tina who is married with four children requested home visits by the probation officer concerning child care issues. During home visits, when the probation officer was able to gain access, Tina's offences were rarely discussed. Task interference presented itself in the form of requests regarding her children's ill health, friends visiting, and seeking welfare advice. If her partner was at home, Tina would insist that it was not possible to speak openly in his presence.

It was against this backdrop that during 1989, probation officers in Miskin, both male and female, questioned afresh how best to work with women offenders who were subject to statutory supervision.

THE CHARACTERISTICS OF THE WOMEN

We began by conducting an examination of the circumstances and characteristics of the women offenders with whom we were working. These were diverse:

1. age range 17-57;
2. living alone or with partners;
3. some childless, one had five children;
4. variety of offences ranging from minor shoplifting to house

burglary/theft of cars/violence/supplying drugs;
5. some carried 'mentally ill' labels;
6. extreme variations in educational achievements;
7. extreme variations in material wealth;
8. previous convictions varied from 0 to 20+;
9. some had experienced three or more custodial sentences/ some had committed their first offence;

Only a few common factors were in evidence. All had committed offences and were subject to probation supervision, and all had low self-esteem and lacked a sense of themselves and of their needs as individuals in their own right.

BASIC PRINCIPLES

Having decided to initiate action to provide a more relevant service for women offenders in Miskin, we began by determining principles to govern a new way of working. These are:

1. Targeting high risk women offenders i.e. those with at least three recent previous convictions.
2. Providing a structured, yet flexible programme with clear objectives and methods.
3. Focusing on offending behaviour and cognition, rather than welfare issues linked with stereotypical roles, e.g. wife, mother, etc. It is offending behaviour and this behaviour alone which provides the authority for probation officers' intervention in the lives of offenders.
4. A directive approach with appropriate use of authority to ensure compliance with the requirements of the probation order.
5. Provision of formal and informal group experiences which offer safe space to explore alternatives to the 'double bind' of their situation in which they are obliged to meet the needs of others yet feel indignant, angry, depressed or powerless that their own needs are not being met.

CHOICE OF GROUPWORK MODEL

Given the above principles, it was necessary to consider carefully which groupwork model to adopt. We initially drew upon a variation of the 'drop-in' ('drop-out') open group model developed by Henry (1988). A minimum number of group sessions was agreed, to be completed within a prescribed period of time. Beyond this contract, women offenders joined and left the group as they wished. Next, because the offender group expressed dissatisfaction with the constantly changing group size and composition, we introduced a 're-formed' open group model (Henry, 1988), which still forms the basis of our practice. A reformed model enables the formal group sessions to move beyond 'formative' issues and into 'performing', as predictability of group membership is increased by no new members being added for a limited period of time (currently five weeks). At the end of that time, a new group is reformed which might include some old and some new members. At first, attendance was on a voluntary contractual basis only, but now, while contracts are still required, some attend voluntarily and others who are considered to be at high risk of custody at the time of sentence attend as a condition of their probation order.

The marginalising of the needs of women offenders has resulted in neither the women offenders themselves nor probation officers having a clear notion of what constitutes an effective programme for supervising them in the community. To develop a clear understanding of those needs, we suggest that it is necessary initially to provide women offenders with an opportunity to discard their prescribed gender roles. In mixed offender groups women are able to avoid working on their own offending behaviour by adopting those roles which meet the emotional and practical needs of others rather than themselves. Our group programmes are therefore led by women probation officers. This is to ensure that nothing detracts from the women developing a sense of themselves outside their stereotype.

All groups are conducted in an activity centre attached to one of the probation offices. On group mornings the centre is closed to all other offenders and male colleagues. The women have the sole use of all the resources it provides, e.g. computer, pool table, table tennis, music centre, telephone, kitchen facilities, and information in respect of employment, education and welfare rights. Creche facilities are available for pre-school age children. This 'separatist' approach initially created tensions with male colleagues. Linda, as manager of the team which housed the activity centre, encouraged discussions about the fears and suspicions experienced by male colleagues, thereby demystifying the process and promoting an increased sense of understanding and trust between men and women workers. Over a period of time the tensions were replaced by acceptance.

Supervising officers, whether male or female, carry overall responsibility for probation orders on women, being fully involved in all aspects of their supervision from referral to post-group review, other than participation in the group itself. This ensures that all colleagues enhance their understanding of the issues faced by women offenders.

THE GROUPWORK MODEL

Key concepts

Figure 1 places the Miskin Model in the context of other models of working with women offenders. The model draws on concepts from both the feminist and welfare or traditionally orientated approaches. It offers the offenders both formal and informal activities. The formal activity is mainly groupwork to challenge and confront offending behaviour, whilst informal approaches are designed to deal with personal issues which may contribute to offending, e.g. use of leisure, education, employment opportunities.

Underpinning and informing all aspects of our model is offending behaviour. As stated earlier, it is this behaviour alone which authorises probation officers to work with offenders who are the subject of probation orders.

The key aims are to:

1. enable women offenders to explore fully the reasons for their involvement in offending, by providing a forum for challenging and confronting their behaviour and its consequences for themselves and others;
2. widen and develop the options available for alternative behaviour;
3. encourage group members to consider strategies for dealing with perceived powerlessness in changing their behaviour.

Group ethos

> ...when women are spoken for but do not speak for themselves
> ...dramas of liberation become only the opening scenes of the
> next drama of confinement (Showelter, 1987, p.250)

The workers aim to create an atmosphere of honesty, openness, sharing and respect for others, which is both challenging and enjoyable. Each member of the group has her part to play in creating an atmosphere requiring the taking of risks. The group

Figure 1
Groupwork models with women in the criminal justice system

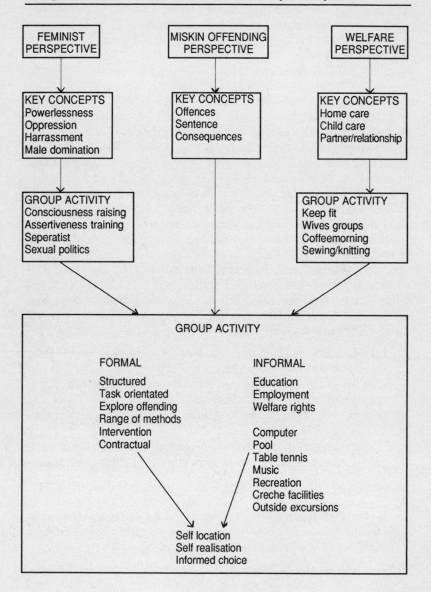

is orientated towards achievement of the task i.e. to fulfil the group contract which is determined during session one. The concept of individual responsibility is promoted at every opportunity. Language which conveys and reinforces helplessness is always challenged e.g. terms such as 'I can't...', 'I must...', 'I need...', are substituted with 'I won't...', 'I choose to...', 'I want...'. Sue would always say: 'I can't stop shoplifting'. When she went shopping alone, she said she felt compelled to shoplift, and believed it was out of her control. The only controlling factor she had was to shop with a member of her family. Only then was she able to avoid her urge to steal. At the first group session she attended she was encouraged to substitute 'I won't...' for 'I can't...'. The effect of saying 'I won't stop shoplifting' was immediate. From that point on she began to take more responsibility for what did or did not happen to her.

Contract

All women offenders participating in the programme do so on a contractual basis with aims and objectives clearly agreed beforehand. The contract is a commitment to herself to work towards breaking unhelpful patterns of thinking and feeling which contribute to her offending behaviour. It provides a sound basis for entry into the group by promoting the offender's sense of individual responsibility and giving the workers permission to highlight those areas of behaviour requiring change.

At the pre-group stage, the supervising probation officer and the offender will agree that group attendance is appropriate. A referral is made to one of the groupworkers and a three-way interview is arranged. The aim of the interview is to negotiate the offender's contract of attendance at the group. During that interview, the following questions in relation to participation in the groupwork programme are discussed: Why?, When?, How?, What?. She and her probation officer will have an opportunity to share aspects of the work they have undertaken together to meet her perceived needs. On this basis, the woman determines her reasons for joining the group and makes a statement about what she would hope to achieve through group membership. She will be expected to share her contract with the other group members at the first group session. The contract is signed and agreed by the three parties and a copy is placed in her probation record.

It is at this point that the offender is given full information about the groupwork programme:

1. no more than eight other women will be involved in the closed group sessions;

2. rules, boundaries and expectations include commitment to attend an initial series of five weekly group meetings from 10.15 a.m. to 12.30 p.m., each incorporating a 75 minute formal group session focusing on offence behaviour;
3. absence from the first session, or subsequently any two consecutive sessions, will result in withdrawal from that series with an opportunity to rejoin when the group is reformed (in our experience to date, a period of 2-7 weeks later depending on demand).

A second category of 'non-negotiable' group membership contract exists which is defined by the court at the time of sentence. A woman offender who attends the group on a compulsory basis follows a similar process to that described above. At the time of sentence an additional requirement of attendance at group sessions will have been inserted into the probation order. This condition may only be made with the agreement of the offender and will only be suggested by the probation officer preparing the social inquiry report in cases where the court, due to the gravity of the offence or the offending history, is seriously considering imposing a custodial sentence. Attendance on this basis involves ten sessions, and unacceptable absences may result in return to court for failure to comply with the condition.

In our experience, groups containing a mix of both voluntary and compulsory attenders do not hamper achievement of the group task. Each shows an equal capacity to make use of this model.

After the initial group involvement, a second three-way interview will take place to review whether or not the contract has been met. The offender will be given an opportunity to determine how the next period of her probation order will proceed, which may or may not result in further attendance at a re-formed group.

Planning and preparation by the workers

The model places great emphasis on proper planning and preparation. Full staff meetings involving all women probation staff in Miskin take place two weeks before the start of each programme to delegate essential tasks both practical, e.g. ensuring adequate material resources for the children, tea/coffee, transport; and professional, e.g. staff development, methods of groupwork intervention, skill sharing, co-leadership, issues which may be anticipated, review of the professional literature available.

THE GROUP SESSION

Each session is divided into three phases: beginning, middle and end.

Beginning: (approx 15 mins)

The aim is reorientation into the group and to provide an opportunity to share 'burning issues'. All participants including the workers 'check in'. Each 'check in' is time limited and if there is an issue requiring work during the session, detailed consideration at this stage is discouraged, as opportunities will be provided later.

Middle: (approx 45 mins)

A range of groupwork methods are used, largely determined by group need. Whilst the two groupworkers will have a suggested framework or plan of group activity which might be appropriate on the basis of the group contract and issues emerging from the previous group session, this framework is not imposed upon the group members: flexibility, spontaneity, the ability to think on one's feet are crucial skills/professional qualities for groupworkers.

In one group session there was a disagreement over how to proceed. Half the group wanted to spend the session focusing on the influence of friends, whilst the other half wanted to look at the attitude of the police towards women offenders. To work with the process and yet resolve the deadlock, the group was divided into two and each camp took up opposite sides of the room, one worker with each. The task of each sub-group was to consider the opposite point of view and to decide ten reasons why the group should focus on that topic. After 20 minutes the full group reassembled and the points were shared. The focus, however, had shifted to how group members related to one another, and in the wider context how each woman related to others. The exercise developed the skills of negotiation, listening, perspective taking and co-operation with others.

Other methods used to date have included: discussion, role play, brainstorming, trust exercises, hot seat, negotiation, perspective taking, video film material, social skills exercises, experiential role reversal techniques, transactional analysis concepts, guided fantasy, relaxation, sculpting, genograms, assertiveness training and music.

End: (approx 15 mins)

This phase focuses on summarising and evaluating the session. The workers reinforce the key insights engendered e.g. in the session described above, the workers made the point that, when considering the influence of friends and police upon behaviour, it is often easier to externalise the responsibility for difficulties in relationships, rather than acknowledging the part we play ourselves in influencing them.

During this period participants are also encouraged to deal with unfinished business arising from the session and to exchange positive strokes. We consider the giving and receiving of positive recognition to be extremely important as women are generally recognised for 'doing' in accordance with their role, rather than 'being' as individuals in their own right.

It is essential that attendance is recorded formally on case records. The summary and evaluation of each group session includes time for the offender group to agree a statement jointly which is then recorded on each participant's probation record.

INFORMAL GROUP ACTIVITIES

We attempt to provide opportunities and interests which may be unfamiliar in the experience of the women participants. Our aim is to broaden their horizons and to think about and practice skills in a variety of contexts. Increased confidence can result when the women experience and deal with matters they might initially believe to be beyond their abilities.

The activities include: advice/information on welfare rights, education and employment; leisure activities - pool, table tennis, computer, video work, outside visits; informal discussions.

The role of the workers changes in this phase. We intentionally get alongside the offenders on as equal a basis as the professional relationship will allow. For example, Jackie, during a three month period, became an excellent pool player and taught us some techniques to improve our play.

STAFF SUPPORT/DEVELOPMENT/SUPERVISION

A team approach

The women staff group responsible for the planning and running of this initiative quickly realised how crucial it was to work together as a team. We were dependent on one another to develop the model. We shared a vision and a value base but needed to set objectives and determine strategies for achieving those objectives. It was only by co-operating together that this could be achieved. The key principles which influence our work together are:

1. clear objectives and agreed goals in relation to our work with women offenders;
2. sound administrative procedures and regular review and monitoring of our work;
3. firm, decisive leadership based on co-operation, creative conflict, support, trust, openness and confrontation;
4. high priority given to individual development within the team context;
5. sound inter-group relationships with colleagues in the two Miskin teams and in the organisation as a whole. Middle managers have a significant part to play here.

Group leadership

During the five week programme, the two groupworkers meet for one hour prior to the start of each session to review and plan for the group's needs, develop their working relationship, and deal with co-leadership issues. Two leaders provide increased role modelling and group management possibilities, and additional support in dealing with administration such as referrals and reviews. It also enhances staff development and skills sharing opportunities.

A prerequisite of successful co-leadership is the ability of each partner to enter the working relationship with openness, honesty and mutual respect. Effective co-leaders are able to acknowledge and resolve differences and conflicts in their working relationship. We can recall several instances of unhelpful communication arising from the discounting of abilities, perceived power imbalances and a reluctance to ask for what we needed. When these difficulties have been resolved, we have been surprised at how often our process is echoed by that of the group members. These insights enhance our effectiveness as groupworkers.

Consultancy

Our experience of consultancy and its ethos may aptly be described by the following quotation:

> (No one) can reveal to you aught but that which already lies half asleep in the dawning of your knowledge (Gibran, 1975, as quoted by Brown, 1984)

and

...by listening, questioning and testing impressions, the groupwork consultant can focus on issues and draw conflict out into the open so that workers themselves can resolve it (Mullender and Ward, 1989, p.7).

Consultancy is structured into our programme, occurring immediately after each session for up to one hour. It begins with each group leader giving a very brief snapshot of the session and a statement of what is or is not required from the consultant. The process largely revolves around the consultant actively listening to what emerges and responding to requests for feedback or intervention from the consultees. The focus of consultancy is two-fold, partly on process, partly on content. Process issues have tended to focus on over-identification with the offender group: the issues stemming from women working with women. As women probation officers, we are able to identify with women's socialisation issues which hamper self-fulfilment and the achievement of potential. Sometimes, however, they experience us as being one step removed from their everyday reality. This has been an uncomfortable yet enlightening experience for us as workers.

Other processes which have provided a focus for consultancy have included co-leadership issues of the kind highlighted earlier. The relevance of exercises and methods used are also reviewed. If the group has not experienced an aspect of group activity to be helpful, alternative exercises and techniques are considered for future reference.

Selection and training of consultants

During the initial 18 months, consultancy was provided by a member of our working group who had considerable groupwork experience, commitment to the initiative and who also held management responsibility at local level. The potential role conflict was avoided because firm boundaries for the consultancy were discussed and agreed from the outset. Those colleagues who have an interest in developing consultancy skills have an opportunity to do so by observing the consultancy sessions (with of course the agreement of the workers) and practising consultancy in a 'live supervision' situation.

Successful consultancy depends on consultee skills. We have become increasingly aware of the importance of entering consultancy with an ability to acknowledge our personal areas of competence and our limitations; to reflect upon our performance and co-leadership; and with a readiness to receive or give constructive, critical and positive feedback. We have each developed an increased sense of individual responsibility. For example, during early consultancy sessions, the words 'she made me feel...' would be common place. We now realise that co-workers cannot make us feel anything. We may choose anger or frustration in response to the stimulus of a colleague, but ultimately we are in charge of our own feelings.

Staff appraisal

All members of staff involved in running the programmes are offered an opportunity for a formal supervision session at the end of a period of groupwork. The aim is to provide a formal evaluation and appraisal of their work performance for inclusion in locally held personal files, and incorporation in future supervision agreements for their wider professional and skills development.

CONCLUSION

The implementation of this model of groupwork in Miskin has had positive implications for both women offenders and the agency.

Women offenders

Women offenders have been empowered to take more control over the Probation Service resources they are using. An increased awareness of the reasons for their offending behaviour results in an improved ability to state their needs to probation officers and thereby achieve more meaningful, self-determined periods of supervision. They have been enabled to access their own personal resources. Sue's increased confidence resulted in her leaving the area to lead a more independent and, to date, offending-free lifestyle. Karen's previous sense of 'anomie' has been dispelled, and she is engaging in activities in the community which are enabling her to achieve recognition. Although initially her male partner disapproved, these outside interests now enhance their relationship.

The agency

The probation officers

For us the challenging yet enjoyable nature of the work provides a sense of achievement and satisfaction. Our efforts have been acknowledged and supported and we are influencing others both at an organisational and personal level. We have demonstrated that there is still room for 'bottom-up' initiatives in the probation service.

The probation field teams in Miskin

At every opportunity we seek the advice of our colleagues and the ensuing discussions which focus on practice issues, skills sharing and cross fertilisation have generated debates concerning the values which inform our practice. One of our early debates addressed the question of whether a group for women offenders, run by women workers, constituted a form of 'sexism'. The co-operation which is given by other colleagues is crucial to any sub-group of staff who have been delegated responsibility to provide more appropriate service delivery to an identified marginalised offender group.

Middle management

The support, commitment and enthusiasm of middle management has been crucial to the development of this model. Its future ongoing success is dependent on this support continuing. We were fortunate that Linda had responsibility for managing one of the field teams involved and was able to offer support, consultancy and leadership as both a peer and manager. In these circumstances, roles and boundaries require skilled, sensitive and clear gatekeeping. In the same way that the workers establish such clarity with the women offenders in respect of the formal and informal components, Linda was able to establish and maintain boundaries with regard to her role as a peer and also as a manager in the organisation.

Middle management commitment is crucial to:

1. negotiate within the organisation's management structure;
2. take a lead in producing clear discussion documents which highlight the gap in organisation policy, service delivery and resources;
3. ensure that the issues are discussed within the local criminal justice system. If the treatment of women offenders is to be addressed meaningfully, initiatives for working more effectively with them must be shared with sentencers. Our vehicle for this has been the Probation Liaison Committee. It is our experience that the magistracy is receptive to taking advantage of opportunities to discuss women offenders and how their own attitudes might influence the sentencing process.

Senior management

Hankinson and Stephens (1986) state:

It is with regret that we conclude that the current trend within the modern Probation Service is towards more rather than less bureaucracy.

Our work with women offenders in Miskin has overcome bureaucracy and exerted power and influence upon organisational processes from a 'grass roots' level. We therefore challenge the pessimistic conclusion put forward by Hankinson and Stephens (1986, p.33):

> It is often said that a system can be changed by becoming part of it and changing from within. We see little prospect of this approach succeeding within the Probation Service.

In our experience, senior management will support 'bottom-up initiatives' provided they are documented, established on sound practice principles and governed by the aims, objectives and values of the organisation. Steps have now been taken to initiate action to address the gaps in policy and practice in relation to women offenders throughout the Mid Glamorgan Probation Service. The process of empowerment has therefore extended beyond women offenders and women probation officers to the organisation as a whole. This theme will be the subject of another paper.

Footnote

It is fitting for the final comments to be those of the women with whom we were working nine months into the development of the model. At that time only two women probation officers were in post in the Miskin Division. The future of the group was in jeopardy. The women offenders on their own initiative insisted that their statement (below) be brought to the attention of the Chief Probation Officer.

> We want to keep the group going because we get support from each other and understanding, help, advice, friendship and a sharing of problems. We'd rather have two probation officers in the group than one, but if not, one will do, OK Chief.

Marion Jones, Mary Mordecai, Frances Rutter, Mid-Glamorgan Probation Service; Linda Thomas, Lecturer, Department of Applied Social Studies, University College of Swansea (she was with Mid-Glamorgan Probation Service when this chapter was written). This chapter is reprinted from Groupwork, *1991, 4(3)*

16

Groupwork with Women Offenders: A Source of Empowerment for Users, Workers and Agency

LINDA THOMAS

THE CONTEXT

Since the late 1970s the development of British penal policy has been influenced by the increased politicisation of law and order issues. Rising crime rates, increased fear of crime, overcrowded prisons (which have had little effect on reconviction rates), and institutionalised discrimination towards women and ethnic minority groups by and within the criminal justice system have all contributed to the development of Central Government policies. 'Solutions' to the issues have included legislation and a barrage of directives requiring those agencies involved in the administration of justice to offenders to review and revise their work.

The impact upon one of these agencies, the Probation Service, has been significant. It has been increasingly required to transform itself 'from a useful social work agency for meeting the social needs of offenders' to 'an effective service making a genuine impact on the behaviour of offenders' (Faulkner, 1989, p.3). In addition, research published during the late 1980s (Gendreau and Ross, 1987) indicating that the inclusion of certain components in probation programmes for offenders can significantly enhance the likelihood of a reduction in reoffending, heralded a shift away from probation groupwork practice determined by individual probation officer skill and interest.

In this climate it has been necessary for the Service to strive to achieve improved Effectiveness, Efficiency and value for money or Economy. The pursuit of these 3 Es (as they have become known nationally) will continue to shape probation practice during the 1990s.

All 56 Probation Areas within England and Wales have responded by establishing structures to strengthen the management of the Service. The flow of communication within such structures tends to be from the top (Chief Officer grades) to the bottom (main grade probation officers who undertake the face to face work with offenders). Senior Probation Officers, as middle managers, occupy a crucial bridging role between democracy and bureaucracy; policy development and implementation; innovation and standardisation; theory and practice; and 'them and us' attitudes.

The response of probation staff occupying low and middle positions in the line has been mixed. Some, such as Hankinson and Stephens (1986, p.19) concluded:

> ..... that the current trend in the modern Probation Service is towards more rather than less bureaucracy .... It is often said that a system can be changed by becoming part of it and changing from within. We see little prospect of this approach succeeding within the Probation Service.

For them the changes have been experienced as frustrating and debilitating.

Others have welcomed measures to counter previous complacency, inconsistent practice, eccentric standards and lack of accountability. The changes for them provide opportunities to develop consistent, relevant and critically evaluated services to offenders within a clear corporate rather than individual frame of reference. They reframe the apparent and actual problems stemming from new management structures and systems as opportunities to be proactive in influencing service policy and provision, and challenging and testing bureaucratic boundaries.

BACKGROUND DEVELOPMENT

In 1988 against this backcloth, I, then a field team manager working in an 84 per cent male management group, and three women colleagues from my own and a neighbouring field team, decided to collaborate in developing a groupwork model for women offenders. All staff within the two field teams, whose joint probation officer complement was 72 per cent male, were becoming increasingly concerned that whilst pursuit of the 3Es was resulting in improved services for the majority, it was militating against the development of effective services for minority and marginalised offenders such as women. At that time, Mid Glamorgan Probation Service was not untypical in having no policy for working with women offenders who were receiving similar disposals to men, often with fewer previous convictions and for less serious offences (source - Mid Glamorgan Probation Service Information System).

In the absence of specific 'good practice guidelines' and with no clear strategy, women offenders were being worked with on the periphery of mainstream probation provision which had been, and was still being, developed to meet the needs of 17-24 year old white, heterosexual male offenders. Intervention with these women was on the basis of needs perceived by others rather than defined by themselves; the focus being on gender and welfare issues rather than offending. It was not surprising that their response to probation supervision ranged from suspicion, elusiveness, refusal to comply, and payment of perfunctory lip service, to being excessively demanding in respect of welfare issues.

Having decided to 'sail uncharted waters', we agreed that the process which would underpin the development of the groupwork model would reflect and positively exploit line management by objectives, the system already governing mainstream probation provision. New initiatives generated from a 'bottom up' perspective which ignore the frame of reference influencing the thinking of management do so at their own peril! I would suggest that such initiatives are less likely either to survive on a long term basis or to make the crucial but necessary shift from a peripheral position to one which might influence practice and policy within the agency as a whole.

In initiating the Miskin Model (Miskin is the name of the criminal court administrative area served by the two probation field teams, Pontypridd and Porth) our main aim was to develop a model of groupwork intervention for women offenders which was Effective, Efficient and resulted in Empowerment. It was acknowledged from the outset that Economy was unlikely, as providing equal access and non-discriminatory practice to offenders whose needs cannot be met within mainstream provision will be costly in both staff and material resources. The term empowerment is in these circumstances more appropriate, as grafting new perceptions onto well established yet ineffectual practice requires persistent, well managed and strategically creative processes which empower the workers, women offenders and the agency alike.

Workers

Initially the balance of effort, enthusiasm and commitment lay with the workers. We carried the vision and energy to develop more relevant and effective provision for women offenders and to influence agency policy. If the layers of a highly structured line-managed agency are to be penetrated and influenced, the middle manager has a crucial role in harnessing available energy and vision within well considered and clearly documented action planning.

The women offenders

An absence of what constituted universally agreed efficacious groupwork practice with women offenders required that they contributed to the development of the groupwork model. Any model would be invalid without their commitment to participate in its construction. Such participation would result not only in the accessing of their own personal resources, but also in being able to exercise more control over the probation service resources available to them.

The agency

It was anticipated that words translated into concrete actions, and concrete actions translated into local achievements communicated to senior management, would result in the development of a policy and strategy which ensured equal access to groupwork provision for women offenders throughout the agency. If and when this occurred, then the agency too had been empowered.

Figure 1 illustrates diagrammatically the integrated dynamic and developing relationship between workers, women offenders and agency, which resulted as each at various stages became involved in the process of creative empowerment.

The parties are represented by shapes as follows:

☐   The workers

◯   The women offenders

◯   The agency

The relative heaviness of the figure perimeters relates to the amount of effort being made in developing or reinforcing the work.

The four phases span a 2 year period:

Phase 1 - 0-6 months
Phase 2 - 6-12 months
Phase 3 - 12-24 months
Phase 4 - 24 months +

In keeping with the pursuit of the 3Es theme, I have ascribed to each 'Phase' words beginning with the letter E which epitomise the key actions or otherwise of one or more of the three parties at that point in the developmental process. The Es are distributed according to the type and source of input.

In the remainder of this paper I shall expand upon the essential features of the 3Es assigned to the different Phases, each of which formed a small yet essential plank in promoting the development of provision for women offenders.

PHASE 1

Workers —Explore the gap in provision
—Establish a commitment to work together to
—Eliminate the gap

You see things and you say 'Why'
But I dream things that never were
And I say 'Why Not? (George Bernard Shaw, 1921, p.7)

Workers - explore
During the *forming* stage of a team's life when there is uncertainty about how to proceed, exploring and analysing the issues involved from multi-dimensional perspectives will pay dividends. Thorough groundwork at this stage will increase the probability of those involved establishing a solid foundation upon which to build their practice and co-operate together as a team. The workers will also be better placed to challenge organisational boundaries constructively, and to form coalitions with others later when institutional resistance will need challenging. Often an innovation which initially receives support will, following successful implementation, make demands later upon scarce resources, and may thus in retrospect appear not so attractive if it becomes someone else's problem. Answering the questions below, which are not exhaustive, will assist in this phase:

1. Why develop a new model of groupwork practice?

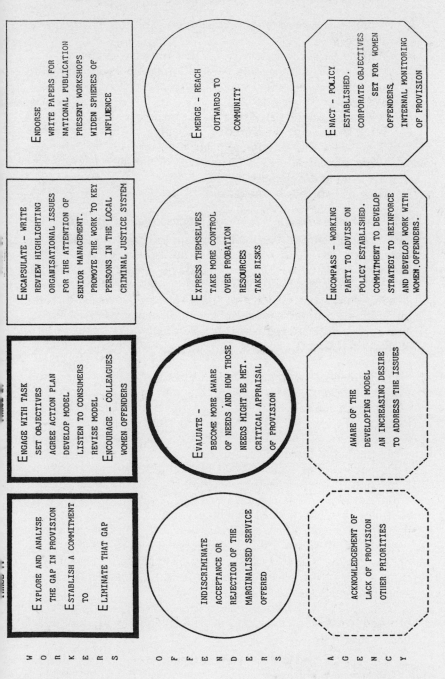

ENDORSE
write papers for
national publication
present workshops
widen spheres of
influence

EMERGE – REACH
outwards to
community

ENACT – POLICY
established.
CORPORATE OBJECTIVES
SET FOR WOMEN
OFFENDERS.
INTERNAL MONITORING
OF PROVISION

ENCAPSULATE – WRITE
review highlighting
organisational issues
for the attention of
senior management.
PROMOTE THE WORK TO KEY
PERSONS IN THE LOCAL
CRIMINAL JUSTICE SYSTEM

EXPRESS THEMSELVES
TAKE MORE CONTROL
OVER PROBATION
RESOURCES
TAKE RISKS

ENCOMPASS – WORKING
PARTY TO ADVISE ON
POLICY ESTABLISHED.
COMMITMENT TO DEVELOP
STRATEGY TO REINFORCE
AND DEVELOP WORK WITH
WOMEN OFFENDERS.

ENGAGE WITH TASK
SET OBJECTIVES
AGREE ACTION PLAN
DEVELOP MODEL
LISTEN TO CONSUMERS
REVISE MODEL
ENCOURAGE – COLLEAGUES
WOMEN OFFENDERS

EVALUATE –
become more aware
of needs and how those
needs might be met.
CRITICAL APPRAISAL
OF PROVISION

AWARE OF THE
DEVELOPING MODEL
AN INCREASING DESIRE
TO ADDRESS THE ISSUES

EXPLORE AND ANALYSE
THE GAP IN PROVISION
ESTABLISH A COMMITMENT
TO
ELIMINATE THAT GAP

INDISCRIMINATE
ACCEPTANCE OR
REJECTION OF THE
MARGINALISED SERVICE
OFFERED

ACKNOWLEDGEMENT OF
LACK OF PROVISION
OTHER PRIORITIES

W O R K E R S

O F F E N D E R S

A G E N C Y

2. What is the view of the consumers, in this case women offenders?
3. What are the characteristics of the women offenders?
4. What service provision is being offered, has been offered in the past, for this client group locally and nationally? Has it worked?
5. What values and principles will inform practice?
6. What is the current thinking informing groupwork in this field (academic, societal, legislative)?
7. What statistical evidence is available to inform or reinforce the need to develop provision?
8. How will success be measured?

Establish a commitment to work together to eliminate the gap

The notion of team and teamwork within the Probation Service is widely acknowledged to be highly desirable, yet it so often remains an elusive academic concept which bears little resemblance to the reality of day to day working life in 'teams'. The reasons for this are too numerous and complex to detail here, but taking Tuckman's model of group development (Tuckman, 1965) one significant contributory factor in my view is the failure of probation teams to move beyond *storming* and *norming* to *performing*.

As a group of workers about to engage in risk-taking and experimentation we were aware that our success depended on establishing sound teamwork and a shift from 'I'/'me' to 'we'/'us' thinking, feeling and behaving. During our own *storming* phase we did not smooth over the often heated discussions, nor did we avoid conflict in the name of support. True co-operation requires a degree of conflict, which if worked through creatively results in constructive collective action targeted towards the achievement of agreed goals. It is crucial during this phase to distinguish between creative and destructive conflict. Conflict becomes destructive when rumour and hearsay replace facts, personalities intrude, and threats to individual perceptions result in defensiveness. This is best dealt with by examining together the causes, clarifying assumptions, expectations and roles, and reaching consensus about future actions.

The essential components of effective teamwork which ultimately assisted us to *perform* and develop the Miskin Model of groupwork for women offenders were:

1. clear aims and goals incorporating systems for regular review and monitoring.

2. firm decisive leadership, and interpersonal relationships based on co-operation, creative conflict, support, trust and openness.
3. prioritising of both team and individual development.

PHASE 2

Workers   –Engage with task
                 –Encourage others
                 –Offenders - evaluate

All things are to be examined and called into question. There are no limits to thought (Hamilton, 1964, p.10)

Workers - engage with task, encourage others
Engaging with the task initially involved building on Phase 1 by setting objectives which were clear, achievable, acceptable, measurable and time limited. These goals were governed by principles which targeted risk and need, not determined by gender issues but by offending behaviour which is the probation officer's sole authority to intervene in the lives of her clients. A structure was provided which maximised the opportunity to comply with supervision requirements and offered both formal and informal group experiences.

Objective setting was followed by strategic planning to define a programme of action to achieve the desired results. At this stage little was forthcoming from the women themselves to inform the pilot groupwork model: they had a restricted sense of themselves as individuals in their own right having unique needs, and so had little notion of what they required from an effective probation programme. We therefore produced an initial model on the basis of perceived need determined from information obtained during Phase 1.

It was fundamental to this model to encourage and respond to constructive, critical feedback from the women offenders involved. It was also necessary to encourage formal and informal discussions with other colleagues to explain, debate and consult on the issues being addressed. Close collaboration and communication with all colleagues, whether or not they were closely involved in referring women offenders to the programme, was crucial, as was reinforcing and consolidating the learning achieved during the group sessions.

Offenders - evaluate

Within nine months of its inception the initial groupwork model devised by the workers was being reviewed, reappraised and modified to take into account the views of the women offenders themselves and the insight being gained - by them and the workers - into their offending behaviour.

The participants were experiencing a unique opportunity to engage with probation officers in a group setting which focused on the thought processes underpinning offending. As a consequence the potential trap of collusion with a system which pathologises women offenders for not conforming to their gender stereotype was avoided. As they shifted from what they perceived as a position of powerlessness towards taking, and experimenting with, opportunities provided to express opinions, so their feedback both positive and negative became increasingly direct.

Evaluation should be a proactive rather than reactive process; therefore simply to express discontent, with its inherent danger of becoming entrenched, is insufficient.

Whilst comments such as 'This is a load of ...', 'That was alright' and on one notable occasion 'You lot couldn't organise a .... up in a brewery!' were initially encouraged and accepted, group members soon came to realise that clear, direct and succinct expression of why they held that view, coupled with suggested solutions, achieved better results. Soon evaluative comments such as 'That exercise was useful because I now realise that I don't listen to other people but I expect other people to listen to me' and 'I didn't enjoy that at all, you didn't explain it properly at the start .... OK, I know I should have said something then, I will next time' were more commonplace, and an important step towards empowerment had taken place.

PHASE 3

Workers   —Encapsulate
Offenders   —Express themselves
The agency   —Encompasses the work achieved

> We must each look into ourselves
> And so find the courage
> To break free
> From those concepts of ourselves
> Which we have allowed
> To predetermine

What we are
And what we should be
Or what we should remain
(Rosenthal and Wiley, 1975, p.32)

Workers - encapsulate

Successful passage through this phase requires that the commitment and resolve of the workers, particularly the middle manager senior probation officer who occupies the most critical role,
remains intact.

Having achieved progress this far, many groupworkers fail to
take the next and often most important and difficult step —
initiating a process which ensures that the work is acknowledged
and action is taken within the parent organisation to address
policy gaps and disseminate the practice. If all opportunities, no
matter how limited, are both taken and made, then progress is
possible even within the most highly structured bureaucratic
organisation.

The production of a formal, comprehensive written review of
the work undertaken, highlighting gaps in policy and good
practice with women offenders, was well received by senior
management. We also capitalised on the fact that during this
period the Probation Inspectorate were undertaking a 'Thematic
Inspection' of the effectiveness of probation provision for women
offenders, and on the Home Office's increasing concern about
institutionalised discrimination against women and black
offenders.

Alongside the proactive stance being taken within the agency
we produced information for sentencers explaining the nature
and aims of the groupwork. For the first time, key persons within
the local system e.g. magistrates, court clerks, solicitors, were
debating women offenders and their treatment. One Probation
Liaison Committee meeting (a discussion forum for magistrates
and probation officers) was devoted entirely to a presentation of
the groupwork model; it provided opportunities for both magistrates
and probation officers to participate jointly in group exercises designed
to raise awareness of how and why women offenders suffer
discrimination. The response of the magistrates was very positive,
one said 'I've learned something about myself today'.

Offenders - express themselves

Women offenders involved in the programme were also
developing a sense of empowerment: they were moving beyond

'self location' towards 'self actualisation'. Their own resources were being accessed to enable the modification of rigid thinking, and the conceptualising of alternative ways of reacting to interpersonal difficulties. For example, during a short period when the future of the groupwork sessions was in jeopardy due to recruitment issues, the group members on their own initiative drafted a letter to the Chief Probation Officer.

Their suggestion that the group structure be amended was accompanied by well considered cogent reasoning involving the application of alternative thinking and an increased awareness of the consequences of their behaviour for themselves and others. Some were beginning to extend their horizons beyond the groupwork sessions. They responded positively to a request from a BBC researcher to meet and discuss with them the treatment of women offenders in the British criminal justice system; the meeting was successful and mutually beneficial to both the researcher and the group members.

The agency - encompasses the work

If new initiatives are to achieve pivotal influence, links must be established between senior managers and the innovative practice. The receipt of our formal written review produced a rapid response. Women offenders were placed on the agendas of management meetings where the contribution of a newly appointed Assistant Chief Probation Officer, a woman who shared my commitment, cannot be overestimated.

The undertaking to develop widespread effective provision for women offenders, which had already been forthcoming informally, was formalised and a process began which was to culminate in an organisational strategy to reinforce and develop groupwork with women offenders. This involved the establishment of a steering group with the delegated task of producing an advisory document on implementing policy and strategy to govern work with women offenders.

PHASE 4

Workers   – Endorse
Offenders   –Emerge
The agency –Enacts

> What we call the beginning is often the end
> And to make an end is to make a beginning
> The end is where we start from (T.S. Eliot, 1972, p.896)

Workers - endorse

My three probation colleagues and I have endorsed our work by writing papers for publication, being invited to present workshops at conferences, and expanding our spheres of influence and opportunities to promote and share aspects of our work. Like them, I am far from complacent because the development of effective work with women offenders has barely begun; there is still much to learn, to hear and to achieve.

Progress can only be sustained in a culture of continuous critical review and modification. A determination not to allow the limitations of today's practice to govern tomorrow will result in increasingly relevant models of work being developed for all client groups.

Offenders - emerge

Experience indicates that the model has the potential to be effective. Although quantitative measurements of independently researched 'success' are not yet available, most women attending the programme reported improvements in self esteem, assertiveness and self confidence, with corresponding reductions in re-offending. One woman accessed her personal resources to the extent of leaving the area to lead a more independent and, to date, offending-free lifestyle. Others have become involved in furthering their education or community activities, providing positive recognition of a kind not previously experienced.

The agency - enact

A policy and strategy for women offenders now governs practice in Mid Glamorgan Probation Service. In 1991 a corporate objective on work with women offenders was introduced for the first time. A working party established to advise on intensive probation packages for women offenders has reported, and Marion Jones has adapted an intensive cognitive skills training programme being offered to men, for use with women offenders : this programme will be the first of its kind to be available in the UK. As already stated, these first steps mark only the beginning of what is likely to be a long term process as:

> There are very few human beings who receive the truth complete and staggering by instant illumination.
> Most of them acquire it fragment by fragment on a small scale of successive developments, cellularly like a laborious mosaic.
> (Anais Nin, in *Bartlett's Familiar Quotations*, 1969, p.858)

CONCLUSION

My own experience and that of the team which developed the Miskin Model of groupwork for women offenders suggests that 'a system can be changed by becoming part of it and changing from within' (Hankinson and Stephens, 1986, p.19). Creativity and innovation can become tangible outcomes both in terms of shifting agency climate and stimulating the development of new policy and strategy within the Probation Service. I doubt if this could be achieved by individual probation officers working with individual offenders. The key to empowerment is the purposeful use of the opportunities for support and sharing which are only available within a group.

The process from vision to reality is not without its obstacles, but it is possible when the workers involved apply themselves to the task as a team, and with courage, dedication and persistence. Successful empowerment like successful groupwork requires that energy and vision be harnessed into clear, focused, purposeful activity, in this case setting objectives whose achievement was guided by action planning, regular review and a team approach. Positive proactive rather than negative reactive behaviour, within rather than outside the frame of reference influencing the course of agency policy, is likely to be more potent in promoting action which reinforces and develops the work on a corporate level.

The role of middle managers cannot be underestimated, as they are relied upon for the effective transmission of messages from the 'bottom' to the 'top' in a line management system. Neither 'bottom up' nor 'top down' initiatives will prosper within that structure unless something happens in the middle. Our experience confirms that it is possible to make things happen, develop something new, and set free workers' creative energy in the 'modern' Probation Service. May 3E thinking live on!

Acknowledgements
I would like to thank Marion Jones, Mary Mordecai and Frances Rutter for contributing to the planning of this paper.

Linda Thomas, Lecturer, Department of Applied Social Studies, University College of Swansea (she was with Mid-Glamorgan Probation Service when this chapter was written).

17

The Telford Motoring Offenders Education Project

KATHRYN HUTCHINS

INTRODUCTION

The Telford Motoring Offenders Education Project (MOEP) is a programme run by the Shropshire Probation Service for motoring offenders aged 17 and over. The first Shropshire MOEP was set up in Shrewsbury in response to the concern of the courts, the Probation Service, the Police and the local community about escalating motoring-related crime. Following the success of the project at Shrewsbury, the programme was extended to Telford where motoring offences were also on the increase. Between 1987 and 1990, for instance, reported cases of taking a vehicle without the owner's consent rose in the Telford area by 89 per cent; over the same period incidents of theft from vehicles rose by 62 per cent; and, between 1989 and 1990, reported excess alcohol cases increased by 35 per cent. These figures confirmed an impression that our court lists were filled with motoring offenders, many of whom were in the 16 to 21 years age range, and that some form of intervention aimed at helping them to become responsible legal road users was needed.

Traditionally probation officers have worked with offenders on a one-to-one basis but recent years have seen developments in offence-focused and issue-based groupwork. Experience here and elsewhere (Hamilton and Oulds, 1990) shows that many motoring offenders commit their offences with others and that peer pressure is influential. Thus an approach which provided an opportunity for constructive peer challenge and influence seemed most appropriate. The MOEP was therefore designed as a groupwork programme which could be a component part of an overall probation order (in which other, traditional methods might still be applied). Using a groupwork model also facilitated the involvement of other community members and agencies, such as the police, magistrates and insurance company staff as well as others. More will be said about these community links shortly.

From the start it was intended that the MOEP would have an educational focus; in addition its form would be such as to ensure that the participants' offending activities would also be challenged. The latter was especially important in view of Shropshire's aim of targeting resources on offenders with an established pattern of offending who were at risk of custodial sentences or further offences. We believed local courts needed to be convinced that what was on offer provided a means of addressing the particular matter which brought the offender before the court. Thus, unlike several motoring projects elsewhere in Britain, the MOEP programme was not designed to involve clients in 'banger' racing, motor repair or driver re-training. Instead the approach has been to take clients through various aspects of what they need to know and do to become legal road users, whilst confronting them with the consequences of repeated motor offending - for victims as well as themselves.

The MOEP programme has evolved over time, in the light of contributions and comments from workers and participants. For this reason the description which follows is not a 'snapshot' of the MOEP at one point in time but consciously reflects and incorporates what we have learned, and are continuing to learn through our growing experience.

SETTING UP THE PROGRAMME

Setting up the MOEP has involved a whole variety of considerations, from community involvement to agency practicalities, from membership of the groups to the content of the sessions and the materials needed to work on and address the topics covered in the content. These are discussed below.

Community involvement
Recent Home Office papers, including *Supervision and Punishment in the Community* (1990a) and *Crime, Justice and Protecting the Public* (1990b) place emphasis on concepts of partnership between the Probation Service and local community-based agencies and resources. An important aspect in the development of the MOEP to date has been the active support and co-operation of the police, magistrates and an insurance

firm. The involvement of these contributors has been central in the provision of materials, equipment and expert information on sentencing, motoring law and insurance. Moreover, we have found that the group members enjoy discussion with 'real' people who are prepared to enter into debates and give accurate information. More recently we have presented the MOEP to our local branch of the Institute of Advanced Motorists and that resulted in offers of help from the County Council Road Safety Officer. This positive response from individuals and community groups to plans for work with motoring offenders has been particularly gratifying, and is reflected further in the readiness of local media (press, radio and more recently television) to publicise the MOEP and related work. We enlisted help from a trainee BBC TV crew to make a video showing two youths stealing a car, crashing it and going to court. This has been especially useful in helping us develop offender-focused material which is realistic. It provides a visual means for engaging clients who might otherwise be unable to cope with group discussion or self disclosure.

Agency practicalities

Mention has already been made of agency policy in targeting resources on offenders at high risk of further offending and/or a possible custodial sentence. But there are practical considerations in mounting programmes like the MOEP which also have to be taken into account. In particular, the Telford programme represents a heavy commitment for its two probation officer co-leaders and we have found from experience that there is a need to negotiate some workload relief for the staff running the course. (Equally, though, the pressure of running groups extends beyond the co-leaders and impacts on colleagues who may be called on to cover other essential work). We have also found it important to facilitate involvement of colleagues as co-leaders so as to widen knowledge of the MOEP and increase a sense of ownership by workers. Co-leadership and involvement helps workers sell the MOEP to potential clients and sentencers. But to do this we needed an easily accessible database with details of the programme, timings of exercises, lists of resources needed, etc., so that any colleague could use the materials. Programme details are stored on an easily revised word processor disc, and workers are encouraged to add to or alter the basic package over time in the light of special client need, experience, or development of new resources.

Membership and attendance

Potential members for the MOEP are identified by an agreed referral system operated by the two Telford probation teams, and on request from Shrewsbury. Attention is focused on motoring offenders in the 17-25 year age range who are also assessed by 'Risk of Custody' scales (see Bale, 1987; 1988; MacLeod, 1988 for a discussion) as being at high risk of custody and/or re-offending. However we have occasionally taken clients outside of this age and risk range and have found older clients helpful in challenging some younger members' attitudes. For high risk clients, attendance at the MOEP is included as a condition of the probation order. This means that their attendance is compulsory but, mindful of the compulsion/voluntarism debate which is going on in the probation and social work literature (Raynor, 1978), we have begun to consider voluntary membership. Currently, though, we require a doctor's note in case of illness. Two unacceptable absences lead to breach action (i.e. a return to the court with fines or re-sentencing as a possible outcome); acceptable absence usually results in being put back to the next available course.

We have taken the optimum size of a group to be 6-12 members and for the two groups offered so far, ten referrals to Group 1 led to five completions and 14 referrals to Group 2 led to seven completions. All the members in Group 1 were disqualified drivers with related 'no insurance' charges and one 'drunk driving' charge. They had all been to prison for driving offences in the past, and analysis of their known criminal records revealed between 1 and 3 sets of motoring convictions (which in one case added up to over 90 offences). One member had bans totalling over 18 years. Members of Group 2 were similarly heavily convicted and included a person convicted of causing death by reckless driving. Seven out of the nine starting Group 2 had previous custodial experience, and one had avoided custody on appeal. The general view amongst members was that they believed they would have been sent to custody had the MOEP not existed.

Equal opportunities considerations

There are equal opportunities issues associated with the MOEP. Shropshire is a predominantly rural county with centres of population in the county town of Shrewsbury and the rapidly expanding new town of Telford. Day-to-day probation fieldwork is based in three field team offices (two offices in Telford and one in Shrewsbury) and smaller offices in the outlying rural team areas. This has implications for service delivery in that while Telford and Shrewsbury have groupwork and video facilities and good access to public transport, the same is not true for the outlying areas. Thus we have used volunteer drivers, travel warrants and bus fares to try to overcome transport problems. On a different equal opportunities point, the MOEP materials have been designed to take account of the varying levels of literacy amongst group members, and some is suited to one-to-one work.

We aim to make the MOEP as widely available as possible to suitable candidates although, as Buckley and Williams (1991) have pointed out, serious motor offending is a predominantly male activity and I am not aware of any female referrals to the group. Our area has a relatively small ethnic minority population, and we are aware that minority group members may have special needs if referred to what has until now been an all white, all male group (with the exception of female group leaders). In fact, we have had only one referral of a client from an ethnic minority and that client was dealt with in another way by the courts. Further research is undoubtedly needed to identify what happens to female and ethnic minority motoring offenders in our courts and when we prepare social inquiry reports.

Content of the sessions and relevant material
The MOEP has been designed as an eight session programme run on a two-nights-a-week basis for four weeks. The eight sessions are structured as follows:

1. *Introduction*: rule setting; confidentiality; Highway Code - road use.
2. *Attitudes*: input from police; video quiz; discussion.
3. *Documentation needed for legal driving and responsible vehicle ownership*: factsheet; input from police on road safety and police equipment.
4. *Personal offending analysis*: costs to self and others; victim perspective; trigger videos.
5. *Insurance, uninsured driving and driving whilst disqualified*: input from insurance assessor on why you need it; what it does and does not cover; how the costs are worked out; how to get it; consequences of uninsured driving for self and others.
6. *Alcohol and driving*: quiz; influences on driver ability; try out breathalyser equipment.
7. *The role of the courts*: input from magistrate; discussion on

what they take into account; sentencing exercise based on video and anonymous social inquiry reports; sentencing exercise and discussion.

8. *What to do after accidents and course review*: where do we go from here; future plans; personal target setting; follow up Highway Code quiz; client feedback (written and in discussion for the less literate) on how they found the MOEP course; helpful/less helpful parts, likes and dislikes, comments etc.

We have found it essential to use a variety of methods and materials to encourage full participation by group members, so we make use of exercises, trigger videos (including our 'in house' video) and material from the commercial *Road User* educational package produced by the Strathclyde Regional Council. We also use methods based on McGuire and Priestley (1985), such as brainstorms, full and small group discussion, paired work, alcohol and Highway Code knowledge tests, attitude quizzes, and a chance to use police equipment such as the breathalyser and speed gun. Flipchart and video equipment is needed, as are notepads, pens and copies of the Highway Code for each member.

We have also made cautious use of very emotive material. A chilling reminder of the consequences of unsafe driving or casual attitudes to safety is brought home by handling motorbike helmets from fatal accidents. This needs to be done very sensitively and leaders need to be aware of potential problems in this area, when, for example, referrals are received in respect of clients charged with death by reckless driving. Potential course organisers also need to consider the gravity of offence that their courses will seek to address, as mixing very serious offenders with those charged with lesser matters can risk some people cutting off and not seeing the course as relevant to their own situation. It is important to check this out at the referral stage before the group begins.

PROCESS EXAMPLES

Obviously groups differ and there is not a 'typical' occurrence in the process of any programme. But the following examples will perhaps help to illustrate what the MOEP is like and how it seems to have a productive impact on its members.

A 20 year old with a long history of driving while disqualified came to realise that, in doing so, he was uninsured and putting other road users at risk of considerable loss if he caused them an accident. He was able to challenge a 43 year old with an equally bad record of disqualified motoring, who was sent to MOEP for drink driving charges. The younger member was effective in confronting the drink driver's poor attitude to driving while unfit through alcohol, because his aunt had been killed by a drunken driver and he was able to bring that experience up in the discussion. Both were able to explore their opposing ideas of the sort of risks their illegal driving posed to others as well as themselves, and the leaders felt the peer confrontation was particularly effective. Group members bring to the MOEP their own ideas of a hierarchy of offending and drink drivers tend to be regarded as particularly irresponsible; they can, however, helpfully remind other members that uninsured, unsafe driving, or car theft are equally unacceptable and risky to other people.

During the group, individual attitudes to road safety and basic road knowledge are questioned. We seek to hold a balance between challenging offending, and educating members in a way that will, we hope, help them to adopt safer, more responsible attitudes when they go on the road again. One member was delighted to finish the MOEP without having a court case pending for banned driving, after years of being repeatedly disqualified. His probation officer said the MOEP gave encouragement to him to get through the ban without reoffending, so he can now get back on the road legally.

FOLLOW UP

Following each session, the group leaders record how the session went and, in particular, note the participation of each group member. These notes contribute to a final write-up on each member which they and their supervising probation officer each receive. This ensures that the group experience for the member can feed into any subsequent work on probation as is seen to be appropriate.

CLIENT FEEDBACK

Feedback from group discussions and individual question sheets can be used to inform developments of the programme. In response to comments we are actively reviewing the video material, and are considering involving a speaker from Victim Support or other ways of demonstrating the victim perspective (possibly by video). Noting that some people have wanted more input, we have been investigating other road training and motor-related education programmes to which suitable group members can be directed as a follow-on from the MOEP.

EVALUATION

We do not yet have the benefit of a computerised information system but hope that, by monitoring referrals, completions and re-conviction at timed intervals, we can get some indications of the impact of the MOEP on high risk offenders. So far the scheme we have devised is as follows. Supervising officers are asked to note progress and any re-offending and new sentencing details on a form circulated three months after the group and, from then on, every six months while the client remains in contact with the Probation Service. The first two reviews on MOEP Groups 1 and 2 (at three and six months post-group) have been collated; of 12 clients completing groups in August 1990 and December 1990, seven are known not to have been reconvicted, one has since been sentenced to detention in a young offender institution, two have received suspended sentences, and two are awaiting court appearances. All these new convictions included motoring, which is disappointing, but it needs to be remembered that the MOEP is targeted on those with a high risk of re-offending and custody. With more experience of the MOEP we hope to be able to increase its impact.

On a more positive note, we would hope to use successful completion of the MOEP, and lack of further offending, to support applications to the courts to discharge or convert orders early on grounds of good progress. If it becomes possible to extend provision for motoring offenders to incorporate driver retraining, we may also seek to support clients applying to courts for early return of their driving licences, as a regular problem tends to be that offenders have difficulty staying off the road when subject to lengthy bans, with the result that they continue to drive while banned and, thereby, while uninsured.

SOME FINAL COMMENTS

Community involvement adds variety to the resources normally available to probation staff. The expertise and enthusiasm shown by police, magistrates, insurance staff and other offers of help received give grounds for optimism that the MOEP will continue. In this sphere of work one is faced by problems arising out of entrenched attitudes to motoring and all that driving represents, as well as the financial and social implications of car theft, drunken, uninsured and disqualified driving. Through a variety of means, the MOEP seeks to examine the consequences of ignorance and bad attitudes to driving for offenders and others. The influence of peer pressure and discussion available in a groupwork approach, coupled with economies of scale of information-giving sessions, offers a level of challenge, debate and discussion it would not normally be possible to achieve on an individual basis. As it stands, the MOEP combines offence-focused, confrontative work, with an educative approach, seeking to enable members to make informed choices about their future driving behaviour. The balance is not always easy to hold, not least because of strongly established male attitudes to vehicle use (see Buckley and Williams, 1991); however, individual work carries on after the MOEP, building on the coursework programme and the member's response to it as detailed in the group leaders' report on their progress. Although complete in itself, the MOEP thus informs other work under the overall probation order. We would not see the MOEP as providing all the answers to the problems posed by illegal or inconsiderate road users, but we hope it goes at least part way to offering such motorists the chance to reconsider how they will act when, as they invariably do, they go back on the road.

Kathryn Hutchins, Staffordshire Probation Service. This chapter is reprinted from Groupwork, *1991, 4(3)*

18

Handling Conflict:
Groupwork with Violent Offenders

ROB CANTON, CAROLYN MACK AND JEFF SMITH

The groupwork experience which this paper describes was part of the client course tradition of the Nottinghamshire Probation Service. This tradition has its origins in the approach to problem solving developed by Priestley, McGuire and their colleagues in the late 1970s which has been so influential in modern probation practice (Priestley, McGuire et al., 1978; Despicht, 1987). Although this course was designed by the authors, it drew heavily on the experiences of our colleagues and in its turn, perhaps, has made its own contribution to the development of an established groupwork programme.

The four day programme, 'Handling Conflict', was made available to those clients of the Service who identified this issue as a problem for themselves. Although a violent response is by no means the only way in which conflict may be handled inappropriately, it was our expectation that most of those referred would have convictions for violent offences.

VIOLENT OFFENDERS

Constituting some 15% of all prison receptions in England and Wales in 1988 and 23% of the average custodial population at any time (Home Office, 1990, p.11), violent offenders are often explicitly excluded from proposals to shorten sentences, increase remission or extend parole. Even groups who favour substantial reductions in levels of imprisonment often try to make their case by reference to the large numbers of non-violent offenders in custody, conceding, so it seems, that custody may be appropriate for those convicted of crimes of violence.

Home Secretaries assure Parliament and the electorate that the courts respond robustly to offences of violence against the person. The numbers of violent offenders in custody increased by almost one-third between 1983 and 1988 (Home Office, 1990, p.12), while the average sentence for violent crime increased by 12% between 1980 and 1988 (*The Guardian*, 13 May 1988). Politicians are somewhat more reluctant to notice that, far from reducing violence, these increases have gone step by step with substantial rises in the incidence of crimes of violence.

Any attempt to influence the level of offending by increasing sentence length is based on a flawed understanding of the relationship between crime and the penal system (Canton, 1987). In the particular case of offences of violence, there is reason to think that dependence upon imprisonment is more likely to be harmful than merely irrelevant.

Although this view cannot be defended here in detail, it is grounded in an understanding of the development of violent incidents and the characteristics of some regularly violent people. It has been well said that: 'Violence feeds on low self-esteem and self-doubt and prison unmans (sic) and dehumanises; violence rests on exploitation and exploitiveness ...' (Toch, 1969, p.266) Prison culture presents no challenge to that ethos: rather, it is itself a powerful symbol of violence and oppression.

It is the work of Hans Toch that begins to suggest a more considered response and two of his insights were especially influential in the design of this course. Violence can be analysed as a 'game' (in the technical sense), often involving a complex transaction between offender and victim. One may see the other as hateful or threatening and act accordingly; the other reciprocates, reinforcing the original preconception. This kind of analysis gives a violent incident a context and so makes it intelligible rather than random. Secondly, Toch's typology of violence suggests that the origin of violence commonly lies in the interaction between a person's self-image and how others behave to confirm or to threaten that image. Violence of this character, 'falls firmly [therefore] within the province of social skills training' (McGuire and Priestley, 1985, p.111).

A further dimension is suggested by the work of Sykes and Matza. Their seminal paper on 'techniques of neutralisation' emphasised that the value systems of offenders, so far from being alternatives or inversions, are often very close to conventional values. Offenders interpret their conduct to themselves and to other people in ways that seek to justify their behaviour (Sykes and Matza, 1957). It is our experience that many violent offenders will appeal to various techniques (of which denial is just one) to account for themselves. These interpretations need to be challenged creatively. Certain kinds of challenge will elicit more persistent denial or superficial compliance. Enduring change can only take place when it is acknowledged that denial and other techniques have a function (Sheath, 1990). Groups can generate precisely this compelling combination of challenge and support towards change.

The principle of 'voluntarism'

In many areas, attendance at an 'offending behaviour' group is a formal requirement of a Probation Order. It is an irony that so many of those running these groups would claim the influence of Priestley and McGuire (Despicht, 1987), although their view of this was unequivocal:

> Voluntary participation is in fact the linchpin ... Participants in a problem-solving process must be free to join or not to join in the first place, free to stay or leave at any time subsequently, free to accept or reject any activity which is on offer, and free to make whatever use they deem fit of the results of any of the exercises they choose to complete (Priestley and McGuire, 1978, p.12).

Thus the invitation for referrals to this course began by emphasising that attendance would be voluntary. There are certain decisive general considerations. The course is an educational undertaking and there is at least an uneasiness, if not a contradiction, in the idea of coerced education. Moreover, it was our intention to make demands upon the participants: insistence on informed consent and commitment gave the authority to proceed. It immediately established an atmosphere of acceptance and tolerance within the group: attendance was an indication of a sincere resolve to engage with personal difficulties and this commanded respect.

Brown notes that: 'Paradoxically, control systems in which the members carry power are likely to be more successful than those which are imposed on them' (Brown, 1979, p.51), while our experience precisely confirmed that:

> By starting with a group of people who ... share a central concern, and by allowing them to set the direction and objectives of the group - acknowledging the skills, knowledge and abilities they already possess and working with them in partnership - the groupworker can help them not only to reach an

understanding of their key problems but also to identify and use methods of successfully tackling those problems (Mullender and Ward, 1985, p.156).

There is also something about the character of their offending that makes the principle of voluntarism even more relevant in working with violent people. If this tendency is related, as has been suggested, to self-image, compulsory attendance is precisely the wrong start: coercion and constraint inhibit the process of examining self-identity; instead, they elicit denial and defence. It seems to us to be necessary to start, though not indeed to finish, by providing a setting without threat or discomfort and this may well be incompatible with compulsory attendance.

THE COURSE

Preparation, introduction and ground rules

Applicants were interviewed by a course leader in the company of the referring probation officer. Their right to decline to attend was emphasised, but assurances were given - that their interpretations were to be taken seriously, that it was for them to set their specific objectives, that they would not be judged or denounced - which would mitigate anxiety and enable them to attend, confident and receptive.

A sense of control and responsibility was also enhanced by the assurance that it was not the purpose of the course to tell people how to behave. It was hoped to challenge the common feeling that violent incidents are unavoidable. This is more than a general sense of fatalism. Toch writes of violence-prone people who 'scan human contacts assiduously for the possibility of threatening implications' (Toch, 1969, p.229). The dynamic of the group would enable this 'blind area' of motivation to become public (Douglas, 1976, p.118) and, by deepening understanding of the context of violence, allow a different interpretation and thus a different response. So far from telling people how to behave, then, the course was intended to increase the range of behaviour and the opportunity of choice.

The three group leaders had anticipated working with about twelve people in the four consecutive days of the course. The average daily attendance was eleven, although not everyone attended the whole course. It happened that almost all participants had significant records of violent offending. Some had been made subject to Probation Orders recently; others had committed serious offences in the past and were on licence. Two of the group members had taken life.

Structure and content

The course followed the familiar structure of assessment, setting objectives, learning and evaluation (Priestley, McGuire et al., 1978). There is an inevitable tension between the need to prepare a planned programme and, on the other hand, to leave enough flexibility to enable participants to set their own objectives. The course was shaped by three general aims which were felt to be sufficiently broad to accommodate most individual objectives:

1. to help people to understand the origins and context of conflict and its deterioration into violence;
2. to help people to identify those circumstances in which they are most likely to meet or to initiate violence;
3. to help people learn to assert themselves effectively and appropriately.

After a formal welcome, the group leaders went through the ground rules for the programme again. We checked that people were there because they had chosen to be and affirmed our own view that this represented a personal commitment that demanded respect from everyone involved in the group. The boundaries of confidentiality were discussed. Although we hoped that the learning from the course would be developed in individual work with their probation officers, it was for group members to determine what dialogue there was to be between the course leaders and the supervising officers.

Personal folders were distributed (checks had been made at the referral stage to anticipate difficulties about literacy) so that people could retain their own notes and handouts. Introductions followed and, in a paired exercise, participants helped each other to speak about some of their expectations and reasons for attending.

Assessment

The group watched a video - an extract from a well known television comedy - in which a sequence of misunderstandings led to an exchange of blows. A 'brainstorm' followed in which people tried to identify exactly what had led up to the incident and the many ways in which any one of those involved could have prevented a violent outcome. Although this was a deliberately light-hearted opening, it already marked out some of the themes that were to be developed over the next few days: the potential for violence from misunderstanding (and the corresponding value of explicit and assertive communication), the context and development of a violent incident (it does not 'just happen'), the pointlessness of finding someone who is to blame and the wide range of alternative strategies for avoiding violence.

This part of the programme, which included more large group discussions and another brainstorm ('What is conflict?') was at a very general and safe level. The attempt was to establish a unity of purpose within the group and a culture of acceptance and cooperation which were felt to be preconditions of effective challenge at a later stage. For now, it was important to establish an unthreatening setting so that retreat or defence became unnecessary.

Setting objectives

Setting of objectives must involve more demands. Exercises, questionnaires (retained by the participants in their personal files) and discussion in smaller groups and in pairs began to enable a more precise identification of the problems on which people were to choose to work. While this necessarily involved more personal attention, the extent to which people were to share their objectives remained within their own control.

One exercise was the 'Feelings Thermometer'. Given a sheet of paper with a sketch of a thermometer, participants were asked to record something that made them 'boiling mad', something that was mildly irritating and perhaps two or three things that they would rate between these extremes of 'temperature'. The 'Anger Inventory' lists a number of possibilities (Somebody is staring at you. You are trying to concentrate and someone is making a lot of noise. Someone makes a mistake and blames it on you.) which are to be given a score between 1 (It would not especially bother you) and 5 (It would make you very angry).

One participant disclosed in the small group that he had scored every situation with a 3 and that it was a silly exercise: he was either angry or he wasn't - he did not know what it was to be slightly angry. This man, in other words, saw his own anger not as a rising thermometer but as a switch. This must give a frightening sense of powerlessness. He had killed someone years ago and did not know, he said, whether or not 'it' might happen again. For much of the remainder of the course, the group helped him to work with his objectives of learning to understand more about how violent situations develop and how to interpret a context, so that he would be able to make his choices before the critical point. His 'blind area' - something about him which was apparent to others but mysterious to himself - was illuminated by this support. As Douglas puts it, 'The enlargement of the public area increases awareness and opens behaviour to an element of conscious choice in areas previously restricted or out of such control' (Douglas, 1976, p.118).

It was in this phase that the group was first introduced to role play, which was to be used extensively as an indispensable part of the course. The transactional character of violent incidents makes role play a powerful learning experience. The method is most effective when the role play is immediately followed by group analysis and discussion (Argyle, 1972). The introduction to role play involved the recollection and role-playing of incidents of conflict that had been appropriately managed. As well as making for a comfortable introduction to the experience of role play, this was a reminder that everyone - even the most violence-prone people - handle (probably most) incidents of conflict with a measure of control and success. In any process of assessment and objective-setting, moreover, it is important to remind people of their strengths and the possibility for finding solutions from within their own resources (Mullender and Ward, 1985).

This small group exercise was among the least successful sessions of the course. Our own familiarity with the practice of role play makes it easy to overlook how uncomfortable and strange a demand it can make. More thought needs to be given to how role play is to be introduced. (Perhaps a more tightly structured scene would be easier than a recollection of one's own.) Nevertheless, it was a measure of the group's unity and commitment that, despite this unpromising beginning, it was possible to reintroduce role play at a later stage to much more rewarding effect.

Learning

The learning phase began with the theme of 'reading people', attempting to facilitate a more sophisticated interpretation of other people's behaviour. A first exercise involved handing round photographs, cut out from newspapers and magazines, and inviting people to tell the group as much as possible about the person in the photograph. This made the point that we often form impressions of people before any kind of communication takes place and these preconceptions can shape the whole subsequent encounter (Satir, 1972). Communication was explored in the well-known game in which a message is passed along a chain and, usually, ends up distorted, though often with some recognisable elements. An exercise to demonstrate non-verbal communication was immediately followed by a role play, presented by the group leaders, in which verbal messages of interest were persistently contradicted by non-verbal messages of detachment. The group was helped to see the value of unambiguous messages and the unease that can be evoked by paradoxical injunctions or double binds.

As part of the exploration of alternative strategies for handling conflict, there was some assertiveness training - mainly role played 'rehearsals' and analysis in small groups - although this, like a number of other sessions, was suggestive rather than systematic. An exercise that worked particularly well was a brainstorm of excuses and responses. Taking an example familiar to most participants, we asked the group to think of as many excuses as possible that the Department of Social Security might advance to explain why their payment had not arrived in the post, and then to think up assertive and imaginative rejoinders to those excuses.

Violence was addressed directly in a session in which the group analysed a filmed incident. Learning from earlier sessions was exploited to show:

1. the assumptions and prejudices that people brought to the encounter;
2. the development and escalation of the conflict;
3. the transaction between the persons involved and the various points at which either person could have redirected the dispute;
4. the aggressor's complete failure to gain his purpose.

Alternative strategies were discussed and experiment made in role play.

A session was included that looked at the physiology of aggression - what chemical processes are taking place in the body in a state of arousal. An earlier exercise had demonstrated individuals' need for personal space and this was developed to show that it is not uncommon for the body to react to threat and for feelings of discomfort to be experienced before this has been apprehended by the intellect (McGuire and Priestley, 1985, p.85). There is a need for a greater awareness of what evokes anxiety and how that anxiety is experienced before it becomes acute and gives rise to behaviour that is experienced as uncontrolled.

Another session gave information and prompted questions about alcohol. The association between alcohol and aggression is so much an aspect of the experience of many participants, and so undermines the judgement and skills necessary to manage conflict appropriately, that alcohol was prominent in many discussions. Participants were made aware that there is ready access to courses which address the issue of alcohol directly. It is to be noted, however, that the observed correlation between drinking and violence is likely to be evidence of something rather more complex than a simple cause-effect relationship (Walmsley, 1986).

A final learning sequence involved an exercise in which the group looked at a number of cases that had been reviewed by the Criminal Injuries Compensation Board and were asked to award a sum of money (McGuire and Priestley, 1985). (Many examples are to be found in the Board's reports.) The participants' assessment involved careful and demanding reflection on the many ways in which violence can be damaging. By this time, group members had the confidence to challenge each other to think of implications for victims that they had hitherto denied or which had otherwise been unacknowledged. Although there was no analysis in the large group of any incident in which a group member had been personally involved, there was some degree of confrontation as people began to make connections between these cases and acts of their own. To be effective, confrontation 'must take place in a safe environment where members of the group feel secure enough and trusting enough to accept that the pressure being applied has ultimately a beneficial awareness-creating end' (Douglas 1976, p.127). By that time, as it seemed to us, just such an environment had been established.

Evaluation

This phase consisted mainly of a review of how lessons from the course could be retained and developed. Participants were encouraged to share their insights with the referring probation officer, although this was within their own control. All the participants wrote letters to themselves, addressed and sealed an envelope and entrusted it to a course leader to post to them after six weeks. In small groups and in pairs, people set tasks for themselves and thought of how to apply their learning to actual and potential conflicts in their lives.

The participants' evaluation of the course itself was fulsome, although most remarks were too general to enable specific suggestions for improvement to be inferred. While it would be unhelpful to be complacent, social workers and probation officers have not been good at heeding consumer opinion and the least that can be said is that the response was encouraging.

From the authors' point of view, it seemed that much more thought needs to be given to the difficulty of introducing role play. It has already been suggested that our own familiarity with the practice of role play may have led us to introduce the idea too cursorily, failing adequately to appreciate the diffidence that many would experience about participating - perhaps especially when assertiveness had been identified as a problem by several members of the group. A confident demonstration by the group leaders, a clear explanation of the point of role play and an opportunity to practise with some 'safe' and predictable scenarios might have helped group members to find the confidence to explore this way of learning with more imagination and creativity.

We are also aware of our relative neglect of the gender dimension to violent offending. As the course progressed, it became increasingly apparent that a propensity to violence was, for many of the male participants, closely bound up with their understanding of how they are expected to behave as men, their very idea of what it is to be a man. Although we tried to enable people to express these thoughts and to encourage a creative challenge to them, a gender perspective did not inform the course from its outset and future initiatives should ensure that this is addressed systematically.

A related point is that we are doubtful that the group was of value to the few women who attended. We took our material to be gender-neutral, but this was not the case. It is, moreover, not unlikely that the women participants had been the victims of abuse by men and their involvement in a group in which men were expressing aggressive and sexist views may have been distressing for them and should not in any case be taken for granted. Our experience suggests to us that women's violent conduct is often associated with experiences of abuse and oppression and needs to be explored with other women alone.

A project that sets an objective, shared by facilitators and participants, of reducing offending should devise a means of determining whether or not that objective is met. This is clearer to us now than it was when the course took place and we are not in a position to assess the impact of the course on rates of reconviction. There is no doubt that information about subsequent convictions during a follow-up period would be valuable, although the interpretation of the findings would not be straightforward. It is important to be clear that reconviction is one among several criteria for evaluation: it is not the only one. The project would not be invalidated even by a high rate of reconviction. Again, all participants were under regular supervision and all were highly motivated. Were the rate of reconviction to be low, it would be impossible to disentangle the influential factors and claim that it was the course that was responsible. Finally, the rate of reconviction should be set against rates achieved by other penal measures, notably imprisonment, rather than against some ideal figure. By 'a high/low rate of reconviction' should be understood 'a high/low rate of reconviction compared with imprisonment'.

DYNAMICS OF THE GROUP

This was a short-term, intensive, task-focused, closed group. Much of the work, moreover, was undertaken in (shifting) smaller groups or even in pairs. These characteristics involve a very different dynamic from that which might be expected in other groups. An advantage is that some of the dysfunctions (which many general texts on groupwork describe) were not apparent. The corresponding disadvantage, of course, is that the exposure and working through of some of these difficulties are themselves rich sources of learning which were not available to these participants.

Inevitably, there was competition for leadership and standing, although the aggression of some of the younger men was tempered by their deference to more experienced members. (One young man told another group member: 'I've learnt a lot from you and I listened because when I saw you I thought you were really hard.')

While the social skills tradition is, deliberately, not reflective or introspective and tries to keep to task, the dynamics of the group generated some powerful learning opportunities. The conflicts which emerged within the group itself were used to illustrate some of the origins of conflict in the ordinary transactions of life. The idea of 'psychological trading stamps' (see, for example, James and Jongeward, 1971, pp.210ff.) was introduced to explain how it is that people can end up experiencing hostility that might 'really' have been directed at others. At a later stage, a group member's expression of anger was analysed in this way and he was helped to express his 'unfinished business' (Douglas, 1976, p.117). Similarly, responses to challenge or criticism could be modelled by the group leaders, and successful and functional responses by other group members were reflected back to the group.

There was little that was innovative about this course. Many of the exercises offered to participants were plundered directly from McGuire and Priestley (1985) in a way that pushed to the limit their generous attitude towards plagiarism, and anyone planning a similar project should begin with the fifth chapter of Offending Behaviour.

Nor is it put forward as a paradigm. What was amply confirmed for us by this experience, though, is that the Probation Service should affirm with confidence that the large majority of violent offenders can and should be dealt with non-custodially. The Probation Service is acquiring the skills necessary to work with serious offenders and has no need to compromise its social work values by opting for coercion. It is simply unnecessary, as well as counter-productive, for it to seek to supervise more intrusively for the sake of something called credibility. Everything that we know about violence and the influence of custody suggests that it is prison, not probation, that must defend its claim to be realistic.

Rob Canton and Carolyn Mack, Nottinghamshire Probation Service; Jeff Smith, Leicester Probation Service. This chapter is reprinted from Groupwork, *1992, 5(2)*

19

Groupwork Programme
for Male Sex Offenders:
Establishing Principles for Practice

MALCOLM COWBURN

Barker and Morgan (1991) report that most probation services in England and Wales are now providing some form of groupwork programme for sex offenders. The prison service strategy for sex offenders is largely based around a groupwork 'treatment programme' (Home Office, 1991). Groupwork is the most publicised form of therapeutic work with sex offenders (e.g. Cook et al., 1991; Hawkes, 1992 are two of the recent contributions to the rapidly growing body of literature in this area). Yet rarely are the underlying values which inform the aims and objectives, and shape and content of these programmes made explicit. Erooga, Clark, and Bentley (1990) have argued that programmes of treatment/work for sex offenders need an explicit value stance '... professionals need to set goals based on theoretical assumptions and values' (p.189). Similarly Salter (1988) expresses the need for treatment programmes to be informed and directed by an overall 'philosophy' (pp.66-67). In a previous paper (Cowburn, 1990, pp.158-159), I described the value-base which underpinned the groupwork with adult male sex offenders in Nottinghamshire, England. This has developed and is updated in what follows.

AN EXPLICIT VALUE BASE

The importance of developing and articulating a clear value base is illustrated by the following anecdote, which may be familiar to many groupworkers. Whilst running a group with nine sex offenders one of them expressed the opinion that all women want to be raped. All the other group members supported him vocally. However, because the workers involved in leading the group had spent time expressing and developing their values and attitudes about this area they were able confidently to confront and challenge this statement. In the work of Nottinghamshire Probation Service, workers have developed the following statements about male sexual violence:

1. Men are responsible for their sexual behaviour.
2. Men can control their response to sexual arousal.
3. Sexual offences are a misuse of power.
4. Sex offences are rarely isolated incidents and do not 'just happen'.
5. Victims of sexual abuse are harmed by the experience whether or not additional physical violence is part of the offence. We would, therefore, take issue with both practitioners and theoreticians who speak of the 'consensual paedophile', the 'non-violent sexual offender', and 'incestuous relationships'. Such terminology minimises the non-physical use of power and denies the harm and damage experienced by the victim. The use of such language implies an uncritical acceptance of the offender's version of what happened before, during, and after the offence, and could, therefore, collude with both the offender's view of himself and his offending behaviour.
6. In white dominated society there are very negative views of black sexuality, which describe black men as predatory and black women as promiscuous. Anti-racist practice must recognise and challenge this by confronting practitioners' and offenders' use of these stereotypes.
7. In white dominated society, racism inhibits black sex offenders talking about their offences in predominantly white groups.
8. Some homosexuals are convicted for their part in sexual acts with consenting peers.
9. In heterosexist dominated society the pressure of homophobia may make it impossible for homosexuals to participate effectively in programmes of groupwork.
10. In heterosexist dominated society there are very negative views of homosexual people, which see them as 'unnatural'. Anti-homophobic practice must recognise and challenge this by confronting practitioners' and offenders' use of these stereotypes.
11. Both research and practitioner experience indicate that convicted sex offenders significantly underestimate - in the

early stages of working on their offending behaviour - the number and type of offences which they commit.

12. Research and experience show that some sex offenders are reconvicted for fresh offences for over 20 years after their first court appearance for sexual offences.
13. Studies of the prevalence of sexually assaultive behaviour indicate that many more sex offences are committed than are ever reported to the appropriate authorities.

Without this wider perspective on sexual offending it is very tempting to understand sexual violence as being a problem of a few 'deviant' individuals who merely need a discrete package of 'treatment' to solve the problem. As practitioners, however, we rarely come into knowing contact with the invisible majority of sex offenders unless, perhaps, we are being victimised (or victimising) ourselves. The issue for us is how does this wider view of sexual offending affect our practice with convicted sex offenders? There are two principal ways in which it can influence the way we work:

1. Of necessity, it places sexually assaultive behaviour centrally within human experience, rather than seeing it as 'deviant' acts of a deprived or depraved minority. This necessitates workers examining their own values and attitudes with regard to their own gender-identity, sexuality and sexual behaviour. For example it may be important for workers to reconsider their attitudes to pornography. Is pornography a legitimate expression of sexual freedom? Or does it embody values and attitudes which are identical to those of the sex offender and which primarily objectify and oppress women and children ? Also what understanding of male sexuality does pornography represent? (These issues are discussed more fully in Cowburn, 1991).

2. It also fundamentally challenges a traditional social work position; namely, belief in and respect for our clients' understanding of their experience. To accept, uncritically, the understandings and values of men who have committed sexual offences is to collude with the sexist power structures of our society which create the climate in which the majority of sexual offences remain unreported (see for example, Levy, 1991) for a full discussion of date rapes). Those which are reported are often dismissed as 'not serious'. In her study of 114 convicted rapists Scully (1990) found that many of these men considered that their biggest mistake was not that they had committed their crimes but that they were caught for them.

GROUP LEADERSHIP ISSUES

If we accept that sexual offending has its roots in the use and abuse of power, then all methods of work must address gender, race and sexual orientation. We must look at how men's attitudes towards white women and white children and black women and black children underpin their offending. It is important to acknowledge how these views are often supported by society as a whole, through the assumption of white male heterosexual superiority. In a programme of groupwork these issues may occur both directly as a specific part of the programme, and indirectly in so far as discriminatory and pejorative statements are likely to be made at different times by various offenders.

It is crucial therefore that a leadership team has spent time together not only agreeing a common set of values which inform their operation, but also how they will confront and challenge racist, sexist and homophobic language and behaviour during the group sessions. Generally if there has not been discussion and agreement prior to running sessions these issues will either be ignored or single group leaders will feel isolated and vulnerable in taking on these issues. Mistry and Brown (1991) note, in discussing race issues for black/white group leadership teams:

> When the focus of the group programme is not anti-racism but another topic ...black/white co-workers in mixed groups face [issues] ... arising from the fact that race is not the 'official' topic (p.108).

They pertinently comment:

> Often the issue of how far to challenge the introduction of racist stereotypes or unrelated racist comment in the group raises interesting discussions. Our experience is that *white co-workers tend to talk about the choice whereas for black co-workers there is no choice but to challenge in the group* ...(emphasis added, p.108).

It has been suggested elsewhere (Cowburn and Wilson, 1992) that the stigmatising forces of racism and homophobia, widely present in society, inhibit black and gay men from participating fully in groupwork programmes. When considering putting together a team to run a groupwork programme [and selecting the group membership] these possibilities need to be addressed actively. The recruitment of black men and black and white women and gay men as workers, however, should not be undertaken on the basis that they have sole responsibility for challenging the abuse of power that sexism, racism and heterosexism represent. They may have a contribution to make in enabling a particular perspective to be acknowledged, but the responsibility for these issues remains equally with all workers.

GROUPWORK AS A SPECIFIC THERAPEUTIC TOOL

Groupwork is merely **one** means of working with sex offenders. It should be used to achieve specific therapeutic targets which are best approached by using a group. There are some areas of work - for example changing sexual fantasies or initial work on a persons own abuse - where a group-based approach may not only be ineffective but may be harmful.

As practice has developed it has become increasingly apparent that in the past some programmes have provided individual work with offenders in groups.

If group members are given exercises which involve them in writing and thinking through issues in isolation, the valuable resource of the group is lost for that period. It is helpful to ask three questions of every session or exercise in a groupwork programme:

1. Is the exercise being done in a way that utilises the potential for positive influence of the whole group?
2. If not, can it be done differently to utilise the group?
3. If not, should the exercise be done before the course, after the course, during an evening as homework, or not at all?

These questions focus planning of programmes of groupwork: consequently exercises that require group members to work privately on their motivations, attitudes and feelings can be excluded.

SEQUENCE OF A GROUPWORK PROGRAMME:

Any piece of groupwork with sex offenders should include a specific selection phase, an assessment phase, a work/treatment phase, and after the programme is completed it should be evaluated.

Selection

Selection is the process of choosing certain sex offenders to work in an intensive manner on their offending behaviour. A number of factors are relevant:

1. *in the offender*: motivation, acceptance of responsibility, willingness to change, level of perceived risk, age, number and type of previous convictions for sexual offences ;

2. *in the agency*: appropriate aims, objectives and strategies, appropriately skilled staff, sufficient and varied resources, including access to informed supervision/consultation. Without appropriate resources, it is clear that work with sex offenders can only be limited and inadequate.

There are three tiers in the process of selecting offenders with whom to work. The first tier relates to the agency policies about which offender groups are deemed to be priorities for intervention, the second tier is concerned with the motivation of the offender and their suitability for a programme of groupwork, and the third tier addresses offence-related issues.

First tier–priorities for intervention
Agency strategies related to working with sex offenders need to identify:

1. The number and type of people with current convictions for sexual offences;
2. The number and type of people with previous convictions for sexual offences;
3. The groups of offenders to be given priority attention–this decision could be based on:

   • the nature and type of offence;
   • the stage in the penal process;
   • the number of previous convictions for sexual offences;
   • the perceived risk to the public;

4. The type of services which it is prepared to resource for these groups.

The second tier–motivation and suitability for groupwork
It is important to establish whether or not the offender considers his behaviour to be a problem and, importantly, one which he wishes to change. If he does, the next question to be addressed is what level of responsibility does he accept for his behaviour? Many offenders will acknowledge that their behaviour is a problem–either because of their victim(s)' acting out behaviour or because of society's views–neither position accepts any personal responsibility for the harmful behaviour. Without the motivation to examine critically and to change both his attitudes and behaviour undertaking of a programme of work is a futile exercise.

Additionally, in the context of groupwork, the offender has to be willing to participate fully in the programme.

Third tier—offence-related issues

The level of risk to the public may be a significant factor in determining whether to work with an offender.

Similarly, if an offender is indicating strong motivation to re-offend (for example, through expressions of anger, or attraction), but also asking for help in learning to control his behaviour, this may at least require further assessment.

On this level, it is also important for workers planning programmes to make statements about whether their groups will be for single or multiple offence types.

Assessment

It is essential that as a part of any structured groupwork with sex offenders a full assessment of issues related to their offending behaviour occurs. During assessment a detailed life and sexual history should be obtained. Additionally, it is also important to begin to obtain information about the following areas:

1. what responsibility the man accepts for his offending behaviour;
2. his pattern and type of offending;
3. the level of risk which he poses;
4. what attitudes (social and sexual) he has to children, women;
5. how he views himself as a man and what he understands and accepts is 'normal' male behaviour;
6. how he understands what his victims experienced whilst, and as a result of being abused;
7. how he understands his own sexuality and what particularly arouses him;
8. his level of sexual knowledge.

Assessment is not a process which is engaged in once at the beginning of a programme of work. Regular re-assessment should be an essential feature of all programmes. Having obtained an initial picture relating to the above areas it is then possible to plan a longer term piece of work addressing each area according to the priority given to it.

Work / Treatment

This phase in a programme of work will address the various targets identified in the initial assessment (including matters which may have emerged during the taking of personal histories - for example the offender's own experience of abuse) and redefined in subsequent reassessments. In an ideal setting a wide range of methods and therapeutic techniques will be used, involving workers from other disciplines (e.g. survivor-focused services, psychologists, psychotherapists, etc.). It is not possible to specify how long this period of work should last, but given the experience from the USA and some European projects it is unlikely to be less than 12 months [see Knopp (1988) for a full description of 12 treatment facilities in the United States; similarly there is a project in Rotterdam, Holland which works with incest offenders for a minimum of eighteen months (Cowburn, 1991, pp. 103-107).

Evaluation

Evaluation involves examining the effectiveness of a project, model of treatment, focusing on the work itself after a programme has been completed. It draws on a range of sources, including monitoring data (for example checks for reconvictions), verbal and written reports by a variety of people, and research findings. Whilst it is important to evaluate the offenders' views of a programme/treatment, it is crucial for practitioners to make their own evaluation.

Unless appropriate evaluation constitutes an integral part of the work itself, it is hard - if not impossible - to know:

1. whether a piece of work is successful in relation to a particular offender or a group of offenders;
2. whether particular processes are more appropriate than others;
3. whether resources are adequate;
4. whether a particular multi-disciplinary approach is effective;
5. whether the work discriminates against any group of offenders on grounds of gender, race, sexual orientation,mental or physical abilities;
6. whether the worker-team dynamics contribute to or detract from the success of the work;
7. and ultimately whether the objectives of the work have been fulfilled.

Looking at current levels of evaluation of probation-led programmes, Barker and Morgan (1991) state:

> In general, though there are some striking exceptions, monitoring and evaluation of programmes is rather sketchy and inadequate. For the great majority of programmes, monitoring consists of daily/weekly reports on progress for the offender's supervising officer. A smaller number of programmes collect statistics

on the numbers of offenders passing through the programme, the types of offences they have committed and the sentences they have been given. Just over a third of the treatment programmes are carrying out evaluation of their work, some using psychological testing before and after treatment, and some involving follow-up studies of reconvictions. Because of resource restrictions, evaluations tend to be incomplete and therefore inconclusive (p.176).

In practice, often due to time and other resource limitations, the work is planned and done without adequate evaluation and monitoring components [see Furby et al. (1989) for a rigorous critique of earlier attempts at evaluation]. However, it appears to be unethical to begin a programme of work in this way, since the workers involved cannot be clear why they are doing what they are doing, and what positive or negative effects the work is having on the offenders, or staff, or on others.

(For a more detailed discussion of evaluation and other topics discussed here, see Cowburn, Wilson et al.'s publication *Changing Men: A Guide to Working with Adult Male Sex Offenders,* 1992)

MODELS OF PROGRAMME DELIVERY

Although the aims and objectives of the work in Nottinghamshire have not significantly altered in that we continue to have the reduction of offending behaviour as our overall aim, we have now expressed these in a more systematic manner, recognising the necessary logical sequence of selection; assessment; work/ treatment; and evaluation. We have also, however, restructured the programme to extend over a period of eleven months.

In a previous paper (Cowburn 1990) I described the rationale behind changing the method of programme delivery of sex offender courses in Nottinghamshire. Briefly it was considered that changing the programme delivery from one evening per week over a 13 week period to a more intensive schedule delivered over ten days would have a stronger impact on group-members. Unfortunately appropriate methods of evaluation were not devised and the validity of the hypothesis could not be adequately tested. At the present time there does not appear to be any research data which has explored the differential effect and validity of these different forms of programme delivery. However, the Sex Offender Treatment Evaluation Programme (STEP), which is funded by the Home Office as part of its brief is currently comparing treatment programmes which use either one of the two different forms of programme delivery.

In Nottinghamshire a probation service working group was convened to develop the groupwork practice with sex offenders. They identified the following areas of dissatisfaction with the programme as it was then operating:

1. The programme was considered to be to be far too short. Workers felt that by the end of the two week block course, they were just beginning to engage with groupmembers beyond their denial. Additionally with the course finishing and group-members dispersing, the power of the group dynamic was lost just after it had become established as a genuinely critical force.
2. The brevity and the intensity of the ten day course sometimes provided more problems for the referring probation officers than it solved. Offenders would appear to make substantial progress whilst they were undertaking the programme - particularly in accepting responsibility for their offences, and in acknowledging the harm done to their victims. However, after the course had finished probation officers were sometimes at a loss as how to maintain the momentum created by the group. The problem had two aspects: many officers considered that they did not have sufficient knowledge or experience of this area to continue an in depth programme of work. Also, the very absence of the group caused a substantial reduction in offenders' willingness/ ability to sustain their work.
3. Although the ten day programme raised many issues for offenders, these could only be dealt with briefly and in most cases superficially. Such issues (for example a man's own victimisation) were generally directed to the referring probation officer who was often also unable to address them fully.
4. Workers increasingly felt that the programme was good at challenging offenders' denial and minimisations. In effect the programme de-constructed the men's world view of themselves (particularly with regard to their offending behaviour, but also in relation to their sexuality, and themselves as parents), but it did not help to reconstruct their sense of self. This insensitivity was perhaps most starkly highlighted in the manner in which offenders' own victimisation would be dismissed as not relevant to the

programme, and possibly a tactic to avoid addressing the content of the programme. Alice Miller (see particularly *Banished Knowledge*, 1990) in her work has repeatedly shown how the behaviour of therapists with adults, who have been abused as children, often mirrors or repeats the behaviour of the disbelieving or abusing adult.

5. Relapse prevention and future supports after the group programme had finished were virtually non-existent.

The working group devised the following 'modular model' of groupwork provision for adult male sex offenders. Figure 1 shows the components and the sequence of the work in the proposed model. The programme will be piloted in the forthcoming year.

Assessment module

This would be similar to the first week of the courses currently operating in Nottingham. It will address the areas outlined above. It would be full time (10am-4pm) for five days, and staffed by four workers (two female/male pairings; and ideally two black and two white workers).

All of the other modules would be staffed by a mixed gender pairing (with the possible exception of some of the sessions in modules 4 and 5).

Cycle of behaviour module

This will address issues related to offenders' pattern of behaviour (see Erooga et al., 1990 for a fuller description of this concept). It would consist of six half-day sessions held weekly. Emphasis would be placed on the process of targeting (the use of power to control), and exploration of how victims are identified, isolated and abused.

Victims

Six half day weekly sessions. The intention is to help offenders develop an understanding of the consequences of abuse for the victims. Techniques employed may include victim video/audio tapes , role play, and straight teaching from people who work with victims.

Sex education, gender identity, power and sexuality

Eight half day weekly sessions. Focuses upon male identity, sexual orientation, sexual knowledge, human development, what

Figure 1 The proposed model for reorganising work with male sex offenders in groups

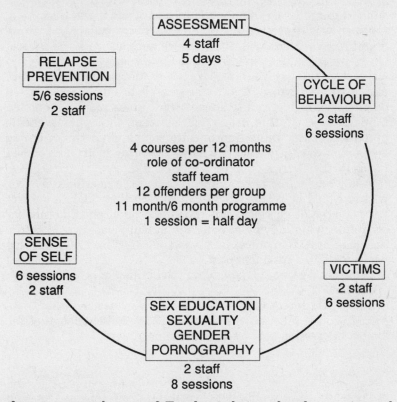

does pornography mean? Emphasis being placed on notions of power and consent.

Sense of self

Six half day weekly sessions. Intended to help offenders develop a positive sense of themselves as men. It may be that if there were sufficient victims of abuse in the group that this specific issue could be addressed. Social skills and assertiveness training may also form part of this module.

Relapse prevention/risk assessment/termination

Five half day weekly sessions. The themes central to this module will have already occurred in earlier modules. These sessions will be based on the work of Pithers et al. (in Salter, 1988), and will consolidate previous learning into explicit risk assessment and relapse prevention packages.

In concluding the programme the possibility of developing a support group for the men who had completed it was discussed. Concern was expressed about how such an open-ended group might be resourced. Also, although we were aware of the work of Giarretto et al. (1990) in relation to the Parents United self-help support groups, we were also aware of Marshall et al.'s (1990) unequivocal statement that there were clear indications that sex offender self help groups did not work and should be stopped immediately. At this stage we consider that the referring probation officer is the appropriate source of post-programme support, although we acknowledge that this is an area which needs further work.

A key role in this programme is that of the co-ordinator. This person would be responsible for ensuring that module leaders were aware of issues from earlier modules. S/he should also offer consultancy and advice to both the module leaders and to the referring probation officers. It was envisaged initially that this post should be a specialist post, however the amount of resources put into the post would depend on the number of programmes in operation.

Ideally this programme will combine the impact of the block-period groups with the sustained support and challenge of the longer one session per week programmes.

CONCLUSION

Groupwork with sex offenders is continually developing, as is all work with this group of offenders. It is important that the work is informed by a clear value-base, that the sequence of selection, assessment/treatment, and evaluation are all core parts of any programme, and that groupwork is recognised as one of the therapeutic tools to be used in working with these offenders.

Malcolm Cowburn was with Nottinghamshire Probation Service when this chapter was written. He is now a Project Leader, National Children's Homes.

References

Ahmed, S. (1991) 'Developing anti-racist social work education practice' in CD Project Group (ed.) *Setting the Context for Change*. London: CCETSW.

Ainley, M. and Kingston, P. (1981) 'Live supervision in a probation setting', *Social Work Education*, 1(1).

APP Archives and Annual Reports, 1976-91

Argyle, M. (1972) *The Psychology of Interpersonal Behaviour*. London: Penguin.

Ashe, M. (1991) 'Meeting prisoners' needs through groupwork', *Groupwork*, 4(3), pp.277-283.

Audit Commission for Local Authorities in England and Wales, 1989.

Badham, B., Bente, M. and Hall, P. (1988) 'Nowt to do and always getting into trouble', *Groupwork*, 1(3), pp.239-251.

Badham, B., Blatchford, B., Mcartney, S. and Nicholas, M. (1989) 'Doing something with our lives when we're inside', *Groupwork*, 2(1), pp.27-35.

Bale, D. (1987) 'Using a risk of custody scale', *Probation Journal*, 34(4), pp.127-131.

Bale, D. (1988) 'Summing up for the defence', *Probation Journal*, 35(1), p.17.

Ball, K., Davill, M., Eastwood, S. and Holt, J. (1987) *Worth the Risk!? Creative Groupwork with Young Offenders*. West Yorkshire Probation Service and Hilltop Practice Development and Publications Unit (Save the Children Fund).

Barker, M. and Morgan, R. (1991) 'Surveying probation practice with sex offenders', *Probation Journal*, 38(4), pp.171-176.

Barr, H. (1966) *A Survey of Group Work in the Probation Service*. London: HMSO.

Beck, E.M. (1980) *Bartlett's Familiar Quotations*. Boston: Little, Brown and Company.

Becker, S. (1989) 'Poor women' and 'Keeping a poor woman down'. *Community Care*, 12 & 19 January.

Behroozi, C. (1992) 'Groupwork with involuntary clients: remotivating strategies', *Groupwork*, 5(3).

Berkman, A. (1912) *Prison Memoirs of an Anarchist*. New York: Mother Earth Publications.

Berne, E. (1961) *Transactional Analysis in Psychotherapy*. New York: Grove Press.

Bertcher, H.J. and Maple, F. (1984) 'Elements and issues in group composition' in Glasser, P. Sarri, R. and Vinter, R. (eds.) *Individual Change Through Small Groups*. New York: The Free Press.

Bion, W. (1961) *Experiences in Groups*. London: Tavistock.

Blagg, H. and Smith, D. (1989) *Crime, Penal Policy and Social Work*. London: Longman.

Brown, A (1979) *Groupwork*. London: Heinemann Educational.

Brown, A. (1984) *Consultation: An Aid to Successful Social Work.* London: Heinemann.

Brown, A. (1986) *Groupwork*. Second Edition. Aldershot: Gower.

Brown, A. and Caddick, B. (1986) 'Models of social groupwork in Britain: a further note', *British Journal of Social Work*, 17, pp.535-543.

Brown, A. and Caddick, B. (1991) 'Editorial', *Groupwork*, 4(3).

Brown, A. and Clough, R. (eds.) (1989) *Groups and Groupings: Life and Work in Day and Residential Centres.* London: Routledge.

Brown, A. and Seymour, B. (eds.) (1983) *Intake Groups for Clients: A Probation Innovation.* Bristol: SAUS.

Brown, A., Caddick, B., Gardiner, M. and Sleeman, S. (1982) 'Towards a British model of groupwork', *British Journal of Social Work*, 12(6), pp.587-603.

Buckley, K. and Williams, T. (1991).'Driving with Rambo', *NAPO News*, 30 (May/June), pp.12-13.

Buckley, K. and Wilson, C. (1989) 'Empowering women', *Probation*, December.

Burney, E. (1980) *A Chance to Change: Day Care and Day Training for Offenders.* London: Howard League for Penal Reform.

Burney, E. (1982) *Learning how to Change: A Therapeutic Programme for Young Offenders.* APP Day Centre Ltd.

Caddick, B. (1991) 'Using groups in working with offenders: a survey of groupwork in the probation services of England and Wales', *Groupwork*, 4(3), pp.197-214.

Canton, R. (1987) 'Working at the margin, campaigning at the centre', *Probation Journal*, 34(3).

Carlen, P. (1988) *Women, Crime and Poverty.* Open University Press.

Carlen, P. (1989) 'Feminist jurisprudence or women wise penology?', *Probation*, September.

Carlen, P. (1990) *Alternatives to Women's Imprisonment*. Milton Keynes: OUP.

Carlen, P. and Worrall, A. (eds.) (1987) *Gender, Crime and Justice.* Milton Keynes: Open University.

Coleman, D. (1989) *Review of Probation Training: Final Report*. London: Home Office.

Collins, S. and Behan, D. (1981) *Social Work with Young Offenders.* London: Butterworth.

Cook, D.A.G., Fox, C.A., Weaver, C.M. and Rooth, F.G. (1991) 'The Berkeley Group: ten years experience of a group for non-violent sex offenders', *British Journal Of Psychiatry*, 158, pp.238-243.

Cook, R.D. (1988) 'A non-residential therapeutic community used as an alternative to custody', *International Journal of Therapeutic Communities*, 9(1).

Corey, M.S. and Corey, G. (1987) *Groups: Process and Practice.* Monterey: Brooks/Cole.

Cowburn, M. (1990) 'Work with male sex offenders in groups', *Groupwork*, 3(2).

Cowburn, M. (1991) *Sex Offenders in Prison: A Study of Structured*

References

Interventions Designed To Change Offending Behaviour. Unpublished M.Phil. Thesis, Nottingham University.

Cowburn, M., Wilson, C. et al. (1992) *Changing Men: A Guide To Working With Adult Male Sex Offenders.* Available from Nottinghamshire Probation Service.

Crow, I. (1987) 'Black people and criminal justice in the UK', *The Howard Journal*, 26(4), pp.303-314.

Davies, M. (1989) *The Nature of Probation Practice Today.* Norwich: University of East Anglia.

Davis, G., Boucherat, J. and Watson, D. (1987) *A Preliminary Study of Victim / Offender Mediation and Reparation Schemes in England and Wales.* Home Office Research and Planning Unit Paper No. 42. London: HMSO.

Denman, G. (1982) *Intensive Intermediate Treatment with Juvenile Offenders.* Lancaster University.

Despicht, K. (1987) *Specificity in Probation Practice.* University of East Anglia Monograph 56.

Donnelly, A. (1986) *Feminist Social Work with a Women's Group,* Social Work Monograph 41. Social Work Today/UEA.

Douglas, T. (1976) *Groupwork Practice.* London: Tavistock.

Douglas, T. (1979) *Group Processes in Social Work.* Chichester: Wiley & Sons.

Douglas, T. (1983) *Groups: Understanding People Gathered Together.* London: Tavistock.

Duguid, S. (1987) 'To inform their discretion', *Proceedings, College Programmes Behind Bars: Models for Higher Education*, Yahara Centre, Madison, Wisconsin, pp.12-13.

Duguid, S. (1986) 'Selective ethics and integrity: moral development and prison education', *Journal of Correctional Education*, 37(2), pp.60-64.

Earnshaw, J. (1991) 'Evolution and accountability: ten years of groups in a Day Centre for offenders', *Groupwork*, 4(3), pp.231-239.

Eldridge, H. and Gibbs, P. (1987) 'Strategies for preventing re-offending: a course for sex offenders', *Probation Journal*, 34(1), pp.7-9.

Eliot, T.S. (1972) 'Tb Little Gidding V' in *New Oxford Book of English Verse 1250-1950.* Oxford: OUP.

Ernst, S. and Goodison, L. (1982) *In Our Own Hands: A Book of Self-Help Therapy.* London: The Women's Press.

Erooga, M., Clark, P. and Bentley M. (1990) 'Protection, control, treatment: groupwork with child sexual abuse perpetrators', *Groupwork*, 3(2)

Faulkner, D.E.R. (1989) *The Madingley Papers II.* University of Cambridge: Board of Extra Mural Studies. Papers presented to a seminar for Probation Committee members at Madingley Hall Cambridge, 20-22nd February 1989.

Fletcher, H. (1988) *Racism, Representation and the Criminal Justice System.* London: NAPO.

Forsyth, D. (1990) *Group Dynamics.* Monterey: Brooks/Cole.

French, J.R.P. and Raven, B. (1959) 'The bases of social power' in Cartwright, D. (ed.) *Studies in Social Power.* Ann Arbor: Institute for Social Research.

Garvin, C. (1981) *Contemporary Groupwork*. Englewood Cliffs, New Jersey: Prentice Hall.

Garvin, C. and Reed, B. (eds) (1983) 'Groupwork with women/groupwork with men', Special Issue, *Social Work with Groups*, 6 (3/4).

Gawlinski, G. and Graissle, L. (1988) *Planning Together the Art of Effective Teamwork*. Bedford Square Press, p.59

Gendreau, P. and Ross, R.R. (1987) 'Revivification of rehabilitation: evidence from the 1980s', *Justice Quarterly*, 4, pp.349-407.

Giarretto, H. and Einfield-Giarretto, A. (1990) 'Integrated treatment: the self help factor' in Horton, A.L., Johnson, B.L., Roundy, L.M., Williams, D. (eds.) *The Incest Perpetrator: A Family Member No One Wants To Treat*. Newbury Park, Ca: Sage.

Gibran, K. (1975) *The Prophet*. London: Heinemann (originally published 1923).

Hadjipavlou, S., Murphy, S. and Green, G. (1991) *Report of a Scrutiny of Probation In-Service Training*. London: Home Office.

Hamilton, E. (1964) *The Greek Way*. Chapter 1. New York: Norton.

Hamilton, R. and Oulds, G. (1990) Unpublished notes of a workshop entitled *Working with Motoring Offenders*. Presented at an Inter-Disciplinary Day Conference, Haigh Hall, Wigan. Organised by Greater Manchester Probation Service and Regional Staff Development Office (Northern Region).

Hankinson, I. and Stephens, D. (1986) 'Ever decreasing circles: practitioners and probation bureaucracy', *Probation*, 33(1) March.

Harding, J. (1982) Victims and Offenders: Needs and Responsibilities. NCVO Occasional Paper No.2. London: Bedford Square Press.

Hare, A.P. (1962) *Handbook of Small Group Research*. New York: The Free Press.

Hawkes, C. (1992) 'An integrated approach to the preparation of social enquiry reports concerning child sexual abusers' in *Beyond Containment: The Penal Response to Sex Offenders*. London: Prison Reform Trust.

Heap, K. (1977) *Group Theory for Social Workers*. London: Pergamon Press.

Henry, J. and Walker, D. (eds.) (1991) *Managing Innovation*. London: SAGE Publications.

Henry, M. (1988) 'Revisiting open groups', *Groupwork*, 1(3), pp.215-228.

Home Office (1982) *Criminal Justice Act 1982*. London: HMSO.

Home Office (1984) *Probation Service in England and Wales: Statement of National Objectives and Priorities*. London: HMSO.

Home Office (1986) *Criminal Statistics for England and Wales* 1985. Cmnd 10. London: HMSO.

Home Office (1988) *Punishment, Custody and The Community*. London: HMSO.

Home Office (1988) *Tackling Offending: An Action Plan*. London: HMSO.

Home Office (1989) *Risk Prediction and Probation: Papers from a Research and Planning Unit Workshop*. Research and Planning Unit Paper 56. London: HMSO.

References

Home Office (1990) *Crime, Justice and Protecting the Public: The Government's Proposals for Legislation*. London: HMSO.

Home Office (1990) *Supervision and Punishment in the Community*. London: HMSO.

Home Office (1990) *Partnership in Dealing with Offenders in the Community*. London: HMSO.

Home Office (1991) *Criminal Justice Act 1991*. London: HMSO.

Home Office (1991) *Treatment Programmes for Sex Offenders in Custody: A Strategy*. Home Office, Prison Service, Directorate of Inmate Programmes.

Home Office (1992) *Draft Probation National Standards*. 16 March. London: HMSO.

Home Office CCETSW (1990) *Requirements for Probation Training in the Diploma in Social Work in England and Wales*. Joint paper from the Home Office and the Central Council for Education and Training in Social Work.

Hudson, B. (1987) *Justice Through Punishment*. London: Macmillan.

Hutchins, K. (1991) 'The Telford motoring offenders education project', *Groupwork*, 4(3), pp.240-248.

James, M. and Jongeward, D. (1971) *Born to Win*. Signet Books.

Johnson, D.W. and Johnson, F.P. (1975) *Joining Together: Group Theory and Group Skills*. New Jersey: Prentice-Hall.

Johnson, D.W. and Johnson, F.P. (1991) *Joining Together: Group Theory and Group Skills*. Second Edition. New Jersey: Prentice-Hall.

Jones, M. (1953) *The Therapeutic Community: A New Treatment Method in Psychiatry*. New York: Basic Books.

Jones, M., Mordecai, M., Rutter, F. and Thomas, L. (1991) 'The Miskin model of groupwork with women offenders', *Groupwork*, 4(3), pp.215-230.

Knopp, F.H. (1988) *Retraining Adult Sex Offenders: Methods and Models*. New York: Safer Society Press.

Levy, B. (ed.) (1991) *Dating Violence: Young Women in Danger*. Seattle: The Seal Press.

Lewis, P.J. (1980) *Psychiatric Probation Orders*. Cambridge: Institute of Criminology Occasional Paper No.6.

Mackintosh, J. (1991) 'The Newcastle Intensive Probation Programme: a centralised approach to groupwork', *Groupwork*, 4(3), pp262-276.

MacLeod, D. (1988) 'Bale's risk of custody scale: some critical comments', *Probation Journal*, 35(1), pp.15-16.

Mair, G. (1991) Paper given at the British Society of Criminology Conference, York University, July 1991.

Marsh, J. (1976) 'Philosophical considerations of prison education: "pro and con" ' in Reagen, M. and Stoughton, D. (eds.) *School Behind Bars*. New Jersey: The Scarecrow Press Inc.

Marshall, W.L. et al. (1991) 'An optimistic evaluation of treatment outcomes with sex offenders', *Violence Update*, 1(7), pp.8-11.

McGrath, J.I. and Altman, I. (1966) *Small Group Research*. New York: Holt, Rinehart & Winston.

McGuire, J. and Priestley, P. (1985) *Offending Behaviour: Skills and*

Stratagems for Going Straight. London: Batsford Academic and Educational Press.

McLoone, P., Oulds, G. and Morris, J. (1987) 'Alcohol education groups: compulsion v. voluntarism', *Probation Journal*, 34(1).

McWilliams, W. (1990) 'Probation practice and the management ideal', *Probation Journal*, 37.

Miller, A. (1990) *Banished Knowledge*. London: Virago.

Mistry, T. (1989) 'Establishing a feminist model of groupwork in the probation service', *Groupwork*, 2(2), pp.145-158.

Mistry, T. and Brown, A. (1991) 'Black/white co-working in groups', *Groupwork*, 4(2), pp.101-118.

Mullender, A. and Ward, D. (1985) 'Towards an alternative model of social groupwork, *British Journal of Social Work*, 15, pp.155-172.

Mullender, A. and Ward, D. (1989) 'Challenging familiar assumptions: preparing for and initiating a self-directed group', *Groupwork*, 2(1), pp.5-26.

Mullender, A. and Ward, D. (1991) *Self-Directed Groupwork: Users Take Action for Empowerment*. London: Whiting & Birch.

Nation, D. and Arnott, J. (1991) 'House burglars and victims', *Probation Journal*, June.

National Association for the Care and Resettlement of Offenders (1986) *Race and Criminal Justice*. London: NACRO.

National Association of Probation Officers (1988 and 1989) *Probation Practice Committee Briefings on The Use of Schedule 11 Conditions Day Centres*. NAPO Policy Guidelines.

Nin, A. (1943) (1969) 'The diary of Anais Nin. Volume III Fall 1943' in Barlett, J. (ed.) *Bartlett's Familiar Quotations*.

Northumbria Probation Service (1989) *A Strategy for Tackling Offending by Young Adults - Action Plan*.

Northumbria Probation Service (1991) *Intensive Probation Unit Annual Report 1990-91*.

Papell, C. and Rothman, B. (1966) 'Social groupwork models: possession and heritage', *Journal for Education for Social Work*, 2(2), pp.66-77. Reprinted in Specht, H. and Vickery, A. (eds.) (1977) *Integrated Social Work Methods*. London: George Allen Unwin.

Papell, C. and Rothman, B. (1980) 'Relating the mainstream model of social work with groups to group psychotherapy and the structured group', *Social Work with Groups*, 3(2).

Patten, J. (1990) 'Foreword' to *Annual Report, APP Day Centre Ltd, 1989-90*.

Patten, J. (1990) 'Keep away from the college of crime', *Farnham Herald*, 9 March.

Perls, F. (1971) *Gestalt Therapy Verbatim*. Des Plaines: Bantam.

Preston-Shoot, M. (1987) *Effective Groupwork*. London: Macmillan.

Preston-Shoot, M. (1989) 'Using contracts in groupwork', *Groupwork*, 2(1), pp.36-47.

Priestley, P. and McGuire, J. (1978) *Social Skills and Personal Problem Solving*. London: Tavistock.

Priestley, P. and McGuire, J. (1983) *Learning to Help*. London:

References

Tavistock.

Priestley, P. and McGuire, J. (1984) *Social Skills in Prison and the Community: Problem Solving for Offenders*. London: RKP.

Priestley, P. and McGuire, J. et al. (1978) *Social Skills and Personal Problem Solving: A Handbook of Methods*. London: Tavistock.

Prochaska, J.O. and DiClemente, C. (1982) 'Transtheoretical therapy towards a more integrative model of change', *Psychotherapy: Theory, Research and Practice*, 19, pp.276-278.

Public General Act (1972) *Criminal Justice Act 1972, Chap. 71*. London: HMSO.

Public General Act (1982) *Criminal Justice Act 1982, Chap. 48*. London: HMSO.

Raynor, P. (1978) 'Compulsory persuasion: a problem for correctional social work', *British Journal of Social Work*, 8(4), p.411.

Raynor, P. (1985) *Social Work, Justice and Control*. Oxford: Basil Blackwell.

Raynor, P. (1993) *Social Work, Justice and Control*. Second Edition, Reprint. London: Whiting and Birch Ltd.

Rojek, C. and Collins, S.A. (1987) 'Contract or con trick?', *British Journal of Social Work*, 17, pp.199-211.

Rosenthal, S. and Wiley, J. (1975) *A Time of Blossoming - A Zen Philosophy of Love and Human Development*. Cardiff: The British School of Bompu Zen.

Ross, R.R., Fabiano, E. and Ross, R.D. (1986) *Reasoning and Rehabilitation : A Handbook for Teaching Cognitive Skills*. Ottawa: Cognitive Centre.

Ryan, M. and Ward, T. (1990) 'Restructuring, resistance and privatisation in the non-custodial sector', *Critical Social Policy*, 30.

Salter, A.C. (1988) *Treating Child Sexual Offenders and Victims: A Practical Guide*. London: Sage.

Satir, V. (1972) *Peoplemaking*. Science & Behavior Inc.

Scully, D. (1990) *Understanding Sexual Violence: A Study of Convicted Rapists*. London: Unwin Hyman.

Senior, P. (1985) 'Groupwork with offenders' in Walker, H. and Beaumont, B. (eds.) *Working with Offenders*. London: BASW/ Macmillan.

Senior, P. (1991) 'Groupwork in the Probation Service: care or control in the 1990s', *Groupwork*, 4(3), pp.284-295.

Shaw, G.B. (1921) *Back to Methuselah A Metabiological Pentateuch*. Pt.l. Act 1. London: Constable & Co.

Shaw, M.E. (1971) *Group Dynamics*. New York: McGraw Hill.

Sheath, M. (1990) ' 'Confrontative' work with sex offenders', *Probation Journal*, 37(4).

Showelter, E. (1987) *The Female Malady*. London: Virago Press.

Smith, P. (1980) *Group Processes and Personal Change*. New York: Harper & Row.

Smith, P. (1983) 'Management of assaultive behaviour', unpublished work mentioned in Kaplan, S.G. and Wheeler, E.G., 'Social skills for working with potentially violent clients', *Social Casework*, June.

Sykes, G. and Matza, D. (1957) 'Techniques of neutralization', *American Sociological Review*, 22.

The Road User. A package of videos and discussion notes aimed at young people. Produced by British Institute of Traffic Education Research and Strathclyde Regional Council, Scotland, 1985. Published by British Institute of Traffic Education Research, Kent House, Kent Street, Birmingham, B5 6GF.

Thorpe, D., Smith, D., Green, C. and Paley, J. (1980) *Out of Care*. London: Allen and Unwin.

Toch, H. (1972) *Violent Men*. London: Penguin Books.

Tuckman, B.W. (1965) 'Developmental sequence in small groups', *Psychological Bulletin*, 63(6), pp.384-399.

Vanstone, M. (1986) 'The Pontypridd Day Training Centre: Diversion from Prison in Action' in Ponting, J. (ed.) *Alternatives to Custody*. Oxford: Basil Blackwell.

Walker, H. and Beaumont, B. (1981) *Probation Work: Critical Theory and Socialist Practice*. Oxford: Basil Blackwell.

Walmsley, R. (1986) *Personal Violence*. Home Office Research Study 89. London: HMSO.

Ware, P. (1983) 'Personality adaptions (doors to therapy)', *Transactional Analysis Journal*, 13, pp.11-19.

Weaver, C. and Fox, C. (1984) 'The Berkeley sex offenders group: a seven year evaluation', *Probation Journal*, 31(4).

Whitaker, D. (1976) 'Some conditions for effective work with groups', *British Journal of Groupwork*, 5(4).

Whitaker, D.S. and Lieberman, M.A. (1964) *Psychotherapy Through the Group Process*. New York: Atherton Press; London: Tavistock.

Willis, A. (1986) 'Help and control in probation: an empirical assessment of probation practice' in Ponting, J. (ed.) *Alternatives to Custody*. Oxford: Basil Blackwell.

Woodcock, M. (1979) *Team Development Manual*. Aldershot: Gower

Worrall, A. (1990) *Offending Women - Female Law Breakers and the Criminal Justice System*. London: Routledge.

Yochelson, S. and Samenow, S. (1976 and 1985) The *Criminal Personality*. Volumes I and II. Northvale, New Jersey: Jason Aronson Inc.

Zimbardo, P.G., Ebbensen, E.G. and Maslash, C. (1977) *Influencing Attitudes and Changing Behaviour*. Second Edition. Reading: Addison-Westley.

Subject Index

Author Index